DEAN BUTLER

PRAIRIE MAN

MY LITTLE HOUSE LIFE & BEYOND

CITADEL PRESS
Kensington Publishing Corp.
www.kensingtonbooks.com

CITADEL PRESS BOOKS are published by

Kensington Publishing Corp.
900 Third Ave.
New York, NY 10022

All Kensington titles, imprints, and distributed lines are available at special quantity discounts for bulk purchases for sales promotion, premiums, fund-raising, educational, or institutional use.

Special book excerpts or customized printings can also be created to fit specific needs. For details, write or phone the office of the Kensington Special Sales Manager: Attn. Special Sales Department, Kensington Publishing Corp., 900 Third Ave., New York, NY 10022. Phone: 1-800-221-2647.

Library of Congress Control Number: 2049932266

ISBN-13: 978-0-8065-4329-1

First Citadel Hardcover Edition: July 2024

ISBN-13: 978-0-8065-4331-4 (ebook)

10 9 8 7 6 5 4 3 2 1

Printed in the United States of America

Contents

Foreword

I FIRST MET DEAN BUTLER WHEN I WAS, AS WE SAY ON THE PRAIRIE, "a sprig of a girl." I'd been told by Michael Landon that the role of Almanzo Wilder had been cast and in a few years' time, I (as Laura) would have a husband.

Well, I was immediately flooded with all sorts of emotions. Curiosity mixed with anxiety but above all, excitement at the prospect of growing up while getting to play, as I had read in Laura's books, one of the great love stories of all time.

The day came for Dean and me to meet. I'm still not sure what I was expecting but it was definitely not the grown-up MAN who stood in front of me. I was a gawky, goofy teenager, still growing, and here was this tall handsome guy who DROVE A CAR!!

I hadn't even been on my first date yet. I wasn't even shaving my legs yet and this guy had clearly been shaving his face . . . for years!

All my anxiety, curiosity, and excitement immediately turned into intimidation as I wondered how I was going to "fall in love" with this grown-up person. Well, all that anxiety and worry was absolutely for naught. Dean could not have been kinder, sweeter, or warmer.

FOREWORD

Dean was also so eager to please. He was eager to please Michael Landon and Kent McCray, our bosses, but he was also eager to please the rest of us. Especially me. So much so, that I could feel it, and it disarmed me immediately. I knew deep down, with Dean, that I was safe and nothing untoward would ever happen.

I knew it even if sometimes my very young self lost sight of that for a moment or two as I emotionally navigated our characters' courtship, romance, marriage, and the birth of our children all while still not being old enough to date or shave my legs or get my ears pierced. All that happened when I turned eighteen, but still, in so many ways, I was very immature and, consequently, I could sometimes be a bit snippy toward Dean. Unfairly so. But what can I say, I was just so young.

Well, I'm not so young now and looking back, I am amazed by how gently and consciously Dean approached our on-screen romance and me. I don't know any other actor who had to deal with playing a romantic relationship with such a young leading lady. In fact, I don't think that relationship could be filmed at all these days. But that's a story for another time.

This is about Dean and his integrity and kindness. His talent and good humor. His gentleness and strength. I am so honored to have been asked to write this foreword. It is my hope that once you read this book you will come away knowing a bit more of the Dean I know, and you will understand why I am so blessed to call him my friend.

—Melissa Gilbert

"**O**H MANLY . . . !"

I roll my eyes and start to laugh at the familiar sound. I turn to my left and there, once again, is Dean Butler standing at the autograph table, with his ever perfect posture, surrounded by a group of positively giddy middle-aged women.

Someone has once again invoked his romantic TV nickname, descended from the long-ago term of affection used by author Laura Ingalls Wilder for her beloved husband Almanzo. They say the real Almanzo Wilder was quite handsome. I really don't know, but Dean certainly is.

And apparently no one is ever going to let him forget it.

Certainly not today's group. Yes, today they're close to my age, women who clearly grew up watching the show in its first run. But the ages vary. I've seen much younger women who were not born when the show first aired, the rerun generation, staring at Dean with the same breathless, elated look.

It's HIM. The man they've adored since girlhood, their first love.

Dean, possessed of an iron determination to remain gracious, no matter how embarrassing the situation, nods and smiles.

Dean has always been great with the fans. Charming, patient, happy to answer seemingly any question. Modest and unfazed by the fuss people make over him.

Except when this happens.

Slowly, the color rises up from his neck into his face. Being as fair skinned as he is, there's just no hiding it. Then, some of the women sigh and begin to blurt out things like, "He's STILL gorgeous!"

And once again, Dean Butler blushes.

Not just slight pink either. I've seen the poor man go red as a beet.

Of course, this only drives the women crazier.

I myself am always torn between feeling my heart break in sympathy for him and laughing hysterically.

But I have to ask, who is this man, who after FIFTY YEARS since the run of our show, can still inspire such adoration? And who is this man who, after all these years of this sort of carrying on, is still modest enough to blush?

Can he really be that innocent? He certainly was when I met him way back in 1979. He joined our cast to play the long-awaited husband of Laura Ingalls. I'm not sure we really gave him a proper welcome. (I feel kind of bad about that now. Sorry, Dean!)

But Melissa Gilbert and I were, well, a couple of snotty teenage girls. Teenage girls who had grown up in Hollywood, in show business, in show business FAMILIES at that. And Dean . . . hadn't. He was new to the business. And to us, seemingly new to Planet Earth. Although he was several years older than us, he seemed younger somehow. Sadly, I have to say, we kind of "gave him the air" back then, rolling our eyes at his wide-eyed naïveté.

Now, of course, it's been talked about endlessly that Melissa G, at the time, was terribly freaked out about having to kiss Dean. As experienced as she was in Hollywood and show business, at fifteen she was still completely inexperienced when it came to boys. Also, her mom insisted on watching. *Ewww.*

But to me, it seemed they could not have picked a less threatening, more innocent and adorable creature to do the job. I didn't know that he'd already played THE boyfriend in the TV movie of Judy Blume's *Forever*. It was as if he was destined to be everybody's first love.

Years later, I noticed this pattern. I asked him about it. "Let me see if I have this right. You were Michael in *Forever*, Almanzo on *Little House*... then GIDGET'S MOONDOGGIE, Buffy the Vampire Slayer's DAD, and then you went to Broadway where you were ... Rapunzel's Prince??? You were THE GUY. The primary male relationship to ALL of these beloved female characters? That's a rather oddly specific career trajectory, don't you think? Was this a PLAN?"

He assured me it wasn't. I believe him. Who would come up with a crafty scheme to steal girls' hearts like that? Certainly not this guy. But how has he managed to remain unsullied by Hollywood, still able to approach the world with a little bit of that wide-eyed wonder we saw all those years ago?

Now you finally get to find out. I can tell you this book is a great read. But ... *shhhh*, don't tell Dean I said that. He'll just blush.

—Alison Arngrim

Introduction
Prairie Man Begins

IT'S RAINING HARD OUTSIDE. SOUTHERN CALIFORNIA IS ON THE RE-ceiving end of an unusual and intense "atmospheric river." Even if it wasn't time to write, the patter of the rain on the roof might wake me up.

But it *is* time to write. It is precisely 5:16 AM on Tuesday, January 10, 2023. I'm in front of my computer, ready to begin a new adventure. The house is quiet; Katherine is asleep, as is Benny, our one-year-old Cavachon.

This is going to be my time to commune with my keyboard and my memories. I have given myself six months to write this book, and I've planned out a schedule. I will write every morning, starting before dawn even as the days grow longer. Until July 1—my deadline—there will be no packing, no long drives, no airports, and no hotels. This is an adventure that will unfold entirely at this dining room table, my fingers on the keyboard doing something I thought I would never do: write a memoir.

I am quiet and purposeful. Not quite quiet enough: when I start the coffee and turn on the lights, Benny appears to investigate what is going on so early. Benny issues a low protective bark to let me know he's concerned and scratches the door to go outside. I curse under my breath. This is *my* time, Benny. Didn't you get the memo? I've got a book to write! Will Benny let it happen as planned? If the last year has taught me anything, probably not. That, of course, will be part of the adventure. It suddenly occurs to me that Laura Ingalls Wilder wrote nine *Little House* books, all of them without a computer. She almost certainly had more distractions than I do, and if she hadn't persevered, I wouldn't be writing this book.

I can cope with Benny. I take a few sips of dark roast, step out into the rain with Benny, and smile as he does his business and races back indoors. I dry us both and watch as our pup heads back to snooze on the bed.

Now, my time.

There are classes and courses to help you write a memoir. I'm sure those are great for the right sort of person, but that's not how I work. I'm just jumping in, as I've done so often in my life. My spontaneous decisions haven't always worked out (as I'll explain), but I believe this one will. There are two reasons for my confidence. One, I have a contractual obligation to the publisher. Two, the deadline I've imposed on myself. I can't overstate the importance of having deadlines—especially with real consequences in place for not meeting them. You must put yourself in the position of the legendary NASA Flight Director Gene Kranz. As Kranz says in Ron Howard's *Apollo 13*, "Failure is not an option."

I like writing about other people. I've done it for documentaries, for entertainment, and for biographical features. I'm fundamentally curious about human beings, and I like to tell stories. Like most people I've written short blurbs about myself for resumes and bios. That's a necessity in this business. People need to know you have the experience and insight to deliver for them. Writing about myself in a format like this is different. I tried keeping a diary as a boy but couldn't stick with it. Now, I have a deadline to keep so I must begin. It is awkward and uncertain, but it is also exciting.

I'm writing on a Mac. I've had Macs since the first Apple personal computer appeared in 1984, forty years ago. I have never been a good typist, or a particularly good speller. I love the way computers make writing into an endlessly forgiving process, one where my constant stream of typos can be corrected with the touch of a button. My high school and college papers had been smeared with Wite-Out (if you're under forty, you may need to look that up). The computer's capacity to identify and fix mistakes as if they had never happened seemed like magic, and I love writing even more. Now, the software can intuit the words I'm struggling to write and correct my spelling as I go. I'm setting off on this project with the most sophisticated technology in human history.

I've been writing on computers for forty years. Go back forty years before the first Mac appeared, Laura Ingalls Wilder was still writing her books on yellow tablets in longhand. That's not so very long ago. I know, candidly, that if I had to scribble this out in longhand, I would not write a memoir. In that case, failure *would* be an option. I'm grateful it isn't.

With my indispensable keyboard, I'm going to share reflections on my life. I'll touch on noteworthy events and influences; give insight into personal, intimate, and professional relationships; and explore some family history. This is also, of course, a book about a time gone by in American television, and in the coming pages, I'll share my recollections and experiences about some of the most remarkable people whose work ever appeared on the small screen.

As I sit here to write—it's still dark and rainy outside—I realize you'll learn more about me than I ever wanted anyone to know.

I'm hoping this book will not only offer a deeper understanding of Dean Butler but reveal the lives and influences of those who shaped him. The truth is that I am everyone I've ever met. I think that's largely right. A big part of this project is telling the story of those interactions. Some names you will know, some you will wish you knew; some have been with me every step of my life, while others shaped me unknowingly through the sheer force of their talent and accomplishments.

A book like this relies on a good memory—and people to help you remember! A memoir also relies on sound judgment. We've all read (or at least heard about) celebrity memoirs that share too much. It's easy to generate more heat than light, and to hurt a lot of people unnecessarily to sell books. At the same time, readers deserve an honest, intimate account of a life. I believe I'm at a place to thread that needle. I am at my core a private person. I won't be sharing every detail of my life. At the same time, I'm shaped by the totality of my experiences. So, in a very real sense, you will get all of me.

The first memory I'll share is just a few years old.

It was a beautiful late spring Midwestern morning in 2017. After addressing a group of some three hundred third and fourth graders (and their parents) at Frankenmuth High School in Frankenmuth, Michigan, I was backstage collecting my things; I had a few minutes before a public breakfast and a second speech.

The children weren't supposed to make their way to the make-shift dressing room that had been set up for me. Somehow, one determined little girl snuck her way back, and poked her head around a curtain. She had tears in her eyes. She was freckle-faced and strawberry blonde, and she wore a smock dress not unlike those worn by pioneer girls on television. She looked incredibly fragile as she looked up at me. She opened her mouth, but before she could say anything, her big blue eyes overflowed with tears.

I froze. I didn't know the cause of this emotional outburst; I wondered if I should call a teacher. This little person's body language made clear that whatever was going on, she was going to tell me all about it.

"You didn't call on me to ask my question," she sobbed. The emotion of this sweet nine-year-old was desperately genuine. I pulled up a chair and sat down so we could be face to face. I've had many of these quiet encounters with *Little House on the Prairie* fans through the years, but rarely with one so young and so overwrought with emotion.

"I'm sorry I didn't call on you. What would you like to ask?"

She wiped her eyes, managed to catch her breath, and then, very directly asked a simple question. "Do you have any regrets?"

I wasn't quite ready for that one. In the moment, I replied, "Of course, I have regrets."

Who doesn't have regrets? As I looked at this little girl—whose name I don't remember but whose question I will never forget—I realized that she was very serious. *Little House* had gone off the air twenty-five years before she'd been born, but my answer mattered desperately to her. My mind swirled: I have a mental litany of "woulda coulda shoulda" moments that go back to when I was this child's age. Now, I was sixty-one. It would have been wildly inappropriate to unload decades of regrets about my family, my relationships, and my career.

The right words came in the nick of time. "Of course, I have regrets, but *Little House on the Prairie* isn't one of them."

I meant what I said to that girl, and I mean it now as I sit to write. This memoir will be organized around a unique association and career in television that has defined me for nearly half a century. It is a connection that has put me in homes in every large city, small town, and rural farm across the country—and around the entire world. During the window of time that I was most active as an actor, network television was truly the most awesome content delivery technology on Planet Earth. Television was culture's shared experience. The Internet allows each of us to curate our own media experiences; we watch "our shows" at a time of our choosing, not a network's. That's progress, but what's lost is the remarkable unifying power of a shared, simultaneous, nearly universal television experience.

Though I appeared on television before and after, I am defined by my role as Almanzo Wilder. I am writing this book now because I am finally ready to write it—and because the fiftieth anniversary of the show's debut on NBC is rapidly approaching. (I am far from the first *Little House* cast member to write a memoir, and I may not be the last. I am, as I'll discuss later, the first *male* on-camera cast member to write a book. How important that is will be for you to decide as you read further.) This memoir is my contribution to the fiftieth anniversary, and it is written with immense gratitude at having been a part of something so indelible, so loved, and so admired.

This memoir is also the extended, and perhaps overdue, answer to the "Frankenmuth question."

One last note—no one should write a memoir alone. Or maybe someone should, but not me. I'm grateful that many of my living *Little House* family members and others have agreed to participate in this project. They've shared their perspectives with me in conversation, and you'll be hearing from them throughout this book. Thank you to Melissa Gilbert, Alison Arngrim, Trip Friendly, Susan Sukman McCray, William Anderson, Sam Haskell, and Rick Okie—and so many others!

The rain has stopped, for now, and Benny is ready for an actual walk. I'll get to it.

Thank you for taking this journey into the past with me.

CHAPTER 1

"I Come of Sturdy Stock"

WHEN I REMARKED TO THAT LITTLE GIRL IN MICHIGAN THAT *Little House* wasn't one of my regrets, her face transformed. It was like a switch had been thrown. That's all she needed to hear. That beaming child stepped forward and wrapped me in a hug. I was touched by her genuine emotion, but her question about regrets was a big one. What do we *do* with our regrets? They can inspire us or shatter us, that much I knew; at least in part, they define us.

As I sit to write this first chapter, the first regret that comes to mind is the entire bag of Peanut M&Ms I ate after dinner yesterday. I had more than one trip to the bathroom last night, searching for Tums and other stomach remedies. Overindulgence meant that 5:00 AM came even earlier than it normally would. That might seem like an unnecessary "overshare," but I know that a voracious sweet tooth runs in my family. And family is where this chapter needs to start.

I am a fifth-generation Californian. That's unusual in Los Angeles, where it often seems like everyone has come from somewhere else to pursue their dreams here. My family has been in the Americas since the seventeenth century. You're not reading my memoir for genealogy, of course. But my family history has shaped my life in ways it has taken me years to understand, and it is a vital part of my story. My family history also parallels that of the real-life man behind my most famous role, and that's a good place to start.

Almanzo James Wilder's family arrived in North America in the 1630s. My earliest American ancestors arrived in that same decade. Almanzo's father, James, was born near Milton, Vermont, in 1813. His parents, Abel and Hannah, eventually moved their family to the Salmon River Valley, two miles from the village of Malone in the state of New York. In 1840, James bought the land on Stacey Road and built the farm where his son Almanzo was born in 1857. That farm, which I have visited many times, still exists today as a historical landmark.

To search my own family history, I don't have to go far. Three steps from my dining room table, an old, brown book sits on a shelf. Titled *Genealogy and Recollections*, it was written by my great-great-grandfather Albert Alfonso Moore. Hard bound on heavy bond paper, the book was privately printed in 1915. I own one of only a dozen surviving copies.

A.A., as my great-great-grandfather was known, wanted to share family history with his living descendants. He also cast a keen eye on the future, hoping that those born long after he was gone would take an interest in the stories he shared. A.A. opens his book with words I know will resonate with those who have loved *Little House on the Prairie*. Laura Ingalls Wilder and my ancestor each had similar hopes:

> *I, Albert A. Moore, first of three of that name, write this*
> *for my descendants, by reason that, as I judge, they should*
> *know more fully who they are and of what lineage, and*
> *learn somewhat of the part taken by their ancestors in the*

*fine, fierce, stirring days of old, and the hardship and peril
they endured in building the commonwealth.*

The *Little House* books, as much as any other works of American literature, have given millions of modern readers insight into the "fine, fierce, stirring days of old." Laura Ingalls Wilder is among a select group of writers who have captured the hardship and peril our ancestors endured. I imagine at most only a few hundred family members have read my great-great-grandfather's words—a tiny fraction of those impacted by the *Little House* stories. Yet these accounts have so much in common. One small commonality is that they have each shaped my life.

I had never read the *Little House* books or seen a single episode of the *Little House* series when I began the meetings, readings, and hopeful imaginings that would bring me to Big Sky Ranch in Simi Valley on May 22, 1979, for my first day of shooting as a member of the *Little House on the Prairie* cast.

When I climbed onto the bench seat of the buckboard and took up the reins for my first shot, I had never driven a team of horses. I knew nothing about the real life of the man I was playing or the man who was responsible for putting me into this incredible position. I came into Michael Landon's world on that day with a clean slate. My slate wouldn't stay clean for very long. In less than an hour, I had nearly driven the team of horses into a tree and then asked a question that Michael heard not as the nervousness of a young actor on his first day but as a challenge to his judgment and skills as a director. Michael laughed off nearly killing the horses as a problem that could be solved using my double, Danny Doucette.

A few minutes later I innocently asked him if my first scene was "good enough?" His response put my world in slow motion.

"I've only been doing this for twenty years. How the (expletive) do I know?"

We had literally been laughing moments before, and in asking that question I felt like I got sucker punched. It caught me completely off guard. His answer told me many things, but in no uncertain terms and tones he made it clear that when he said, "Cut. Print," that was it. He was telling me that he did not negotiate with actors on performances. Viewed in more generous terms, Michael was telling me to trust him. I wish he'd just said, "I won't ever let you look bad." Actually, he did say that to me at some later point, and it softened the sting of the first lesson, but the memory of that initial rebuke, at a moment of enormous vulnerability, stuck with me through the next five years and for many more years after that.

It was an amazing coincidence that literally one hundred years earlier, in 1879, the real Almanzo Wilder arrived in Dakota Territory with his brother Royal to establish their first homesteads. It was during that first year, while working their claims, that he was first noticed by thirteen-year-old Laura Ingalls who, as she wrote it many years later in *By the Shores of Silver Lake*, was more interested in the pretty team of Morgan horses than in the man who drove them.

There are some fun parallels between Almanzo and Laura and Melissa Gilbert and me.

The real Laura Ingalls was born on February 7, 1867. She was 5' tall with brown hair and blue eyes. Almanzo Wilder was born just under ten years earlier on February 13, 1857. At his full height he stood 5' 8", weighed 150 pounds, and had a tan complexion, brown hair, and brown eyes. Almanzo was just under ten years older and eight inches taller than Laura. They were both born under the sign of Aquarius.

When I met Melissa, I had just celebrated my twenty-third birthday on May 20, stood 6' 1" and was 180 pounds with fair skin, strawberry blonde hair, and blue eyes. Melissa was 5' 3", had turned fifteen just two weeks earlier, and couldn't have weighed more than 110 pounds. She had fair skin, hazel eyes, and auburn hair. I was just under eight years older and ten inches taller than Melissa. We were both born under the sign of Taurus.

Contrary to her character's interests, I came to sense relatively quickly that Melissa herself had no desire to deal with me on any level, even as the scripts called for her to be head over heels infatuated with Almanzo from the moment she laid eyes on him.

"Looking back at our relationship now," Melissa told me recently, "it couldn't happen on television today."

I tell you; it was tough going forty-five years ago. At the time I knew nothing of the scope of adoration that existed all over the world for this homage to family life in the 1800s, and I had very little knowledge of my own family's pioneer history that took place just over two hundred years before my arrival on the *Little House* set.

Another excerpt from my grandfather's book:

> *Captain James Moore was born in Maryland in the year 1756.* [I was born in 1956.] *James Moore settled in Virginia on the banks of the Kanawha River. He took part in the expedition to Illinois in 1778 under the command of Colonel George Rogers Clarke, in which it is generally supposed James served in the commissary department. He was adventurous and daring in disposition. James, with his companions, reached Kaskaskia in Illinois in the fall of 1781. The next spring, he settled at Bellefontaine. It was supposed when these immigrants left the country east of the Alleghenies that little danger need be feared from Indians. It was not long, however, before the savages began to make trouble, and James Moore was elected captain of the company which came to be raised for the protection of the colony.*

(I want to be clear that *savages* is my ancestor's word, not mine. As many *Little House* fans know, there's been controversy about the way Laura Ingalls Wilder depicted Native Americans. Times and circumstances change, and language we once thought acceptable becomes less so. I will say that A.A. Moore, like Laura herself, grew up hearing stories about pioneers who were killed by Native Americans. It was a much more brutal time than most of us can imagine, and the language reflects an awareness of that brutality.)

If I close my eyes, I can see the room where my great-great-grandfather wrote those words more than a century ago. The house he built in 1906 still stands on my family's ranch.

Seven generations of my family have gathered there, and gather there still to celebrate, commune, and remember. Family weddings, Fourths of July, Easter Sundays, cousins' weekends— my relatives and I treasure our time at the place we simply call "the ranch."

In 1979, I became part of a timeless, beautiful story, set in America's romanticized past, as the personification of a farmer and horseman named Almanzo Wilder. Were it not for the woman he married and their daughter, Rose Wilder Lane, Laura and Almanzo's lives, separately and together, would've likely been lost to dusty footnotes in history. I am not a religious person, but I have been blessed, both by the knowledge of my family and by my creative bond to Laura and Almanzo's family history.

The house in which Albert Alfonso wrote of my ancestors was built with wood from an older disassembled family home a few miles to the east. As often as I can, I sit at the old desk where he would've sat more than a century ago. It is a good room for writing; the ceiling is high, and there is an imposing stone fireplace on the south wall. On the far side of the room there are large picture windows, with a view to the northwest. On clear days, you can see the Bay Bridge and the skyscrapers of the City. A.A. wouldn't have seen the bridge or the Salesforce Tower, but he would have seen the familiar fog resting on the Golden Gate and the gentle curves of Mt. Tamalpais. I imagine him looking there for inspiration, then turning back to continue his introduction.

> *When my children shall learn of the sterling character and rude simplicity of the lives of the pioneers, and their unnoted deaths, and graves now in the main forgotten; as descendants of a passing folk, their modest pride should be, that they came from sturdy stock. So, too, in hardship that must come, let them remember that their forefathers slept in the woods, struggled with wild beasts, fought with Indians, French and English; making their clothing, killing their meat, raising their food from the soil, making their candles, living without stoves, lamps, matches, breakfast foods, tinned goods, telephones, sewing machines, railroads, steamboats, telegraph, gas or electric light and power, motor cars; mainly, without any of the helps now deemed necessities, and thus realize that hardship does not of necessity make for unhappiness, but makes for character, sturdy independence, morals, love of home, family and country.*

While Laura Ingalls Wilder would have said it in a more accessible way (and without quite such a whopper of a run-on sentence), I don't think she could have said it any better. A.A. Moore's reminder to his descendants is a reminder that resonates. Hardships do come in this life, but our ancestors had it harder.

I like that phrase my great-great-grandfather uses: "modest pride." It's almost an oxymoron; modesty and pride are usually framed as opposites. For me, that phrase is a reminder that while I shouldn't believe my ancestors were better than anyone else's, I can and should also be inspired by their tenacity and their accomplishments. I am grateful for all the tenacity and struggle of A.A. and my other forebears; I am a beneficiary of so much hard work and sacrifice.

My grandfather taught high school. My grandmother was a member of the Garden Club of America. Both of my grandparents were fortunate to have had trust funds to support their family. The Roedings, my maternal grandmother's people, had made their money in investments and farming. A.A. Moore (my maternal grandfather's grandfather) had made his fortune as a successful lawyer in San Francisco. The Roedings and Moores set aside what they could, not so their descendants could live in pampered luxury, but so that we could have two things that, historically, are very rare: opportunity and security.

Recently, the media has been obsessed with "nepo babies" in the entertainment industry. There's a critical examination of just how many young stars are themselves children or grandchildren of famous actors. My parents were certainly not entertainers. I am the only professional actor in my family. Still, I might not have enjoyed what success I did had it not been for the resources my family had. I certainly didn't grow up in the lap of luxury; frankly, by my generation, the bulk of the wealth that my family had made in the nineteenth century was gone. There was enough money, though, to make it possible for me to pursue my dreams. As my grandmother put it, there was enough for us to say we were "comfortable."

"Comfortable" is the word that first comes to mind when I think about my childhood. Our lives were comfortable. We lived in nice houses, homes that were kept clean and well-furnished. The refrigerator was always full; the lawn always mowed. Our neighbors enjoyed that same level of comfort. There was a great deal of focus on outward appearance—just as the house needed to be tidy, my brother and sister and I needed to be well-groomed and presentable. To some, this might sound banal and superficial. In my family, it was less about how we looked and more about what we were taught was our highest priority: making *other people* comfortable.

Manners were the key to making other people comfortable.

My lessons in manners started early. It started with the handshake. I couldn't have been more than six when I was first taught how to greet someone. I was to stand up straight, look them in the eye, offer my right hand, and say "How do you do? My name is Dean Butler." This greeting was how every first encounter was supposed to begin. My family taught me the precise grip to use when shaking hands—neither excessively limp nor overly forceful. I was told that the response from the other person would be to repeat the phrase, "How do you do? I'm (whoever they were)."

I was taught that this was how nice people spoke and behaved. Acceptable alternatives included "It's nice to meet you" or "It's a pleasure to meet you," but I always went with "How do you do?" I still do use the phrase, all these years later, even though I have noticed that a great many people do not repeat the greeting. I've also expanded my definition of what constitutes "nice." Not everyone shares the same definition of manners or the same focus on creating "comfort." For that matter, not everyone defines "comfortable" the same way.

By the time I was twelve, I was a skilled host. When a friend of my parents or a distant relative came over to the house, I was prepared to follow up my "How do you do?" with "May I take your coat?" and "May I offer you a cocktail?" To use A.A. Moore's phrase, I took at least a small amount of modest pride in my own manners, and I was grateful to have them. It was better than being tongue-tied and uncertain!

In the 1980s, I discovered the work of A.R. Gurney. He wrote a series of devastatingly clever plays about what some of my cousins call "Our Kind of People." Upper-middle-class WASPs have a particular language, an obsession with manners, and a set of assumptions that are easy to mock. Gurney did so effortlessly. He also found the humanity and the generosity that was mixed in with all that affectation. (And yes, older generations in my family did have the WASPy nicknames that delighted Gurney and his audiences. I grew up with cousins whom everyone called Muffy, Tubby, and Bunt—monikers these relatives had received as children but carried with them all their lives.)

Yes, we were formal, and in today's world, that formality seems over the top. All I know is that when I meet someone new, the confidence of having a script for how to behave and make conversation is a precious gift.

Manners were also crucial to helping me through school. I was not an excellent student. I didn't have confidence in my intellectual abilities. Though my parents made it clear that they thought I could get better grades than I was getting, they also emphasized that grades weren't the thing they cared about most. "You may not be the smartest person in your class," my mother told me on more than one occasion, "but you will be the best behaved." To some, that might seem an unreasonable obligation. For me, it was, to use this word again, a comfort. Excellent behavior was a goal within my grasp and my abilities. I was grateful to have a high expectation I could meet.

Though I am a fifth-generation Californian, I was not born in my home state but in Prince George, British Columbia. My father joined the United States Air Force, and his first deployment after his marriage to my mother was to Canada. In the 1950s, as the Cold War ramped up, Americans were deeply worried about a Soviet invasion from the north. The fear was that Russian bombers and troop transports would advance quickly over the Bering Strait, cross Alaska (not yet a state), and move down through Canada to attack the United States. In the face of this danger, the Air Force set up a series of radar installations across the far north, hoping to have an early warning of a Soviet attack. The base was just south of Prince George, then and now the "northern capital of British Columbia." The base closed at the end of the Cold War, but thanks to this accident of history, it is where I was born on May 20, 1956.

Occasionally, someone will describe me as a Canadian-American actor. I do not consider myself Canadian; I spent only the first few months of my life there. In the late 1980s, when so much film and television production began to move from Hollywood to Canada, I seriously considered the value of claiming Canadian citizenship. I was and am entitled to it under Canadian law, and there would have been real value in being able to work creatively in Canada as a Canadian. What stopped me was that I knew that if I made that choice, I would've been all alone among my family. Neither of my parents and no other relatives hold that passport. As you can probably already tell, family is a central part of my identity. If my people weren't Canadian, then it didn't make sense for me to be Canadian on my own.

While I don't remember my earliest days in Prince George, I have photos of me as a tiny baby, only a few days old. We were so far north that it was still bitterly cold in late May. What strikes me most about those first pictures is how strikingly young and beautiful both my parents were. If you skip ahead, you'll see a few of those photos—and later, I'll have more to say about the impact of my parents' beauty on my own life.

Like many families, we have certain names that recur repeatedly. (My mother is one of at least five Mariannas in our family history.) I was the first Dean, and so far, I remain the only one. My father picked my name after seeing James Dean in *Rebel Without a Cause*; my parents had gone to see the movie not long after they found out my mother was pregnant. This was James Dean's last film, released a month after his death. The brilliant young actor had been killed in a car accident in September 1955—a few weeks or so after I was conceived.

I don't know if my father hoped that I would become a version of James Dean. If he did, I hope he wasn't too disappointed. James Dean and I share a common profession, but his anguished, tortured performances embody a very different ideal from the one I portrayed. Then again, we are both blonde, and we both spent much of our boyhoods on ranches and farms. And that spot in San Luis Obispo County where Dean was killed? It's only a few short miles from the ranch where my great-great-grandmother Jacqueline, A.A. Moore's wife, spent her early years. Perhaps that's stretching things too far. I am grateful for the name—but I am a long way from a rebel without a cause. I may be confusing the artist with his roles, but rebellion for rebellion's sake? That's just a recipe for making people unnecessarily uncomfortable.

Of course, life has a way of teaching you that to make progress, you sometimes need to get uncomfortable. You may even, when confronted with injustice or prejudice, need to make someone *else* uncomfortable. I was raised in a family of moderate Republicans—people who worked hard and were polite, to be sure, but also people who had benefited from the status quo. I grew up hearing my father speak dismissively of "deadbeats" who didn't pull their own weight, and I often heard him complain that government was too big and tried to do too much. For a long time, I shared his views. Perhaps that was because I really believed as he did; perhaps I was just being loyal to the family I treasured. Either way, as a young man I was often judgmental of people, particularly those who didn't have the work ethic or the manners I had been taught were so important. Time and reflection have softened me.

I've come to believe that the absolutes that I was so committed to in my youth lack nuance. Things aren't as black and white as I thought they were when I was young. At the same time, I'm troubled by the way in which the rest of the world seems more judgmental than ever. We live in a harsh era, where disagreements in good faith are increasingly rare. In my childhood, I learned a lot about manners. In my years as an actor—and later as a producer and documentarian—I learned that manners alone weren't enough. To be successful, you had to do more than make other people feel comfortable, you had to create environments where everyone can win. "Zero-sum" deals where one party gets everything and the other gets nothing only breed resentment and conflict. Life is way too short for that.

After nearly seventy years on the planet, I'm far less certain about most things than I was in my twenties and thirties. The things I'm still as sure about as ever are my love for chocolate chip cookies; Rocky Road ice cream; a cold Diet Coke; Katherine's cooking (especially those chicken thighs); my old Cadillac; and a woman's legs in high heels.

In other words, the important stuff.

In the end, each of us is a product of our time. I was born in Canada only because of the particular circumstances of the Cold War. I was raised in an "old California" family with a very specific set of values, values that reflected their lived experiences. *Little House on the Prairie* told a timeless story but was also very much a product of the era in which it was filmed. The passing years don't always grant wisdom, but they do grant perspective—and gratitude. I look forward to sharing that gratitude and perspective throughout the coming chapters of this book.

CHAPTER 2

Desperately Seeking Superlatives

MY WHOLE FAMILY WAS IN A SMALL TOWN IN THE DEEP SOUTH IN July 1994. My father had had one too many. He wasn't drunk, but he had consumed more than a few glasses of his favorite white wine. Perhaps it was because it was my wedding. Perhaps it was because he was a very long way from home. No one in my family had been to this green, leafy, humid (and very, very southern) city before. It was as culturally alien from coastal California as you could get. Perhaps it was because my bride's family—teetotalling Baptists—weren't touching a drop of alcohol.

Perhaps Dad just needed some help to say the things he wanted to say.

I'll write just a little bit more about that first wedding later. For now, what matters is that at the reception, my father pulled my bride and me aside. In a tone both confessional and conspiratorial, Dad told us that I had been a "love child." (My younger readers may not recognize the term; it means I was conceived before my parents were married.) Today, issues of gestational timing are no cause for embarrassment. That was not true

14

in the summer of 1955, when I was conceived. My mother was only twenty; my father was her second cousin. My parents' romance was controversial enough in our family. A baby outside of wedlock would have been absolutely unacceptable.

Plenty of people get married only after discovering a baby is on the way. The postwar culture in which my parents came of age was forgiving of a child conceived before a wedding, as long as the knot was tied before a baby appeared. That gave couples at least a few months to work with. (It's an interesting family history exercise to look at the birth date of a firstborn child, and then at the dates of the parents' wedding.) My parents were married in plenty of time for me to come "legitimately" into the world on that Canadian Air Force base. For some reason, the impropriety of the timing had clearly stuck with my father for years. I don't know why Dad brought it up at my wedding. I hope it made him feel better to tell me at last.

I spent only the first six months of my life in Prince George. My parents brought me back to the States in early December 1956—sparing me the full brunt of a Canadian winter. I spent the first Christmas of my life in the small town that I still call home: Piedmont, California. Piedmont, nestled in the hills across the bay from San Francisco, is a leafy enclave surrounded on all sides by the city of Oakland. Piedmont was where my mother was born, where her father and many other family members grew up. None of my family live in the Piedmont city limits anymore, but it remains "home."

None of my family had been with my parents in Prince George when I was born. I was the first grandchild on either side, and my appearance in Piedmont for Christmas 1956 was a very happy circumstance, though not one for which I can take any real credit. It was also an exceptionally well-documented occasion. No baby remembers anything of their first Christmas, but I've seen so many photographs from that time that I can almost convince myself that I recollect the festivities.

My mother's immediate family was passionate about Christmas, and my "big reveal" to the clan happened on Christmas Eve, so it's not a surprise that I have always loved the holiday. There's nothing unusual about loving what is, for most Americans, the most celebratory time of the year. In my case, though, planning for Christmas and executing the "perfect Christmas" has been a huge source of comfort, joy, and pride. Some of my loved ones might even describe it as a mild obsession, one that I can trace all the way back to the first December of my life.

The thing about being a firstborn is that you have no buffers. In your earliest years, you have no approximate peer to share your experiences—and help interpret them. Younger children look up to older siblings; older brothers and sisters mediate the world for second, third, fourth (and later) children. It's a common complaint of younger siblings that there are more photographs of the firstborn. That's probably true in my family too, though I haven't done a "face count" in old photo albums. At the same time, the firstborn gets all the scrutiny—and when they are the first of their entire generation on both sides, they get that scrutiny in spades. In large families, the first of a generation carries the hopes and expectations not only of their parents but of grandparents, aunts, uncles, and cousins galore.

I'm not writing a book about birth order, but I am keenly aware that my life would be utterly different if I weren't the firstborn. I love my brother and my sister and their immediate families, but their lives have been very different from mine. Not all those differences are attributable to birth order—but I'm quite certain some of them are. With my father and uncles gone, I who was once the first of his generation am now the oldest man in my family. It hardly seems possible! I suspect a lot of people my age say that.

As already mentioned, my parents are second cousins. Both my mother and father were the great-grandchildren of Friedrich Christian Roeding and his wife, Marianna Lazarus. Marianna is a recurring name in the Roeding family. It is my mother's name, and it was also the name of my father's mother. A Freudian would have a field day with the fact that my father not only married the cousin he met at a family reunion, but he also married the cousin with his own mother's name. Dad wouldn't have cared about anything Dr. Sigmund Freud would have said, and neither of my parents cared about the objections of those who consider second cousins to be too close to wed.

Though I am in some sense a "double Roeding," I know much less about that side of the family than I do about the Moores—my mother's father's people. In some ways, the Moores and the Roedings had quite a bit in common. Both arrived in California in the early 1850s, drawn by the Gold Rush. The Moores came from Illinois—and before that, from Virginia and England. The Roedings came directly from North Germany; one of my very distant ancestors was a medieval mayor of Hamburg.

You didn't pick up this book to read about genealogy—though I will have more to say later about the points where my own family history intersects with that of Almanzo Wilder. The parallels are real to the point of being almost eerie. I do want to point out that family stories and genealogy aren't quite the same. We all have two parents, four grandparents, eight great-grandparents, and sixteen great-great-grandparents. I have two fewer great-greats because of the Roeding "duplication," but you get the idea. Every generation you go back, your ancestors double. Go back several hundred years, and even with cousins marrying cousins, we all have thousands of ancestors. Yet we end up with one last name (maybe two if our parents hyphenate). We also usually know much more about one or two branches of the family tree than about the rest.

I am a Butler because that was my father's father's father's name. In terms of genetic inheritance, I am more "Butler" than "Moore." In terms of *story*—and in the end, family is at least as much about story as it is about genes—it is the Moores and Roedings who made me who I am.

My maternal grandmother, Margaret, was a Roeding by birth and a Moore by choice. (She and my father's mother were first cousins.) No one other than my parents influenced me more than "Peggy," as she was known to all save her direct descendants. We called her "Grandmother"—never "Grandma" or "Granny." I know how that reads to most people: antiquated and formal. It wasn't out of fear or duty that we called her grandmother; it was out of deep affection that bordered on reverence. Peggy Moore has been my moral compass throughout my life. My grandmother died in 1998, living until I was forty-two. It was my great fortune to have her for so long.

My maternal grandmother embodied the best of both Moores and Roedings. The Roedings had been successful in business for generations; they were notably intense, driven, and long-lived. They were also prone to gloomy depressions that made them less accessible, less communicative, and far less appealing to be around. I remember as a boy of seven going regularly to visit my great-grandfather, Henry Roeding (Peggy's father) in his elegant Russian Hill apartment in San Francisco. We called him "Greatpa," and I don't know that he ever spoke a word to me, or my siblings, during our visits. I always peeked into his study and saw him bent over his desk, his fingers carefully entering numbers on his calculator.

The Roedings were, to put it gently, better with numbers than with people. On the other hand, the money they made helped sustain our family for generations. The grandmother I adored was able to do so many remarkable things with her life in part because she stood on a small island of inherited wealth.

According to the great-great-grandfather I cited in the previous chapter, the Moores were "sturdy stock." They were cheerful, outgoing, generous, and far more demonstrative with their affection than the Roedings. Less prone to prolonged bouts of depression, many of the Moores covered their pains and disappointments with alcohol. They transformed into different and far less pleasant people when drinking. My grandfather, Arthur—a beloved and delightful man when sober—drank himself to death at sixty-two. He is one of the reasons I have, for most of my life, been very careful with alcoholic drinks. I know too well the destruction liquor can wreak.

We called my father's mother "Granny M." As I remember her, she was almost comically downcast. When it came to affection, comfort, and abundance, Granny M was a consistent miser with all three. In my childhood, she stayed with us almost every Christmas, all but embodying the stingiest qualities of Ebenezer Scrooge. My father dreaded her visits because each time his mother arrived, she brought back painful memories of his difficult childhood. I think one of the reasons my dad fell in love with my mother was that she was so filled with love and positivity. The contrast between these Mariannas at the center of my father's life couldn't have been more striking. The bright, fun, loving nature of one made the dark, depressed nature of the other even more jarring. By the time one of Granny M's visits was over, my father was reduced to an anxious, stammering mess.

When I was three, my parents had my little brother, Scott. Barely a year after that, my sister, Meg, was born. When you're the first of your generation, you're in the spotlight. When younger siblings come along, that takes off one pressure and creates others. (To be clear: I adore Scott and Meg, and I am proud of them and the lives they have made. Scott and Meg are both grandparents now, and it's fun to see them transition into that time-honored role with such ease and unabashed delight.) At the time they arrived, though, my brother and sister just seemed like a confusing and unwelcome responsibility.

My mother tells the story of being awakened one night by my baby brother's cries. When she went into the nursery to check on him, she found three-year-old me standing by Scott's crib, desperately trying to push my own blanket through the bars to soothe the wailing infant. Mom thought it was adorable that I was trying to comfort my little brother. I don't recall the incident as well as she does, but I do know that I had some sense that this screaming thing was somehow my responsibility. I mentioned earlier that my family is very focused on making other people feel comfortable. That's delightful for guests—but for a little kid, the obligation to comfort can be a confusing burden.

Elementary school was confusing too. My teachers liked me, as I was a well-behaved kid who was eager to please. The qualities that please teachers and grandparents aren't generally the ones that win popularity contests with other kids. To my endless humiliation, by the time I was in second grade I was best known for my penchant for turning bright red at the slightest embarrassment or upset. I couldn't control my face. I would hear "Look at Butler . . . he's getting red," and it was as if someone poured gasoline on me and lit a match. I would bluster and issue empty threats, getting redder by the second. "You . . . you all need to stop being so immature," I'd yell. I might as well have painted a bull's-eye on myself and invited everyone to take a shot at it. I'm chuckling as I write this, but as anyone who has been mocked in childhood knows, when you're going through it there is no humor in it at all. It was devastating.

Over milk and cookies one afternoon, my mother told me that she had had the same blushing problem when she was a girl in elementary school. "They called me 'little red tomato face,'" Mom told me with a tinge of humorous outrage in her voice, "and I would get madder and madder."

The reality that my affliction was built into my genetic code was not reassuring news. I fought back tears. I declared I couldn't live if my whole life was going to be defined by my red face. Mom tried her best to offer comfort. "If you can learn to laugh it off, they'll stop, eventually." That "eventually" was the killer.

When? When I was twenty-five? I was an object of taunting and ridicule, and it was never going to stop.

I couldn't help my red face. What I didn't realize at the time was that there was plenty else I was doing to make things worse for myself.

Writing a memoir can be eye-opening. It's been nearly sixty years since I was a student at Wildwood Elementary School, and it's only now, as I tell this story, that I realize how much of the bullying I endured was a consequence of my own behavior. I've always cast myself as the good guy who was trying to survive the bullies. (Casting directors came to similar conclusions.) I followed the rules. I respected authority. Firstborn and responsible, I knew how to behave—and in elementary school I made it my job to tell everybody else how *they* should behave. I couldn't wait to tell kids they'd made a mistake. Honestly, red face or no, it's no wonder I got my ass kicked regularly! People were trying to tell me to knock it off. To my own detriment and everyone else's annoyance, my certainty that I was right kept me going despite the bullying.

This need to be right extended to my family. I had a lot to say, much of it mistaken. The Moores have an informal family motto: "Often in error, but never in doubt." I lived up (or down) to that. When I was seven, after listening to me expound for a moment, my grandfather told me I was a "fount of misinformation." He wasn't wrong. I remember the sting of his words as he laughed. It would have been so much easier if I could have laughed with him. I couldn't. I just turned red. Again. But I didn't stop talking.

When someone knows they can't control their facial expressions, they'll often joke, "You can tell I'm not an actor." You might think I'm going to tell a story of how I became an actor to learn how to better keep my emotions hidden. That's not what happened for me. Indeed, my face still gives away my emotions. Casting directors saw that instantly—and they found me parts where that transparency would be an asset, not a liability. A lot of people think acting is about learning to hide things. In my case, my career has involved a lot of "not hiding," and doing it on camera.

Acting didn't rescue me from the misery of being a bullied, tomato-faced, know-it-all. Music did that.

I'm not a musician. I can't play an instrument. Very few people in my family can. My grandfather knew to play just one song on the piano: "Mary Had a Little Lamb." He might have considered me a fount of misinformation when I spoke what came into my head, but he beamed with pride when I stood by that piano and sang to the notes he tapped out. It would be years before I realized that I got much more praise for singing lyrics someone else had written than trying to come up with something clever to say.

Music gave me a vision of a more palatable version of myself. The first step came when Mrs. Higgins, my third-grade teacher at Wildwood Elementary, asked if anyone wanted to be in the school choir. I raised my hand, vocalized a few scales in front of the class without being mocked, and that was it—I was in the choir. It was wonderful to be part of a group, working together to create a sound that was bigger than any of us. Singing in that children's choir was my entry point into a lifetime of creative expression, and it happened because I raised my hand. That's how simple it can be to step into your life.

When I went home after school and told my mother the news of my new career in the choir, she probably hugged me and gave me a kiss while offering unconditional support for this new opportunity. Mom never failed to offer a foundation of love, positive support, and affirmation. She offered it when I was a little boy, and she was herself still very young; she's still offering it today. "I loved performing when I was in school," she told me. "You might really like it, too."

Singing in choir (and *on pitch*) gave me an experience I hadn't had before: I could utter words and notes and be greeted with smiles and clapping rather than mockery. I heard the applause as affirmation that I had done a good job. I was speaking and no one was making fun of me! Singing wasn't about singing, though I did love the tunes. Singing was about being heard and being accepted for what I had to say. I had found a home. It was miraculous—and I signed on for the duration.

We all need to be heard. And I needed to be seen for something other than being a good boy. The praise I got from my mother and grandmother for being a "good boy" had no currency with my classmates. Later in life, there is great (and underestimated) value in being a good man, but when you're a kid, it's all about cut and dried superlatives: Most Athletic, Best Personality, Best Dressed, Class Clown, Most Likely to Succeed. I was none of those things. No one praised "Best-Behaved Boy." Kids did not look up to "The Most Obedient Follower of Teacher's Rules." I craved being "best" at something that mattered to my peers.

Superlative categories of success sound silly as we get older, but as you probably know all too well, they are there throughout our lives. Is that pathetic or is it being honest? Maybe it's honestly pathetic? The categories change as we get older, becoming more nuanced as we seek ways to stand out and be seen in a crowded, competitive world. Truth be told, that's part of what this book is all about; maybe I should call it "Desperately Seeking Superlatives."

I was not the best singer in choir. Singing did put me on a creative path—and it also helped me find my first happy superlative. Choir rehearsals were in the school auditorium, and as in most such auditoriums, there were lights and curtains, microphones, speakers, and projectors. I was captivated by the bright lights and the sound that boomed out of the speakers when someone spoke into the microphone. As I've said, my face always gave away my thoughts; in this case, my face helped me find my first calling. Mr. Gordon, our custodian at Wildwood Elementary School, saw me gaping in wonder at the audiovisual equipment—and took the time to ask me if I was interested in learning more.

Mr. Gordon had been in the Marines. We were all a little in awe of him, and his reputation for being able to maintain and fix every possible piece of equipment that could be found in the school. Mr. Gordon was also a stickler for spit and polish; Wildwood sparkled because of his commitment to keeping it clean. When he asked if I wanted to learn more, I was a little intimidated—but I was also excited.

It wasn't long before I found my superlative: I was Wildwood's "AV geek," the kid who was best at operating equipment. I loved my new role. I not only ran all the movies and slide shows in my own classes, but I was regularly called out to run projectors in other classrooms. I had a newfound purpose, and I was useful in the school in a way that other kids weren't. Nearly sixty years later, and I still love tinkering with machinery. When you're an actor on set, you learn quickly you don't get to touch, much less operate, the expensive equipment that captures your every look and utterance—but I always did what I could to understand the specific technology our craftspeople used. When I became a producer and a documentarian, I got the chance to play with some of that wonderful technology. I still work with those tools today. More often than not, it brings back the excitement I first felt when Mr. Gordon first taught me to "thread a projector."

"AV geek" was preferable to "tomato-face," but my prowess with projectors wasn't enough to stop the teasing and bullying. Each day at school, I felt as if I were walking through a social minefield—humiliation always only a second away. It left me in a state of constant anxiety. Being good at sports would have stopped the ridicule. Athletes are safely atop almost any school's social hierarchy. My father loved sports, and he would have loved it if his oldest had been good with a ball and a bat. I longed for Dad's approval as much as I longed for the bullying to stop. It was not to be.

I tried all the sports. I was mediocre at best. I'd drop passes, travel with the basketball, get hit in the face with a softball in *right field*. Nobody hits to right field, which is why I was there, but one day in practice, Coach sent a pop fly my way. The ball sailed over the top of my mitt and struck me right in the nose. I was already famous for my red face; now I had blood and a pug nose to add into the mix. The teasing was more merciless.

I recognize that I grew up with considerable privilege. There are far worse things than being mocked for being an obedient, clumsy, know-it-all who blushed easily. There are plenty of other men who grow up haunted by the ways in which they couldn't make their fathers proud—at least not in the ways they thought their fathers wanted. And hey, at least I got to be Wildwood's wunderkind of AV equipment. It was a small superlative, but a valuable one. I did have choir. Yet I can't pretend that what I went through in school wasn't painful. More importantly, remembering the unhappiness I endured leads me to remembering how I was able to find a way out of all that misery. Persistence paid off.

The tide began to turn at the end of 1971. I was a sophomore at Piedmont High School, the same school my mother and grandfather had attended. My favorite sport was basketball, even though I was nowhere near good enough to play for the team. Besides, the Piedmont Highlanders were projected to win the league. We had an elite squad, and I was happy just to root for them. Mr. Cochran was my geometry teacher and ran the scoreboard at games—he was a stout man with an Oklahoma drawl. Like many of the best teachers, he was a shrewd observer of young people and keenly aware of what they needed most.

"It's going to be a great season, Butler," Mr. Cochran said to me one day after class. "How would you like to be our official scorekeeper?"

I had no idea what he was talking about, but I caught on quickly. Every high school sport has scorebooks that allow referees, coaches, players, and press the opportunity to see a snapshot of the game. Today, the score is kept on electronic devices, but for decades, it was kept in a paper book with a number 2 pencil. For basketball, the scorekeeper would record field goals, free throws, rebounds, and fouls. (Later, it would include assists and steals.) It's not hard to do—if the scorekeeper pays close attention to the action on the court and doesn't get easily distracted. Maybe Mr. Cochran saw I had an eye for detail. Or maybe he just knew I didn't have many friends who would distract me during games. Either way, it was a fun way to be involved in a major event for our basketball-mad school.

When I showed up for the first home game of that 1971–72 season, I arrived an hour before tip-off and joined Mr. Cochran at the scorer's table to learn how to do the book. It was fun, and once the players came out on the court for warm-ups, much more so. Our gym could hold maybe seven-hundred and fifty people, and it was packed to the rafters. I watched intently as each head coach came to the scorer's table to confirm their starters; I heard the horn signaling that tip-off was imminent. I thought briefly of how many members of my family had sat in this gym: my mother, my aunt Alison, my uncle Stanley, and my grandfather. Piedmont High was in our blood, but no one in the family had sat where I was sitting.

Mr. Cochran turned to me, a broad grin on his face. He pointed to the silver microphone in front of us. In that broad, slow drawl I've never forgotten, he posed a question to which he already knew the answer: "So, Butler, who's going to introduce the starting lineups?"

If this moment had been a movie, the crowd would fall silent, and the gym would go dark. A single overhead spotlight would shine on the microphone. I looked at the mic and then back at Mr. Cochran. I could feel my face flush. I was still staring at

Mr. Cochran when the referee walked over. I turned; he looked me in the eye and said, "Are we gonna do this, young man?"

Mr. Cochran nodded to the mic. I leaned toward it, took a deep breath, and . . . the words came. "Good evening, ladies and gentlemen, and welcome to Piedmont High School for tonight's game between your Highlanders and [whoever it was we were playing]. Let's meet the starting lineups."

Who was this talking? I sounded so . . . so self-assured. As I spoke each starting player's name, the crowd in the gym cheered; the kids who had bullied and teased me for years responding enthusiastically to the sound of my voice. My world changed in a single instant, as worlds somehow will. On that November night more than fifty years ago, I stepped into a new phase of my life. Everything that has happened since can be traced back to that moment when Mr. Cochran pointed me to the microphone.

I remained the announcer for Piedmont High School varsity and junior varsity basketball games until I graduated. I loved every minute of it. Suddenly I had an identity that had nothing to do with my red face. In the affirmation I got from announcing games I began to find a more relaxed sense of humor. I could laugh at myself.

Later in that same sophomore year, I got another window into my future. Piedmont had strong music, drama, and dance programs. Our 1972 spring production was *My Fair Lady*, chosen as that year's show to take full advantage of the considerable gifts of Jim Kelly, rightly regarded as Piedmont High's most talented performer. As I sat in the balcony of Piedmont's auditorium, I was completely swept away by the dramatic and comedic power of Jim's performance as Henry Higgins. He had the audience in the palm of his hand. During the day, he was just another kid I saw in the hallways—but on stage, Jim was magnetic, charismatic, and larger than life. As I watched Jim sing "I'm an Ordinary Man," I started to wonder: *Could I do that?*

Could I stand on a stage and deliver wonderful dialogue and songs? Could I hold an audience for two and a half hours? Just six months earlier, the idea of commanding that kind of attention would've been unthinkable, but a single season of announcing basketball games had altered my sense of what was possible. Yes, I'd been an object of derision for years. That was the old Dean. Watching Jim as Henry Higgins, I realized I could do what he was doing. Maybe not in quite the same way, maybe not quite as well at first, but I understood viscerally that not only could I bear the spotlight, I craved it.

Joining the choir in elementary school had taught me to sing on pitch. Announcing basketball games had shown me I had a gift for public speaking. Watching Jim Kelly perform Henry Higgins brought it home for me: I wanted to perform. I wanted to sing, I wanted to act, and I wanted to be heard.

Watching the lovely Rebecca Powell play an impressive Eliza Doolittle to Jim's Henry filled me with another important realization: pretty girls might really like a guy who could act and sing. I had already found my confidence, much to my surprise. Now, watching Rebecca, I had the motivation.

CHAPTER 3
Growing Up

I WAS SEVEN WHEN I WAS SURE MY FATHER HAD DIED RIGHT IN FRONT of me.

Dad left the Air Force when I was still tiny. Once back in the Bay Area as a civilian, he delighted in serving as a flight instructor, later joining a flying club where he could rent Cessna 150s and 172s for day and weekend flights. He loved to fly and had quickly accumulated over seven thousand hours at the controls. Dad loved to test his skills—and he was also an inveterate risk taker.

On more than one occasion during our long summers at the ranch, Dad would "buzz" the place on his way home from a pleasure flight or a business trip; he'd fly low, dip his wings, and wave. My brother, sister, mother, and I would rush out of the house when we heard an engine low overhead, stand in the dusty driveway, and wave back.

It was a hot August afternoon late in the summer of 1963, and moments before we heard Dad's plane flying up the canyon, we children had been summoned from the pool to get ready for dinner. The Cessna flew over the house and disappeared behind the treetops. Less than a minute later, we were gathered outside as the little airplane returned as it so often did. It flew lower and slower, and just as the plane came over the pool, the tail of the Cessna clipped the top of one of the huge elms on the far side of the water. The airplane dropped like a stone and banked hard to the right, now at full power as it crashed into the branches of a massive hundred-year-old oak tree.

It's been sixty years, and I still remember the whine of the engine, and the horrible sound of twisting metal and tree limbs snapping. Far more than that I remember my mother's singular scream, crying out our father's name: *Peter!*

My grandfather's first cousin, Allan Starr, owned his own ranch nearby. He had seen my father's plane minutes before the crash, and though he didn't hear my dad go into the tree, my mother's scream told him exactly what had happened. From well over a mile away, he came as fast as he could to help.

As high-octane aviation fuel gushed from the crumpled wings into the branches of the tree, the engine was somehow still running at full power. My grandfather, lit cigarette in his hand, walked toward the scene in wonder. He was presumably numb with shock; one spark from the propeller, the engine, or that cigarette might have set off an explosion that could've killed us all. When Cousin Allan arrived, he ordered my grandfather back while he climbed into the tree to turn off the engine—and determine whether my father was alive. No one could see my dad's condition from the ground. If he was alive, he wasn't moving.

As I would hear repeatedly over the years from every adult who witnessed the crash, everyone thought my dad was dead. My grandmother whisked Scott, Meg, and myself onto the back porch. Aunt Alison—my mother's younger sister—and her fiancé were assigned to drive us home to Piedmont to wait for what everyone assumed would be the worst possible news.

I have blotted out the memory of that hour-long drive home. My aunt remembers that my face was ashen, and that I stared out the window, unable to speak. My siblings compensated for my silence. Scott, who had just turned four, talked all the way about how exciting it was that a "cwane" would need to come and get "da pwane out of the twee." My sister, barely three, apparently thought Daddy was "vewwy silly." It is hard to imagine what I was thinking, but every giggle from my siblings must have been torture. *How would I tell Scott and Meg our father was dead?*

We had been home for only a few minutes when my grandmother called. My father was alive; he had a severe concussion but would recover. My aunt says that it was only then that I broke down in tears of relief, my brother and sister regarding me with confusion and wonder.

The Federal Aviation Administration wanted to cut down the oak tree to recover the wreckage, but my grandfather wouldn't allow it. Just as my brother had guessed, a "cwane" had come and pulled the broken Cessna out, piece by piece. The oak tree that caught Dad's airplane still stands and shelters the family on hot summer days, just as it did on that afternoon in August 1963.

Over the years, I've reflected many times that it wasn't just my father who got lucky that day. Just ten minutes earlier, most of the family had been in the pool right beneath that tree. If the plane had come just moments sooner, or my father had been on a slightly different course, three generations of my family could have been wiped out in a staggering tragedy, all the result of a reckless showboating accident.

I was very young, but my relationship with my father was already complicated. Three months before I watched his plane hit the great oak tree, my father shattered something else.

It was my seventh birthday, May 20, 1963. It was a Monday. We were living on Harvard Road in Piedmont. I was excited: there was a birthday party planned for me that day that included my brother and sister, my maternal grandparents, my great-aunt, and of course my parents. I was just coming to understand that birthdays are very special days. All of a sudden, the normal rhythm of your day is interrupted, and extra attention flows your way. There's wrapping paper, a song, and cake. Not every child grows up innocent and safe and loved, but for fortunate little ones, a birthday is a magical time.

Mom had prepared the party perfectly. There was just one thing missing: Dad wasn't home yet.

Finally! I was watching from the window when his convertible Volkswagen Beetle pulled up at last. Now the party could begin! I ran down the stairs to the street to greet Dad at his car and to look for what I was sure would be something special, waiting for me in the backseat. As I looked hopefully through the window, Dad climbed out of the Beetle.

"There's nothing here for you," he said. Dad's tone was harsh, almost mocking. His words hit like a punch in the stomach.

I was just seven, but I already knew how to cover and bluff. "I wasn't looking for anything," I replied instantly. Embarrassment and shame coursed through me. What a fool I'd been, hoping to find a present in my father's car; I had no choice but to bluff and pretend I hadn't cared. I tried to focus on the presents and cake and cards that were there for me and shrug off what wasn't. "There's nothing here for you" would echo down the years, and shape—perhaps unfairly—a lot of my feelings about my dad.

There's a throughline that connects my seventh birthday with the plane crash three months later. In both cases, because of Dad, I had to pretend. I was acting when I professed not to care that there was nothing for me in his car; I was acting when I held in my terror and shock after watching my father fly into the oak tree. My father didn't intend to hurt me in either instance, but both events were painful, and they were both painful because of his carelessness. Both incidents taught me to hold something back and to figure out how to feign something other than what I was really feeling.

* * *

In the early to mid-1990s, I studied acting for five years with Milton Katselas. Himself a product of the legendary Actors Studio, where he had trained under Lee Strasberg and Elia Kazan, Katselas was a master. His classes were always in demand. I came to him just as I was turning thirty-six, my own career very much in flux. I had made a name for myself as a young romantic lead, but I needed something else in my bag of tricks. If anyone could teach me how to go to my next level, it would be Milton. He had a preternatural gift for exposing the shit that got in an actor's way.

I did dozens of scenes for Milton during my time in his class. I felt the growth, and Milton confirmed that progress during some wonderful critiques, which were always empowering. Then one night after a scene—seemingly out of nowhere—Milton declared, "You have a problem with your father."

He didn't *ask* if I had a problem with my father; he *told* me I had a problem with my father. I told Milton I loved my father. Milton told me I needed to tell my father to "eff off."

"That's never going to happen," I said.

The great teacher shrugged. "Well, Dean, that's the problem with your acting. Do with it whatever you want."

I was conflicted because part of me knew he was right, but as usual, I stuffed it. "Would it be enough to tell *you* to eff off?" I wondered. But I didn't say a word.

I've read a lot of memoirs. I've read about some truly awful parents who torment their children in unspeakable ways. Those horror stories can be haunting, but the stories that stick with me are the ones where the relationships are more nuanced than complex. These anecdotes I've told you about my dad may have you hating him on my behalf, but I want to make clear that there was another side to my father. It is true I never felt safe with him the way my brother and sister did. It is true that I desperately needed his approval nonetheless, and I was crushed when I didn't get it. It is also true that sometimes, in ways that really mattered, that approval did come.

The summer before my junior year in high school, my brother and I spent six weeks together in a summer boarding school. Robert Louis Stevenson School (RLS) is a prep school in Pebble Beach, California, next to Carmel on the Monterey Peninsula. These famously beautiful places are just a two-hour drive south of my hometown of Piedmont. I grew up visiting as often as I could; my aunt still lives in Carmel, and it was where my grandmother and her sister spent their final years.

My favorite older cousin, Tom Bishop, had gone to RLS as a teen, so it was especially exciting to think about walking the same grounds he had trod a few years earlier. RLS is coed now, but it was still all-boys in the early 1970s. It had that prep school formality familiar from movies like *Dead Poet's Society*, *School Ties*, and *Scent of a Woman*. Prep schools at that time were very WASPy places, and that was just fine with me: I identified as a WASP and a prep, and I loved the formality of wearing a coat and tie as often as I could.

Along with all the classes and sports that took place that summer at RLS was the production of *Pudd'nhead Wilson*, a play adapted from Mark Twain's 1894 novel of the same title. It's a comedy, built around plots of racial identity, parental devotion, lost wealth, and murder with a fabulous Indian knife.

I auditioned and won the lead role of David "Pudd'nhead" Wilson. We had three weeks to learn, rehearse, build the sets, and present the play. We rehearsed for hours every day. I was doing the work of an actor for the first time, learning lines and blocking. As the lead, I was on stage for virtually the entire play—and had lots of funny lines. (Saying words Mark Twain wrote made that part easy.) All this effort was for a single performance. Because it was a one-off, the theater was jammed—my mother and father among them.

I knew all my lines and everybody else's too. That would prove useful: at one point, when another actor jumped two pages of the script, I felt sufficiently in command to go back and pick up the jumped dialogue that we needed for the story to track. My mother and father were both proud of me, and I basked in that praise. Many others gave positive affirmation. I knew I had to try this acting thing again.

I soon got my chance. Piedmont's drama teacher, Charles Harris, wanted more than just the "usual theater geeks" to try out for shows. My senior year, he came up with an idea to bring more of us on stage: an evening of sketch comedy called "The Piedmont Pit Players Proudly Present Themselves." The idea was to have students do dramatic and comedic readings, sketches, and other short scenes in a two-act structure.

I signed up to do two acts. I did the classic Abbott & Costello bit "Who's on First" with my friend Brad Howard, and a fifteen-minute section of Hal Holbrook's brilliant one-man show, *Mark Twain Tonight*. I rented a white suit, troweled on old age makeup, and sprayed my hair with white Streaks 'N Tips. Determined to look and sound like the best version of a seventy-something man that a seventeen-year-old kid could create, I ambled slowly into the spotlight. For the first time, I was completely alone on a stage. It was thrilling to speak these extraordinary words and intoxicating to hear people laugh. I didn't know quite what I was going to do with the joy I was feeling, but by now, I knew I wanted more of it.

Mark Twain Tonight is a collection of funny, insightful, and satirical Mark Twain stories that Holbrook adapted over the decades for his live stage show. The show and Holbrook's performance were a towering achievement that delighted audiences for sixty years until his death on January 23, 2021. By the end of his life at the age of ninety-five, Hal Holbrook had become Mark Twain in the American consciousness. Watching his ever-deeper understandings and personalization of Twain's unique humor was to witness a master class in storytelling.

* * *

A few months after my Piedmont High performance, our family drove to San Francisco to see Holbrook himself perform *Mark Twain Tonight* at a theater on Nob Hill. The show was set up in the round, so Holbrook had to play to everyone in the house while only actually facing half the audience at any given time. This wasn't an unreasonable challenge for an actor of Holbrook's skill. He had performed in that setup many times before and would many times again. This night was different. His wireless microphone wasn't working. Since Holbrook could only face half the audience at any one time, the failed mic guaranteed that half his anecdotes and punch lines went unheard. It was a tough night for Holbrook and a disappointing experience for the people in the sold-out theater.

After the show, I made my way to the stage door to introduce myself to Mr. Holbrook. He looked exhausted. I gave him my politest, "How do you do? I'm Dean Butler," and told him that I had loved doing a small portion of his play earlier that year in high school. The great actor looked me straight in the eye and said, "If I had enough lawyers, I'd sue every one of you guys for stealing my work."

I must have looked like a deer caught in a very intimidating set of headlights. "Mr. Holbrook, I'm in high school," I stammered.

Hal wasn't chastened. "All you guys are stealing from me," he snarled.

I had no idea what to say to that. "Thank you, I loved your performance," I said as sincerely as I could, and retreated from the stage door.

I can count on the fingers of one hand the number of times that I have been directly threatened with legal action. This was the most memorable of those few occasions. My face did burn its usual red. It never occurred to me that I was committing theft when I memorized and recited Holbrook's "Slow Train, Long Dog" story. It was a wake-up call to the reality that protecting intellectual property is a very serious business. Even high school productions may need to pay royalties to authors. Hal Holbrook didn't see me as a seventeen-year-old kid; he saw me as someone who was stealing his work, and in some sense capable of harming his business. In a strange way, that was cool and flattering.

Months later, I got my biggest high school role, becoming perhaps the WASPiest Tevye in the long history of *Fiddler on the Roof*. *Fiddler on the Roof*, which starred Zero Mostel on Broadway, is the beautiful and moving story of Tevye the Dairyman and his family—and their fight for religious and cultural survival in the Russian village of Anatevka. The original production was directed by Jerome Robbins (for whom I would perform years later) and produced by Fred Coe and Harold Prince—all Broadway royalty. While that production was fraught with tension (Jerome Robbins was a relentlessly demanding taskmaster), the resulting show made history as the first-ever musical to run more than three thousand performances on Broadway. It won nine Tony Awards and inspired five revivals, as well as the 1971 feature film starring Chaim Topal as Tevye.

With Jerome Robbins not present, Piedmont High School's 1974 production of *Fiddler* had fewer creative tensions than the Broadway production. What we did have was lots of devotion to being the best high school show we could be. Mr. Harris moved heaven and earth to give us the best opportunity to succeed, and we did. *Fiddler* is in some sense a deeply Jewish musical— and I had the sense not to affect any stereotypical mannerisms. (On both sides, one Roeding great-great-grandmother of mine was Jewish, but that would hardly be permission to cross a line into caricature.) In the most important sense, though, *Fiddler* deals with universal themes about love and family. I think Piedmont's drama department handled it well.

We had a four-performance run. I didn't just love doing the show. To my great surprise and gratitude, several Bay Area talent aficionados saw something in my portrayal of Tevye and in my presence on the stage. The late Bay Area advertising guru Donald F. Dorward came up to me after one show. Don was the father of my classmates John and Mary Anne. Mary Anne had played Tevye's youngest daughter Chava. Don complimented me on my performance and said, "When you're ready to take this to the next level, Dean, I'm going to introduce you to Ann Brebner." In the mid-1970s, Ann Brebner was the biggest talent agent in San Francisco, while Don was an enormously respected figure in the community. Both my parents knew Don socially and they both appreciated his interest in helping get me started professionally, if that's what I wanted to do.

Don Dorward became a different kind of father figure for me. If he thought I had a future as an actor, then . . . well, anything was possible. My own father did support me, and he did come to my shows again and again over the course of his life. Years later, after he and my mother had divorced, and I was doing *West Side Story* in Tokyo, Dad flew over to Japan to see me perform—and paid for his ex-wife's plane ticket to do the same. That is part of the story too, and I have never forgotten it. Yet it was Don, not my father, who made it possible for me to imagine myself as a professional actor. It was his push that sent me down the road I would walk for the rest of my life.

My dad died in 2007. I loved him, and I knew he loved me, and I am pretty sure he knew I loved him, but I never had the relationship with my dad that my younger brother and sister enjoyed. When my siblings had kids, Dad became a doting grandfather. His six grandchildren adored him, calling him "Kupuna"— Hawaiian for "old wise one." (Dad had spent much of his youth in Hawaii.) He was a very loving Kupuna, and I was glad to see so much warmth flow out of him so easily and naturally. I know I am not the only firstborn son to have a more complicated relationship with his dad than his younger siblings have. I write this book very conscious that my own sometimes strained relationship with my dad is a central part of my story—and at the same time, that relationship is not the full picture of who my father was. I hope I've struck a balance between candor and kindness. My father deserved both.

I never did tell my father to eff off, as Milton Katselas advised. I never told any authority figures to eff off; even as I grew into adulthood and my career blossomed, my training as the good, polite boy somehow stuck. Eventually, of course, there came a time when that politeness would no longer be an asset. Sometimes, doing the right thing does mean standing up and telling someone to eff off. As it turned out, one of the most meaningful "stand-up moments" of my life would come not long after my father died.

The Motion Picture and Television Fund (MPTF) was founded more than a century ago by Hollywood pioneers Mary Pickford, Charlie Chaplin, and Douglas Fairbanks. The goal was to provide care for aging and disabled performers with the promise of "We take care of our own." At its height of service to the community, the MPTF's beautiful campus in Woodland Hills, California, included beautiful gardens, a small hospital, a movie theater, a pharmacy, physical and mental health facilities, dining rooms, a memory care unit, and independent, assisted, and long-term care living spaces. It was a place to live out one's final years in dignity and comfort, surrounded by peers.

My wife Katherine, about whom I will say much more soon, is of course an actress. Her own mother, Catherine "Cay" Cannon, was a lifetime dancer though not an industry veteran. She was not automatically entitled to be part of MPTF, but a personal outreach from my friend Sam Haskell to MPTF board chairman Jeffrey Katzenberg had made it possible. Sam explained to Mr. Katzenberg that both Cay's son and daughter were longtime industry veterans. The practice of accepting the family of vested industry members was not unusual but, in this case, required a push. Many people retire to the MPTF home while still quite independent, and only gradually transition to higher levels of care. By the time my mother-in-law moved into MPTF, she already needed skilled nursing care.

On January 14, 2009, the entire industry was shocked by the board's announcement that MPTF intended to close its Long-Term Care Unit, cut a third of its staff, and relocate all long-term care residents to other facilities. The announcement set off a torrent of protest by industry families, and an explosion of bad headlines from coast to coast that caught MPTF board members and management completely off guard.

One evening, a few days after the closure announcement, Katherine and I sat in a meeting with two hundred industry families and listened to Dr. David Tillman, the MPTF's chief medical officer, explain the organization's justifications for breaking its promise of "lifetime care" for residents. The tension in the room rose like a tsunami; I could feel the wave of anger ready to break.

I had never been in a room this filled with angry people before. As Dr. Tillman admitted that this was entirely a financial decision, the rage grew palpable and dark. I'll never forget the late David Carradine, a member of one of Hollywood's most famous families and star of the '70s action drama *Kung Fu*, leaping out of his seat. He jabbed his finger at Dr. Tillman. "You are throwing vulnerable people out on the street. You are betraying families that trusted you!"

The tsunami broke. The room erupted, and Dr. Tillman hastily excused himself with shouts of anguish and rage chasing him out the door.

Katherine and I were at the back of the room, sitting with former *Dukes of Hazzard* star John Schneider. We took in the scenes of emotional despair playing out all around us. Then, about five rows in front of us, we saw a woman we didn't yet know but would soon discover was Nancy Biederman. While everyone else was enraged or despairing, Nancy seemed calm—a small group had gathered around her and, with urgency and purpose, were starting a discussion about next steps. Katherine and I stepped into that conversation. Within minutes, we had bonded with Nancy and a handful of other long-term care family members, including Andy Susser, Daniel Quinn, Brandy Alexander, Melody Sherwood, and Richard Steller.

Like us, Nancy had an unaffiliated family member in the Long-Term Care Unit. She too was struggling with panic and rage. She also saw that giving into raw emotion wouldn't be enough. Instead of venting, she was telling us what needed to be done so the MPTF would come to its senses.

This conversation was a tipping point moment for me. I was fifty-two years old, and I had never in my life stood up against "the man." I hadn't done it with Hal Holbrook, or Milton Katselas, or countless directors. I hadn't done it with my father. I was the very polite Dean Butler, the guy you could generally count on to go along with whatever seemed proper or right. Now, with the imminent closure of a care facility that meant everything to my wife and mother-in-law, I had had enough. I was ready to tell someone (figuratively) to "eff off," and risk real repercussions for doing so.

Hollywood is a company town. It is led by people who have risen to great power and fame because of their success in movies and television. Many of those people were the leaders of the MPTF, and for all the right reasons. They were the ones we trusted to take care of our families. Now, we were going to take them on—not to destroy them but to persuade them that the human cost of their error in judgment would be far greater than any money they could save through the closure of the Long-Term Care Unit.

Katherine and I joined Nancy's little group. We soon got assistance and advice from James O'Callahan, Esq., a partner in the law firm of Girardi and Keese (made famous by the Julia Roberts movie *Erin Brockovich*). Together, we launched a two-front war. In public, we led protest marches and found experts to get on television and talk about the deadly consequences of transfer trauma. We tipped off *Variety*, the *Hollywood Reporter*, and state public health agencies about MPTF's missteps with our loved ones. We created scathing web videos that painted the industry's most generous, beloved, and respected philanthropists as heartless men ready to throw vulnerable retirees out on the street to save a buck. The likes of Jeffrey Katzenberg, Steven Spielberg, George Clooney, Michael Douglas, Tom Hanks, and others had to have been shocked. We dared to cast these icons as abusers of the aged.

When the Fund held its annual pre-Emmys fundraising gala in Century City, our group picketed, kept away from the party by the Los Angeles Police Department. The cameras captured me at the front of the protest. I was quoted in the industry papers about our fight to shame MPTF into saving its Long-Term Care Unit:

> *When you look at that party, that may well have cost several millions of dollars to put on all by itself just to raise $4 or $5 million tonight, it's hard to imagine that that kind of effort could not be applied to raising $12 million more per year to save that house.*[1]

While we were out protesting, our lawyers at Girardi and Keese fought the second front of the war. They made it clear that they had no desire to destroy the MPTF, but they teased compelling evidence of MPTF missteps over the years. James O'Callahan made it clear that these revelations would be not just embarrassing but ruinous.

Nancy's strategy paid off. Our two-front campaign worked. The Motion Picture and Television Fund cleansed the organiza-

---

[1] Mikey Glazer, "MPTF Pre-Emmys Bash Picketed . . . From a Distance," *The Wrap*, September 19, 2009, https://www.thewrap.com/mptf-pre-emmys-bash-picketed-distance-7427/.

tion of those who had made these ill-advised decisions. The Long-Term Care Unit was saved. The MPTF leaders got a chance to present themselves as heroes in the disaster story they had created. That was fine with us. What mattered was the home and our families. We didn't need to take the credit.

In its account of the protest outside the pre-Emmy gala, *The Wrap* (an industry paper) wrote, "*Little House on the Prairie* actor Dean Butler rallied a banner-toting, candle-waving crowd of activists."[2] You might not think there's anything remarkable about that account. For me, though, rallying a "banner-toting crowd of activists" went against everything I'd ever been taught.

I was raised in a home with a right-wing father who declared that anyone who picked up a picket sign was, in his memorable and oft-repeated phrase, a "commie, hippie, pinko fag." My mother would wince at his language, and sometimes he would soften it to simply muttering that all protesters were "deadbeats." I didn't want to be thought of as a deadbeat. I didn't want to cause trouble. I didn't want to anger my father. I never protested. Until he was gone.

To be candid, if my father had been alive when the MPTF crisis began, I might have participated behind the scenes, but I doubt I would have stood in front of a protest march. I wouldn't have carried a sign or served as a spokesperson for a small band of activists taking on the powerful. That's hard to admit, but it's the truth. As much as I loved him, for as long as he lived a part of me remained that same small boy, doing his best to hide his feelings.

My father's "There's nothing there for you" wasn't just about a missing present in a car's backseat—it was about a whole world of things of which he disapproved. It took me a very long time to realize that, in so many ways, there was "something there" for me in a world and a life he did not understand.

---

[2] Ibid.

CHAPTER 4

Coming into the Light

YOU KNOW THOSE RARE KIDS WHO BOUNCE THROUGH ADOLES-
cence? The ones who are popular and clear of skin? They are
few and far between, and as you've already probably figured out,
I wasn't one of them. I was a mess from thirteen to seventeen. I
was a mass of surging hormones, with emotions and urges I
could not understand, much less control. I knew on some level
that most kids were going through the same things, but I figured
it had to be worse for me than for anyone else, right? I could
feel it in my bones, hear it in my squeaky voice, and see it in the
mirror every day.

The dead giveaway that I was a human catastrophe was the
acne. The pimples happened from my chest and shoulders up
to my forehead. For most of high school, my face and upper
body looked like a bomb exploded on it every morning. There
was no amount of Clearasil, vitamin A, or tetracycline that could
make it better. (I see fewer kids these days with bad acne—something has clearly gotten better. Pun intended.) The cruelest part
of it was seeing those happy few who glided through puberty
without a single zit or a moment of shuffling, stumbling awkwardness.

Announcing basketball games helped me find confidence. So too did being on stage, with the acne often covered by pancake makeup. A different avenue for confidence came my junior year. Our American history teacher, Jane Nelson, assigned the class a group project. We had a great deal of latitude to explore some aspect of the American experience. My friend Joe Leadem (probably the Class of '74's best athlete and an excellent student) and I looked at each other. I don't know if it was Joe or me who said, "We should make a movie," but when the words came out, I was totally sold on doing it. I had no idea, however, *how* we would do it.

I looked over and saw another classmate, Bill Knowland, who was regularly shooting 8 mm movies as a hobby. "Bill will be our cameraman," I said to Joe. I hadn't asked Bill yet—I just somehow knew it had to be so. In retrospect, this was the moment I became a producer. After class, I asked Bill if he'd work with us. He agreed, then asked what the movie would be about. In a matter of seconds, we decided we'd make a gangster movie. *The Godfather* was in the theaters, and the world of the mafiosi was on everyone's mind. Before the bell rang for the next period, we'd green-lit our project. We didn't have a title, a script, or a budget, but we were committed to doing it. (That's the way to get stuff done.) Ms. Nelson approved the project in minutes. Now we had to make the movie.

Our little team, filled with the certainty that only ignorance can provide, went into pre-production. I took out a piece of paper and started writing. Bill estimated the cost of the physical film we'd need to shoot a story we didn't yet know. (I can't take too much of the credit for this, but fifty years later, Bill Knowland is still making movies. He is an experienced director of photography.)

As co-producers, Joe, Bill, and I were responsible for organizing everything in front of and behind the camera. We oversaw the money, the cast, costuming, locations, props, and the craft service (the snacks). The whole project was a dream that we would make real with our imaginations—and willingness to try.

We called our film *The Mobster Days of Al Capone.* Bill Knowland would shoot and edit from a script that I would write and narrate. Together, Bill and I would record as much of a non-sync soundtrack as was possible by overdubbing multiple elements from cassette decks. (If you saw *The Fabelmans,* Steven Spielberg's wonderful coming-of-age drama about his early days as a filmmaker, you saw a demonstration of non-sync sound when Sammy Fabelman showed his movie at the senior prom. The film ran on a projector while the sound played separately on what could have been a once-popular Wollensak reel-to-reel tape deck.) We had no idea how to do it until we figured it out.

We shot over a three-week period on the streets of Piedmont and in our homes. One of the most memorable scenes was a phone booth hit in which Joe (playing Dion O'Banion, Al Capone's underworld enemy) kills a Capone gang member in a phone booth. Joe sped up on the running board of an actual Ford Model T (I have no recollection of where we got the car) and opened fire with a toy machine gun. There was no live ammo or even blanks. Bill shot the attack using stop motion photography and applied bullet hole decals to the phone booth glass. We spattered ketchup on the patient victim as he writhed, a few frames at a time, inside the phone booth. It was almost as memorable as Sonny Corleone getting it on the Long Island turnpike. Francis Ford Coppola would have smiled to see it.

The climactic St. Valentine's Day Massacre was shot in The Garage, a Berkeley classic car shop filled with beautifully restored cars from the Roaring Twenties. There were bodies and fake blood everywhere by the time the big scene was done, but we got it all cleaned up and were home by 10 PM curfews. We were fully satisfied that we'd shot a masterpiece. We had no insurance, no releases, and no contracts. We were flying by the seats of our 501s with no concern about or awareness of risk and liability.

We sent the film off to Kodak for processing. (Younger readers, ask your parents.) When it came back two weeks later, Bill edited the whole thing in his bedroom after school. His editing bay was a small desk, a razor blade, and tape. With a premiere date in our social studies class set and the black-and-white picture assembled, Bill and I stayed up late for several nights in a row recording the narration and music. We used a stand-alone tape deck that would have to start at the right instant for the picture and sound to be in sync.

Of course, it wasn't in sync, but it was close enough to be a huge success in Ms. Nelson's class. I sat behind the projector, a familiar place since elementary school—one eye on the movie, the other on the faces of our classmates as they watched what we had created. As word spread on campus of our cinematic achievement, we ran the film in our packed classroom multiple times during that day. The applause we got from everyone who saw *The Mobster Days of Al Capone* guaranteed us all "A" grades and new status as creative leaders in our school.

Some actors have little interest in the mechanics of making a movie. Others are passionate about it. As for me, I've been utterly absorbed by the nuts and bolts of creating entertainment since Ms. Nelson's class fifty years ago. There is nothing like putting together so many different components to make something magical. It has always given me the biggest rush throughout my creative journey. The learning is in the doing; if the result is great, so much the better, but it's figuring out the process that matters most to me. I could read about it in a book, and today I could take a master class from Martin Scorsese online, but I know I wouldn't get it until I did it myself. There is nothing as valuable as the process of making mistakes, recovering from them, and building on the lessons they teach.

My announcing and acting skills landed me perhaps the most prestigious gig I had in high school: emceeing Piedmont's Leonard J. Waxdeck Bird Calling Contest. *Why am I telling you all these things? "Get to* Little House," *many of you will say. Be patient; it's coming. This is the necessary story of all the things that made me ready to be Almanzo Wilder.*

The contest got its start in 1963 when a student approached Piedmont's very popular biology teacher with a request to "liven things up around here." I never took Waxdeck's biology class, but it was said that he always had the prettiest girls seated up front with instructions to keep their legs crossed to the right. Mr. Waxdeck was a born impresario and a charming rogue; the challenge to "liven things up" played directly to his considerable strengths—and weaknesses.

Well-spoken, attractive students dressed in Brooks Brothers suits and Chanel dresses were recruited by Mr. Waxdeck and committed themselves to preparing and presenting seriously accurate bird calls, complete with Latin nomenclature and lofty tales of where they had first heard the call of their selected bird. It was wonderful showmanship. The secret to the contest's huge success was that it was played absolutely straight, as an earnest demonstration of Piedmont's devotion to ornithology (the science of birds). (Search YouTube for the Leonard J. Waxdeck Bird Calling Contest and see for yourself.)

Nobody played it straighter or was funnier than Leonard J. Waxdeck. His tongue-in-cheek spectacle drew packed houses to Piedmont's auditorium every spring. Judges included first local—and over time, nationally known celebrities. Eventually the winners would perform their calls on the late night television shows hosted by Johnny Carson and David Letterman. The Bird Calling Contest was a perfect fit for Piedmont's upper middle-class aesthetic. It had just the right mix of style and stuffy humor.

The highlight of the event was Mr. Waxdeck's remarks to the

audience at the beginning of each contest. After his own introductory remarks, he'd read a series of actual letters from huge Hollywood stars and cultural icons—always including the president of the United States—in which the famous person would offer regrets that they were unable to attend. It was hysterical for the audience. All the more so because it was utterly authentic. We were all willing players in Mr. Waxdeck's wonderful spoof that left America wondering, "What goes on in Piedmont, and is this for real?"

The contest gave me my first opportunity to be on TV.

The week before the 1974 contest, I went to San Francisco with several of the Waxdeck contestants to do what I came to know as "advance publicity." I had never seen anything like the studios of KGO TV, the Bay Area's ABC affiliate, with all the cameras and lights. It was a magical world. During our segment, which ran barely three minutes, I tried to keep my focus on the host, but I couldn't keep my eyes off the on-set monitor displaying our little group assembled on the couch. I must've looked like a wide-eyed rube. I didn't care—I was in heaven. For me, being in that TV studio was the moment that two core parts of my identity intersected. The "AV geek" I had been as a kid was fascinated by all the lights and equipment; the "seen and heard person" I craved to be as an older teen was in love with the camera.

The space between wanting and doing is filled by the willingness to step forward when opportunity arises. I was stepping forward as fast as I could. When we left KGO's studios, my only thought was getting back to a place like that as often as I could.

Well, not my *only* thought. I'd been girl-crazy since the time the first zits erupted on my red face, but by my junior year, I had my first girlfriend. On screen, my most famous romance was controversial because I was so much older than the actress who played my wife. In real life, many of my most significant loves have been with older women. That pattern started with my un-requited crushes on the likes of Sue Stranski, and it continued with my first real girlfriend: Jayne Rutledge.

When I first met Jayne, she was a senior and I was a junior. Jayne was starring in our production of *Once Upon a Mattress*, and after accepting her invitation, I joined the cast as a member of the chorus. Getting guys on the stage in high school is often a challenge for drama teachers. One of the most successful lures for guys is a girl who has captured their fancy. Jayne captured mine. She was 4' 10", highly extroverted, bursting with energy, confidence, and an incredible singing voice—all perfect quali-ties to play Princess Winnifred, the Woebegone in *Once Upon a Mattress*.

Theater aficionados of a certain age will remember that a Broadway newcomer named Carol Burnett exploded to stardom playing Winnifred in the original Broadway production of *Once Upon a Mattress* in 1959. Like Carol Burnett and others who played Winnifred, including Ann B. Davis (*The Brady Bunch*), Dody Goodman, and Imogene Coca, Jayne Rutledge was a quick, fearless comedic actress with a huge voice. She was cut from an iconic mold.

When I met her, Jayne was being trained in Berkeley by Judy Davis, who the *New York Times* would call "The Stars' Vocal Coach." Davis had become famous supporting the vocal careers of great singers including Barbra Streisand, Frank Sinatra, Judy Garland, Sammy Davis Jr., Mary Martin, and even Jefferson Air-plane's Grace Slick.

Jayne aspired to stardom beyond Piedmont High School, and she had the vocal instrument to do it. Jayne approached every moment of preparation for our production with laser focus and fearless professionalism. I was mesmerized by her talent, and as I watched her work each day in rehearsal and felt our cast com-ing together around her performance, I began to see myself fit-ting into this world of creative expression that had been nowhere in my vision when I entered high school two years earlier.

I was old enough to drive, back in an era when the typical American teen still got their license as soon as they turned sixteen. On one of my first dates with Jayne, I drove her to see the George Segal/Glenda Jackson movie *A Touch of Class*. One of the great things about movies is that we see ourselves in the performances we watch, and it was while watching that film with Jayne that I first thought of what it would be like to act not just on stage but on screen. This was also the first time I dared to put my arm around a girl. She seemed to almost nestle into it, which was thrilling until my arm fell asleep. Not sure how to take my arm away without hurting Jayne's feelings, I was in agony by the end of the movie—but it was a sweet pain indeed. That date marked twin beginnings: my first tentative step toward connectedness and intimacy with a girl—and the first instance of seriously imagining myself on the screen.

I adored and admired Jayne. I was devastated when she graduated with plans to go on to college. But I wasn't heartbroken. That would happen with my first real love and the relationship that changed not only my world but the arc of my life and career.

It was the spring semester of my junior year when I first met Tracy Powell. Our first encounter was a classic "meet cute," and to explain it, you need to remember my ongoing quest to be seen, heard, and accepted. As senior year approached, I longed to be an elected student body officer. At Piedmont, we called it the Board of Control. Before you could be elected, you had to make a speech. That speech was my undoing.

Unfortunately, I had not stopped being a fount of misinformation, as my grandfather had said years earlier. I had just added a healthy dollop of indignation to that misinformation, topped off with self-righteousness. Relatively few Bay Area teens in the early seventies were staunch Republicans, but I was one of them. A decade before Michael J. Fox played Alex Keaton on *Family Ties*, I was a far less humorous version of a high school conservative. Alex Keaton had a poster of Richard Nixon on his wall. I didn't, but as the Watergate scandal burst into the headlines in the spring of '73, I was Piedmont High's most vigorous Nixon defender. (There weren't many.) When I spoke to the student body before the votes were cast for the Board of Control, I was booed off the podium.

This isn't intended to be a political book, but in the 2020s, politics has touched every aspect of our lives. I will note that for me, my adolescent conservativism was rooted in my comfort zone—and that comfort zone was giving voice to authority. It was my slightly updated version of the "good boy" I'd been in elementary school. I suppose part of it was also about pleasing my very right-wing father. Regardless, my politics were just one more thing that made me the furthest thing from cool. The boos from my fellow students were still echoing in my head when Tracy approached me with a warm smile and twinkling eyes. She said something like, "You have really great ideas, but you don't have to be so angry." My first instinct was to inadvertently prove her point: "What! ME? Angry?" My second instinct was to be slightly in awe of this slender beauty with long straight hair so blonde it was nearly white.

Earlier in the convention I had watched Tracy deliver her own candidate's speech with visible ease. She had been clever and funny, and she got herself elected Commissioner of Publicity in a landslide. How did she do that? I was as fascinated with her warm and generous style as with her looks.

Jayne and I remained a couple through the following summer. We were still technically dating when I met Tracy again, days before the first day of class for my senior year. She was at school, fulfilling her duties as commissioner of publicity, putting up beautiful posters that would welcome the student body back in just a few days. The posters were bright and cheerful and welcoming, just the way she was. Jayne was diminutive and perky, and I adored her. Tracy was tall, engaging, and graceful. As we greeted each other in the hallway, I was smitten.

When it came time to write this section of the book, I got on a Zoom call with Tracy. I recalled that meeting in the school hallway. Tracy laughingly told me, "I had a crush in three seconds." I assured her it was the same for me. It's been half a century, and I can still remember feeling what I had never felt before. That "wow" would happen again, of course, including when I reconnected with my wife, Katherine, fifteen years after our first meeting on the set of *Little House*.

I would venture to say that anyone reading this book can remember, probably photographically, the moments when they fell in love. After so many years, while we have gone on to have very separate lives, Tracy and I remain devoted to each other and are very close friends. Connecting with Tracy in the hallway that day was like the moment when I saw the mic on the table at the Varsity basketball game a few years earlier. Once again, there was this feeling of being drawn to something in the spotlight. This time the spotlight wasn't on a microphone, but on a young woman. There was a Peppermint Patty quality about Tracy, without any of the gender ambiguity attributed to the character by today's social observers. Tracy was overtly fun (she spelled it *phun*), genuine, and deeply idealistic. Tracy may not have known it at that moment, but she had just gotten a boyfriend, whether she wanted one or not. The year that followed changed both of our lives as we bonded together in a way that was transformational for me and, she reassures me, for her.

Tracy was one of the chief reasons I chose the University of the Pacific (UOP) for college. I wanted to find a way for us to stay together after I graduated. I was totally in love with her, and the idea of being apart was agonizing. I knew I wanted to go to school somewhere close enough that I could still see Tracy regularly. UOP was in Stockton, eighty miles east of Piedmont. I could come home on the weekends.

Pacific also made sense academically. My grades were average. Almost everyone who graduated from Piedmont went straight to a four-year school, with nearby UC Berkeley and Stanford being the competitive colleges of choice. My mother's parents met as students at Berkeley, and three great-grandfathers went there as well, but I didn't have the grades to get into the state's flagship university. My grades may not have been spectacular, but I was well-rounded: I had the theater and basketball announcing; I was on the Highlander swim team and the staff of the school newspaper. Pacific may have been less competitive than Berkeley, but it was still a respected university. I had family ties to it as well: my ancestor Albert Alfonso Moore had graduated from its predecessor, the College of the Pacific, back before the University of California even existed.

I may not have had the grades for Berkeley, but Tracy did. She enrolled at Cal, and instead of going to parties and football games at UOP, I spent most of my Fridays and Sundays on a Greyhound bus going back and forth between Stockton and Piedmont. Tracy and I made it two years, which is a pretty good run—but ultimately our romantic relationship didn't survive the distance and the changing directions of our lives. That's a common outcome, but no less heartbreaking for being so.

For years after she and I broke up, Tracy was in the back of my mind whenever I found myself dating someone new. She didn't do anything to encourage that. For years, I simply couldn't get over Tracy's fundamental goodness and the memory of how she had loved me. I don't know if I'll ever fully understand why we didn't stay together, but that's okay. It was perfect for what it was, and she and I have both found deep happiness with our respective spouses. For more than fifty years, Tracy has remained a very dear friend and the touchstone to some of my most precious memories. I will always love her because she inspired my young heart, my passion, and the beginnings of my social consciousness. (I would stay a Republican for decades, but Tracy made me far less dogmatic.)

There was one other thing Tracy did: she transformed my acting. In almost every role I've had in front of the camera, I've been defined by my relationship with the woman who is the star of the show. That quality of being a romantic lead was something that casting directors saw at once. It was a quality planted in me by my first real love.

CHAPTER 5
Turning Pro

WHAT I HAD WITH TRACY WOULD DEEPLY IMPACT HOW I APproached the Laura and Almanzo relationship on *Little House*. I can't tell you the number of women (and occasionally men), who approach me even now, saying they dreamed of meeting and falling in love with a man like Almanzo. That people feel that way about work I did remains an amazing gift to me, and I am forever grateful for it.

I was not yet ready to be Almanzo, however. I had a few more steps to climb.

Don Dorward, the celebrated Bay Area advertising executive, had promised to introduce me to an agent after he saw my highschool Tevye. He made good on his promise and brought me to meet Ann Brebner, San Francisco's best talent agent. Ann was a lovely woman with white hair and a distinctive New Zealand accent. Before starting her agency, Ann had built a career for herself as an actress, director, and writer. She famously hosted the first table reading of *Star Wars* for George Lucas, right in her Polk Street conference room. Ann had warm, welcoming eyes when she smiled at me, but there was a no-nonsense, professional energy about her that informed me that she was a serious person to be respected. Like all good agents, she was constantly assessing the level of commitment in her potential and current clients.

After a nice conversation about what was needed from me as a client, she agreed to represent me in the Bay Area for film, television, and commercials. She told me that before I did anything else, I would have to join the Screen Extras Guild. The annual dues, which had to be paid up front, were four hundred dollars. I had a summer maintenance job, and I was making what I thought was great money: ten dollars an hour. I'd need to drop an entire week's paycheck on those dues. Ann told me to be ready for more: if I was fortunate enough to be cast in a speaking role, I'd need to join the Screen Actors Guild (SAG).

In the mid-1970s, most of the opportunities for talent in the Bay Area were background work in crowd scenes for commercials, TV series, and occasional films. There were no auditions; extras were cast from pictures in a book at the agency. My first extra casting was for *The Streets of San Francisco*, a hugely popular series that ran on ABC from 1972 to 1977. The Quinn-Martin series for ABC starred the great Karl Malden and the young Michael Douglas (then better known at that time as the son of Kirk Douglas). It was a terrific show. If you get a chance to find it streaming somewhere, check out one of the coolest title sequences of its time, featuring the wonderful voice actor Hank Simms.

I got quite a taste of reality on my first shoot day. I arrived on the San Francisco Embarcadero for the day's work. I was to be part of a high school charity car wash. I took my sponges and my bucket of soap and took my spot on the line of cars. The guest that week on *Streets* was Greg Morris, who was famous as gadget man Barney Collier on *Mission Impossible*.

It's always exciting for me to see that the people I watch on television are real. I feel like I have a relationship with them because I've invited them into my home to watch their stories.

When we turn on the TV, we are in a very real sense inviting the people we watch into our lives as we're eating, relaxing on the couch, getting dressed, or going off to sleep at night. The actor on the screen doesn't experience the audience at home when they're acting—but I promise you, when they're home in front of their TVs, it's the same for them. Fifty years in television haven't changed that feeling for me.

Karl Malden and Greg Morris were set to do a "walk and talk" with the car wash in the background. The camera was on the dolly tracking ahead of them, and I realized that there was a point toward the end of the scene when they were going to be less than five feet from me as I was washing the car. As I scrubbed, I could see Karl and Greg and the camera out of the corner of my eye. I willed myself not to look and ruin the shot, but I was certain at least part of my body was going to be seen. When the work was done, I was soaking wet and cold—but proud of my debut. All the car washers were released by the second 2nd Assistant Director and my first taste of big-time television was over. The company wrapped up and was gone to the next location as quickly as they had arrived.

I was hooked.

During the remainder of that summer and fall of 1975, the work kept coming. Ann was a marvel. I booked extra work in commercials for Coke, Levi's, and even an ad for motor oil featuring Johnny Cash singing "I've Been Everywhere." For the Coke ad, I was upgraded: I went from a guy in the background to the man in the close-up taking a big swig of ice-cold Coke at the end of the spot. That meant I got a residual payment every time the ad aired; soon checks (albeit small ones) were arriving in the mail. It was my first experience with residuals, and it was a big moment. I wasn't quite making a living as an actor, but I was getting paid for it. I thought of how much it mattered to my father that I "not be a deadbeat."

It felt good to cash those checks.

There were setbacks. For that motor oil commercial, I was going to be featured as a tan surfer guy (something I did every day on *The New Gidget* years later). When the director of the spot saw how pale I was during rehearsals, he downgraded me from "featured" to regular "background." The downgrade meant there would be no residuals.

Being pale and getting sunburned have been one of the annoyances of my life. My brother and sister got great tans. My father tanned. But for my mother and me, with our blonde hair and fair skin, the sun meant burning and peeling. On big sets, my paleness could be overcome with body makeup, which at that time was Ben Nye pancake applied with a wet sponge wherever it was needed. The STP commercial crew was a small unit, and they didn't have any Ben Nye pancake makeup on hand. They found someone in the group with a tan complexion to be the surfer, and he got the residuals.

Months later, I was in the dining room of my fraternity house at UOP. My fraternity brothers and friends were gathered around the TV to see my big moment on *The Streets of San Francisco*. When the scene on the Embarcadero came up, Karl Malden and Greg Morris were there with the car wash in the background. I waited for my big moment—and all I saw was my forearm, for about one second.

"There I am," I called out. Everyone in the dining room cheered. They knew that forearm.

What a disappointment! I washed that car with vigor and energy through multiple takes from multiple angles. All there was of me was a glimpse of my arm, and despite the kindness of my fraternity brothers, it was not instantly recognizable as Dean Butler's forearm. It was clear to me that working as an extra was not a viable path to visibility.

Still, I wasn't going to say "no" to extra work. *Streets* brought me back for another episode. This time, I was a hospital orderly working in the ER. It was a transitional moment for the series.

Michael Douglas had made the decision to leave the show, always a risky move. The television landscape is littered by the names of actors who thought they were bigger than the series that made them household names and left only to find a lot of closed doors as they pursued new opportunities. Michael Douglas is an exception that proves the rule. He's had a wonderful career.

This episode called for Steve Keller (the Douglas character) to be shot and wounded, retire from the San Francisco Police Department, and become a professor at a local college. After being wounded, he was rushed to the hospital. I was one of the orderlies who wheeled him from the ambulance to the emergency room. Douglas lay moaning on the gurney, covered with theatrical blood as we raced him down the corridor again and again. Between takes as we rolled him "back to one" (the mark where the action started), he was funny and engaging with all of us. He thanked us for giving him a "smooth ride" on his last episode. I got upgraded to "silent bit" status, which came with a higher day rate, though no residuals. This time, when the show aired, my face was clearly visible. My friends and family could see me and Michael Douglas clearly in the same shot. I was gratified, but I was hungry for more. I wanted to say a line—and get that SAG card.

I earned that card with my third appearance on *The Streets of San Francisco.* My first episode contained my forearm; my second got my face. My third would get me a real character to play.

The 1976 episode "Castle of Fear" featured the wonderful Pat Hingle as guest star. I was one of a pair of teenage prank callers who were terrifying a paranoid old man (Hingle). After a wiretap, we were caught in the act by Karl Malden and Richard Hatch (Michael Douglas' replacement). I got to shake each of their hands. Cooler even than landing my first real SAG job was seeing my name printed on a dressing room door. That's one of those things that's a true dividing line for an actor.

PRAIRIE MAN

Acting for the camera and acting on a stage are two different skills, and I'll admit that after all this time, I still have a lot to learn about both. I'm far more comfortable on a stage than I've ever been in front of a camera. On the stage an actor must reach an audience that could be sitting more than one hundred feet away. In that situation an actor's energy, intention, and physicality must project well beyond the footlights for an audience to have a satisfying theatrical experience. I've always enjoyed working big.

For the camera an actor is performing for a lens that can, very often, be literally inches from his or her face. The performance is shaped in the actor's thoughts, which are delivered to the audience through his or her eyes. I think most actors would say they prefer one medium over the other. How effective we are in these mediums is a decision that casting directors, producers, and audiences make about us. Watching Karl Malden work up close, I saw a master at acting for the camera. For the first time, I realized what a fundamentally different skill it was.

As an aside, when I think of great stage actors, I think of Jim Dale. In 1980, not long after I had joined *Little House*, I found myself at the St. James Theater on Broadway in New York. Dale was starring in the musical *Barnum*, about the rise of the super-showman P.T. Barnum. Dale had the title role, and his presence on the stage was seismic. He filled the theater with enormous energy. He commanded the space with his performance. His enunciation was perfection. As he sang the show's signature song, "There's a Sucker Born Every Minute," every word was perfectly understood—and with every syllable, a fog of moisture spewed from his mouth. I could only imagine how wet members of the orchestra (who were seated directly below him) would get during a performance. I was sitting far audience right, so I could see into the wings. Whenever Dale stepped briefly offstage, he was clearly soaked in perspiration. A costumer was waiting for him with a towel so he could quickly dry himself (without smearing his makeup) before stepping back out to continue the performance. He held nothing back. I was then a regular on one of the biggest TV shows in America, but watching Jim Dale's performance, I was totally enthralled.

Jim Dale did television and movies, but he is best known for his work in the theater. Co-starring in *Barnum* was a young Glenn Close, who played the showman's wife. Glenn Close is one of those very special actors who has shown throughout her career that she can capture an audience equally on the stage and the screen. It's a rarer talent than we realize. On the stage, it's okay to see the craft and the artistry in real time. The camera doesn't accept that. For the lens, you can only be the character. The craft must be hidden.

When I wasn't running back and forth to San Francisco to audition, I was trying to pay attention to school in Stockton. I spent a lot of time learning about radio performance at KUOP, Pacific's thirty-thousand-watt NPR affiliate. One of my instructors, Dave Streeter, provided students with opportunities to read Associated Press wire copy, do interviews, and practice the art of reading commercial messages. That work reading commercial messages paid off when I auditioned for a Bay Area promotion for McDonald's. Back in 1977, the fast-food giant was just introducing its breakfast service. It needed brief spots for its new McBreakfast Bingo. I booked the job. Ann Brebner told me later I got the job because I was one of the few young guys in the Bay Area who had a sense of how to read commercial copy "to time." Radio gives you a very good sense of exactly how many seconds you have to read something, and you learn to pace yourself.

The McBreakfast Bingo promotion also featured me on a poster costumed as a McDonald's employee holding a McBreakfast Bingo card. When I saw the poster for the first time, I was shocked to see a pimple on my chin. Really? They hadn't added it to the image; it was mine, but I had assumed that the art director of the promotion would airbrush it out. It would've been a simple fix, even in 1977. Presumably they thought a little acne made me look like an authentic teen, but for someone still insecure about his complexion, this was more authenticity than I wanted.

Still, that poster hung in hundreds of McDonald's restaurants all over Northern California. For the first time, I experienced people coming up to me to ask, "Hey, aren't you the guy in the McDonald's ad?" For someone who wanted to be seen and heard that was precious affirmation. I got the same experience a few months later when I did a commercial for the long-gone Mervyn's Department Store for a product called Dura-Jeans. Like McBreakfast Bingo, this was just a regional spot, but during the summer of 1977 it ran constantly. Several times a day, I was approached on the street, with "Aren't you the Mervyn's guy?" I loved it.

In the 1970s, the hierarchy of mass media work for actors was as follows: movies in the theater were at the top, followed by movies made for television, then television series, and commercials were at the bottom. Television has become much more prestigious in the last fifty years, largely because you have to pay for it. In 1977, you paid money to see a movie in the theater or a play on Broadway. Television was free. You bought a set at Sears or Montgomery Ward, came home, plugged it in, pulled up the antenna, and you had entertainment. There was no option to pay more for additional programming. If you lived near somewhere like San Francisco (or New York, Chicago, or any other urban area) you had perhaps seven or eight stations from which to choose: one each of the major network affiliates (CBS, NBC, ABC), a public broadcasting station, and maybe three independent channels.

With the exception of PBS, which paid its bills with taxpayer money and viewer contributions, every station made money solely through advertising. There were no cable bills or streaming services to download, no Sling, no Charter, no satellite dishes or Internet. Consumers paid for the TV programming by watching advertising. Commercial advertisers sponsored the programs that would draw the most viewers, and thus the most potential customers. Commercials were cast with talent that the audience would trust, relate to, or aspire to be like. In a world before Instagram and TikTok, commercial actors were the primary influencers. Your work paid for everything everyone saw. As important as you knew you were as a commercial actor, you wanted to move from influencing people to buy things to being someone that people would pay to see in the theater.

I'm always surprised by how many actors I've met through the years who are horribly uncomfortable seeing themselves on film, posters, billboards, or anywhere. That discomfort with an aspect of professional acting so essential to being a professional actor has always surprised me. From the time my fraternity brothers cheered for my forearm as it appeared for a second behind Karl Malden, I knew I wanted to be seen. My love of acting and my need for recognition have always gone together, and so it's taken a long time to comprehend how others in this business could feel so differently. For years, I assumed that someone who doesn't want to be seen would probably be happier not being an actor. Over time, I've come to realize what some of you may already know: many actors are uncomfortable as themselves. They're fine with being seen when they're immersed in a character, but they don't want to do a talk show, where they must appear as themselves. Without a script and without a role, they struggle. They seem to feel exposed and vulnerable.

Actors could get away with being averse to publicity forty years ago, but in our social media culture of today, being reclusive isn't really an option anymore. Obviously, if you're already a superstar, you can withdraw from the world and wait for the roles to come to you. That describes a tiny handful of actors. Almost everyone else, including names you know well, needs to take on a public persona. In 1977, I wasn't doing talk shows. I wasn't doing publicity at all. My only "interviews" were with family and friends asking me about famous people I might have met. People were stopping me on the street, having recognized me from the Mervyn's or McDonald's ads. They weren't asking for my autograph because they didn't know my name. Still, the recognition felt good. I couldn't imagine it being otherwise.

At the beginning of this chapter, I said that I don't think I could have played the roles I did if it weren't for my relationship with Tracy Powell. By 1977, Tracy and I weren't together anymore, but in ways that I didn't yet understand, she was still influencing me as both a man and an actor.

How many times have we heard actors asked if they are like the characters they're playing? Most actors say that their characters are nothing like them. They insist that whole new personas are being pulled out of thin air and presented as fully formed human beings on the screen. That's a fun way to maintain the mystique of an actor, but I don't think that's the way it works, either for me or anyone else I've met. At the risk of demystifying the profession a bit, we actors are *always* playing some version of ourselves, with physical and emotional adjustments.

Thousands of books have been written about acting; dozens of master classes are available online. At the core of the craft is the reality that actors can only play what they can tap from themselves. There are actors with enormously wide ranges who astonish us with their ability to disappear into a character, but they are still accessing some aspect of their memory or experience. Other actors, those we think of as our biggest stars, are always recognizably themselves, just in different circumstances. Actors are multidimensional not because they can shape-shift but because they have developed and honed an ability to probe and reveal themselves. I'm not going to get drawn into this too deeply, but I know that the characters I've played through the years are all completely me, regardless of the circumstances in which the characters lived.

I was never a young German soldier in World War I, but I played one long enough to get bayoneted by the great Sam Elliott in the NBC miniseries *Once an Eagle*. I was cast as the first person Sam Damon (Elliott) ever killed in action. It's a pivotal moment for Elliott's character, as the young man I play is an innocent boy. I played a guard outside an elegant chateau, with the gorgeous Napa Valley standing in nicely for Northern France. I had no dialogue in the script, but the director, E.W. Swackhammer, gave me a few lines of German to say as I walked my post. I got my first close-up in the instant when I came face to face with Sam Elliott; my face opening in pain, shock, and surprise as Sam drove his steel bayonet into my belly.

I got to spend a few hours with Sam Elliott on set before the scene was shot. Even as a younger man, he had that distinctive deep voice which has become his trademark. He was personable and funny and, as the cliché goes, a consummate professional. He'd never remember that day in the Napa vineyard, but he made a very strong impression on me. Getting killed in *Once an Eagle* by a talented guy like Sam? It was a highlight of my early career. At the family ranch, there were cheers and claps as cousins, aunts, uncles, and others watched their relative die.

In June 1977, Ann Brebner got a meeting for me with a casting director from Los Angeles named Mary Goldberg. It was for a CBS movie of the week. You'd have to be at least fifty now to remember the concept of made-for-TV movies of the week. Some of the most famous movies of the week of the 1970s included *Brian's Song*, *The Autobiography of Miss Jane Pittman*, *Can Ellen Be Saved?* (starring my lovely wife, Katherine Cannon), and *Little House on the Prairie* (which was presented as a movie of the week but was really a thinly disguised, "backdoor" pilot).

Mary Goldberg was looking for Michael. Michael was the male lead in a coming-of-age romance called *Forever*, based on the hugely popular 1975 novel by young adult author Judy Blume. After writing a series of successful books aimed at elementary and junior high kids, *Forever* was Judy Blume's first book for older teens. It was beautifully written, and—by the standards of the day—sexually explicit. It was very controversial at the time, and apparently still is.

Mary Goldberg was an attractive redhead with a great smile. She took pleasure in putting actors at ease, which is something I cannot say about many of the casting directors I've known. She would go on to cast movies such as *Amadeus*, *Deep Rising*, and *Alien*. We had a brief but friendly conversation, and then I did a short reading for her.

When I was through, Mary smiled. "It would be a million to one shot for you to get this, but I think you're perfect for it."

"Perfect for it." Nobody had ever said that to me before. I hadn't yet heard the old aphorism, attributed to William Goldman, that "actors starve to death on encouragement." When I say I was thrilled to be considered, I mean it. At the same time, I figured my odds might be a little better than a million to one. *Forever* was going to be shot in the Bay Area, and the director was a local, John Korty, who had already directed several hit movies of the week.

My first sense that my odds were improving came when Mary asked me to meet with John Korty. I drove across the Golden Gate Bridge to Mill Valley and had a brief meeting with him at his office. I liked him at once; it was clear from the moment we shook hands that he was a really good guy. Two days later, John called me and asked if I'd be willing to pick up Stephanie Zimbalist at the airport. Stephanie was the actress that John and Mary wanted to play Katherine, *Forever*'s young protagonist and Michael's first love. Stephanie was flying up to San Francisco from Los Angeles to do some "mix and match" meetings with her prospective co-stars. A "mix and match" is a chemistry test, to see how actors will work together; in this case, the sessions would be videotaped and sent to CBS executives who would make the final decision.

I took a promotional photo of Stephanie to the airport, just to be sure I'd recognize her. This was back in the pre-9/11 days when we could still meet arriving passengers right at the gate. When Stephanie got off the plane, she was even prettier than her headshot; she was just the kind of girl I would want to fall in love with. I knew I could work with her. She seemed to like me too.

When it came time for the mix-and-match sessions, I tried to avoid thinking about the other guys who'd been flown in to compete for the role. I recognized one: Jeff East, fresh off playing young Superman in Christopher Reeve's first *Superman* film. I gulped hard when I realized who he was. I was in way over my head. I had never done an audition like this before. All I could do was the best I could do.

Auditions don't pay the bills. As I was auditioning for *Forever*, I had a summer job in a menswear shop in Oakland. It wasn't a great shop, but I knew menswear because I had worked in an excellent one several years before.

I was in the store when the phone rang. The manager picked it up and then quickly turned to me. "It's for you," he said.

"Hello?"

"Dean, It's Ann Brebner." A pause. "You got it."

I got the million to one shot.

CHAPTER 6
Forever

THERE IS NOTHING AGENTS ENJOY SAYING MORE THAN "YOU GOT it." When she heard I'd been cast as Michael Wagner in *Forever*, Ann Brebner called my house. My mother told her I was at work, and Ann asked for the number at the store. Mary Goldberg had said I was a million to one shot, and I'd hit that shot. Ann was nearly as happy to deliver the news as I was to hear it. As I had already started to learn, agents rarely called personally, preferring to have assistants provide information about meetings and auditions. I rarely heard from Ann or any of the other agents I worked with through the years when I didn't get a part. I came to understand that agents and managers don't like being attached to bad news. The reality is that for virtually everybody in the entertainment industry, the news is bad most of the time. "You got it" is all the more precious because it is rare. It is a healing ointment for the emotional cuts and bruises that come from not getting the job 95 percent of the time.

My family had encouraged me as an actor, but I don't know if anyone seriously believed I could make a living at it. This first big break was in a movie about a young couple who thought they would last "forever" but soon found out otherwise. There was a lesson in that for me, and for every other creative person. I couldn't count on being able to make a living as an actor forever. Still, after Ann's phone call there was no denying that I had gone farther than many had thought possible, going into a professional world of which my forebears had only dreamed. My grandfather had aspired to be a writer in his younger days and had been encouraged by an agent to move to New York. The challenge was too much for him, and he couldn't bring himself to leave California and the ranch that he loved so much. I don't think he ever forgave himself for failing to embrace the opportunity to fulfill his dream.

Getting cast in *Forever* moved me from one world to another world. Almost every single professional relationship—and most of the significant personal relationships in my life—would come to me because of the opportunities this one film provided.

Most TV movies were filmed in Southern California. John Korty was from the Bay Area, and CBS had agreed to make the film in and around his native Marin County. For a love story like that of Katherine and Michael, it would be hard to pick a more beautiful set of locations than the likes of Mill Valley, Sausalito, and Tiburon just north of San Francisco. Most of the locations were thirty miles or less from Piedmont, so the initial plan was that I would stay at home and commute to and from the set. John Korty worried I'd be vulnerable to fatigue from the long hours of working and driving. At his insistence, I joined the rest of the cast at a hotel in Tiburon for the entire shooting schedule. I was "going on location" to shoot a movie I was starring in—more or less in my hometown. (Like many from the Bay Area, I considered the entire region my hometown). It was all incredibly exciting.

I had to quit my job at the clothing store, and I took a semester off from UOP. I knew I could go back to the former, and I assured my parents I had every intention of returning to the latter.

Ann Brebner had negotiated a good deal for me, but I knew that money (which was more than I had ever made before) would only last so long. Indeed, before I was cast on *Little House*, I would return to working "survival jobs" outside of the industry. Unless you're a trust fund baby, you'll do the same as a beginning actor—and to be honest, many actors keep doing those survival jobs on and off for the rest of their careers.

Before I headed off to that Tiburon hotel, I got a call from the director. John asked about a scene early in the movie when Katherine comes to see Michael play for his high school team. It's an instantly recognizable trope that we've seen in countless romance movies. In *Love Story*, Jenny (Ali McGraw) comes to watch Oliver (Ryan O'Neal) play hockey at Harvard. Adrian (Talia Shire) shows up at the Spectrum to see Rocky Balboa (Sylvester Stallone) box against Apollo Creed in the first movie in that iconic series. In *The Natural*, Iris (Glenn Close) shows up at Wrigley Field to watch Roy Hobbs (Robert Redford) play baseball. *Forever* wasn't quite in that league, but the scene was still vital to the story. Knowing I'd need to sell Michael as a high school athlete capable of impressing a girl, John wanted to know what sport I wanted to play. He offered basketball, tennis, or swimming.

I wasn't a standout athlete in any sport. That's part of what drew me to acting. I wanted to be seen as being good at something. Tennis was out. I'd taken some lessons, but my serve was terrible. I had been a varsity swimmer for three years at Piedmont High, so that was the logical choice. I wasn't fast and didn't have a consistent flip turn, but I was comfortable in the water. I also didn't have the ideal swimmer's body, and my skin was pale as chalk. I could see myself on the blocks, glowing white, surrounded by chiseled and tan swimmers. That would be a very bad idea. That left me with basketball. It was a game I loved. I'd begun my journey as a performer announcing games. This would be my fantasy moment to be a basketball player in a movie. I took it.

One of the things I packed from home before going to Tiburon was my brother's basketball. I planned to practice every morning, jogging and dribbling along the waterfront. Scott, who had been a starting guard on every team he'd ever played on, wouldn't miss his ball for a few weeks. That ball was the last thing I threw into my yellow VW Bug before I left.

As I said my goodbyes, part of me knew I was only driving thirty miles away. Part of me felt like I was moving to the other side of the country.

When I checked into the hotel, there was a message waiting for me from Stephanie Zimbalist. She'd flown up from Los Angeles earlier in the day. She wanted to meet and take a walk together around Tiburon. We needed to build our character relationship. I quickly changed in my room and met her in the lobby. Stephanie looked beautiful and understated, just as she had when I picked her up at the airport before my audition. Seeing her for the second time, my first thought was that she was like a beautiful pearl, finely polished and luminescent. Stephanie was no pinup girl, like Farrah Fawcett of *Charlie's Angels*. Her beauty was rooted in her wholesomeness, her gentleness, and her grace.

As we took that first walk together, my co-star and I told each other a bit about ourselves. It was almost like a first date, which in some sense it was. I had a bit of an advantage, as Stephanie was what we would today call a "nepo baby." I knew far more about her family than she did about mine. She had grown up surrounded by respected artists. Her grandfather, Efrem Zimbalist, had been a classical violinist and her grandmother, Alma Gluck, a famous opera singer. Their son, Efrem Zimbalist Jr., had begun his acting career on the New York stage and made his way to Hollywood, where he was put under contract at Warner Brothers, first for movies and then most successfully for television. I'd loved watching him in his most famous role, as Inspector Lewis Erskine on the long-running ABC series *The F.B.I.* Stephanie adored her father, and she was now proudly at the beginning of her journey to extend her family's artistic legacy.

All these years later, I can still remember that long walk on a sunny Tiburon afternoon. While I had no artistic legacy to match Stephanie's, I related deeply to the pride she had in her family history and her desire to honor that history in her career as an actor. While I was back on my heels as I processed her familiarity and comfort with the entertainment business, there were other moments during our long walk that humanized Stephanie for me in unexpected and disarming ways. That walk seeded a friendship that would grow through the duration of the *Forever* shoot and sustain itself over many decades to come.

As you may know, movies are rarely filmed in order. Stephanie and the rest of the cast had plenty of experience with the standard practice of making movies "out of sequence." I didn't. I was lucky: John Korty was committed to shooting *Forever* in order from beginning to end. For a romance where the intensity of the relationship must grow and evolve from the moment of first meeting to the end of the story this was a nice choice. For me, a novice at moviemaking, it was a welcome gift to be able to play the story as it evolved in the script.

There were more gifts in store. Our director of photography, David Myers, and our camera operator, John Bailey, were two incredibly skilled artists. David was a veteran documentarian, and John would go on to shoot movies like *American Gigolo, Ordinary People,* and *In the Line of Fire.* The rest of the actors were equally impressive. Diana Scarwid, who would play Sybil Davidson, would be nominated for a Best Supporting Actress Oscar a few years later. The roles of Katherine's and Michael's best friends, Erica and Artie, were played by Beth Raines and John Friedrich, respectively. Beth was easy and fun to be around—she was a master animal imitator. John is one of the bravest and most thoughtful actors I've ever met. We became very good friends while working on the film. For more than a year after shooting *Forever,* we'd be roommates in Los Angeles.

From our first meeting, the four of us bonded quickly. Casting directors don't make mistakes, they say, and Mary Goldberg had proved that truism right. Stephanie, Beth, John, and I were right for the parts we played individually, and we were "right" as a group.

The first scene we shot was the party where Michael and Katherine meet for the first time. I was incredibly nervous. I had literally never had a conversation on film before. I wondered how bad I'd have to be to be fired on the spot. Would they call Jeff East? As it turned out, my anxiety gave me the perfect state of mind to play the rush of excitement and terror a young man feels when he tries to talk to a beautiful girl for the first time. I knew that feeling very well. With the camera rolling, I gave myself over to courage despite fear, and with just the right amount of tentativeness, took Stephanie into my arms to dance. We were off and running.

The next scene we shot was the basketball game where Michael shows off for Katherine. This was the moment I would get to show off my minimal hoop skills. The extras with whom I'd be playing were all much better athletes than I was, but to my great relief that wouldn't matter. There would be no full court game; instead, John shot half a dozen pieces of a game that featured me shooting and scoring. That was a novel concept for the kid who years earlier had averaged .07 points per game on the Piedmont freshman team.

Given the pressure of the moment, I was relieved to make nearly every shot I took. My dad was in the stands watching, more than a little amazed that I had gotten this acting opportunity. I like to think it was fun for him to see the son he'd named after James Dean living out a dream that so few will ever experience. When I saw the sequence in the completed movie, I winced. My awkwardness as an athlete was on full display; any athlete watching would know that I couldn't really play. It didn't matter. The scene served its purpose, and for a moment I got to fulfill my dream of being a high school basketball star. That was no small thing for a clumsy guy who had craved that exact affirmation only a few years earlier. What made it even sweeter was learning that five years earlier, that same Tamalpais High School gym had served as the location for the "sock hop" sequence in *American Graffiti*. It was a marvel to imagine that I was working as an actor on the same hardwood where Ron Howard and Cindy Williams had slow danced to The Platters' "Smoke Gets in Your Eyes."

(That Platters reference is a reminder that soundtracks are vital to a film. If you've read this far, you may have already looked for *Forever* on DVD or a streaming platform and been unable to find it. It's not you; *Forever* remains unavailable, though you can find some scenes [including the basketball game] on YouTube. The reason you can't find *Forever* is the same reason you can't find many other favorite little films of that era: music licensing issues.)

Forever was shot entirely on location and not on a sound stage. That means that production was done in real places like Tamalpais High School, the streets of Mill Valley, on tour boats in San Francisco Bay, and the Renaissance Pleasure Faire in Novato. On location, it's almost impossible to control all the real-life conditions that are happening just on the other side of the camera. This isn't a problem visually because the camera is framed on the actors and the director can control what he or she wants to see in the background. The aspect of a location that often can't be controlled is how it sounds. Are there cars speeding by just off camera? Are there airplanes flying overhead? Are there bells, whistles, and alarms that can be heard off camera that distract from the scene being filmed? I first learned about this challenge when we were shooting at Stinson Beach. We had loud waves crashing on the shore, and those sounds weren't consistent with the dialogue that was shot in different pieces over several hours. But would the constant sounds cut with the dialogue that was shot in different pieces over a period of hours? Not likely.

After the beach scene was finished, I was told I needed to go to ADR. I had no idea what that was. My first thought was that it had to be some sort of union thing. Was I in trouble? "No," the assistant director explained with a grin at my naïveté, "ADR stands for Automated Dialogue Replacement. You need to re-record your lines."

If there are extraneous sounds (cars, airplanes, heavy breathing) that a director wants to eliminate in the final audio mix of the picture, actors must visit an ADR or Looping stage to rebuild their dialogue. I had been watching TV and going to movies for years. Everything always looked and sounded perfect. I never thought about how it got that way. Now, having been on a set at the center of the action for the first time, I was getting a crash course in film. There was a lot to learn.

No one wants to do ADR if it can be helped, and when time allows, more takes are shot in hopes of recording audio that can be used. But there are limits to the time that can be spent waiting for quiet on a location, so actors must learn to do ADR well or risk their performance being ruined. If you can hear and see the ADR (and you can when it's bad), the actors or the technicians on the ADR stage have done a poor job. Occasionally, I'll be watching a movie and I'll wince as I hear badly done dialogue replacement. It's amazing how often it still happens.

I've known a lot of actors through the years who claim to be completely uninterested in production and post-production. As they see it, they are paid to show up ready to work when they are called, do their scenes, and go home when the day is over. That's fine: we actors should focus on our craft. At the same time, movies and television aren't theater: they're technical media. It's helpful for an actor to understand the basics of lenses, light, and audio, and if nothing else, to show respect for the craftspeople on set.

A key part of the narrative in *Forever* is Katherine's decision to lose her virginity to Michael. As I noted, Judy Blume had written a bravely explicit novel for young people. We needed to find a way to capture the intimacy between the two lead characters while still staying on the good side of the network's "standards and practices." There were no sex scenes in the movie, but there was lots of kissing and heavy breathing. This was fun to do. Knowing that things could only go "so far" in a made-for-television film made things easier for both of us. I was genuinely attracted to Stephanie, and she made me feel that she felt the same. This was still acting, but it was hardly difficult!

Then came the hot tub. While almost all the movie was filmed in Marin County, we shot several scenes in the Sierra Mountains, near Lake Tahoe. The concept was a montage of a day of hiking, sightseeing, and picnicking in idyllic settings. The montage would lead into an evening scene in a hot tub, cut to Jennifer Warnes' 1977 hit, "Right Time of the Night." I have always loved this song and was blown away when I heard it in the movie for the first time. The lyrics made clear what was supposed to happen in the hot tub:

It's the right time of the night for making love . . .

I remember vividly standing next to Stephanie, each of us in bathrobes over bathing suits. The crew was setting up the hot tub shots. There was a chill in the evening air so we were both eager to get into the steaming hot water. Then our producer walked up and told us something that brought a whole different kind of chill.

Forever was made for American network television. What neither Stephanie nor I knew was that it was common to sell American TV movies into European markets. (This would have been mentioned somewhere deep in our contracts about "worldwide rights," but that's a vague phrase.) The producer explained that European TV had a much more permissive standard about sex and nudity. It would be helpful, he said, if Stephanie took off her top when she went into the tub. He assured her that no American audience would see her breasts, but that it would be helpful to the production's marketing abroad if others could.

Today, there are "intimacy coordinators" on sets when sex scenes are filmed. Today, and indeed for many years, actresses have had paragraphs in their contracts stipulating exactly what body parts will be shown and to whom. This was 1977. This was a TV movie. No one had a cell phone. Stephanie couldn't step away and say, "Hang on, let me call my agent." We were in the mountains. It was after dark. The crew was waiting. To be honest, I believe Marc waited until this exact moment to spring this request, knowing that Stephanie would have to make this decision on her own, without guidance or support.

My co-star had been placed in an extremely difficult spot. John Korty assured her that the scene would be tastefully shot by David and John. As Stephanie told me later, she knew that John was absolutely sincere. The problem was the producer: there was no telling what he'd do with the raw footage and how it might be cut for a European audience. Stephanie would never know who had seen what and where.

Stephanie held her ground. She refused to take off her top. She had to say "No" more than once, and Marc finally backed down.

As we sat in the hot tub, we could both tell Marc was still unhappy. Stephanie and I talked quietly and came up with a solution. She would lower her top just a bit and I would use my upper body to screen her chest from the camera as we hugged and kissed in the bubbling water. Her breasts would not be exposed, but no one could see a bikini top either. Viewers could imagine she was topless. That was our compromise, and my first experience taking control of a moment with another actor. I don't think our producer was fully satisfied with this strategy, but Stephanie gave him something he could use. We played the scene close, so there was no possibility of her being exposed to the lens. I couldn't have imagined handling this situation any other way. When it was over, John smiled at us and nodded his head, proud of how we both had handled it. I don't remember any further conversation with the producer, and though I've never seen a European TV cut of *Forever*, I know that audiences in France or Germany didn't see any more of Stephanie than did American viewers because we didn't let the footage get shot.

It was in this moment in the mountains that I recognized, for the first but not the last time, the extraordinary double standard that actresses face. I am proud that I stood by Stephanie when it mattered, and proud that I helped come up with a solution to the dilemma she faced in that hot tub moment. The most famous moments of my career have almost always involved me playing a supportive partner to a woman who is at the center of the story. I am glad that I could be that professional partner off camera as well as on.

In the end, the movie for CBS turned out beautifully. I believe it achieved what it was designed to achieve, and I think the heart and honesty John Korty brought forth from each of us did honor to Judy Blume's novel. *Forever* was about the importance of balancing the wonders of love and intimacy with responsible choices. I feel fortunate that I had a colleague like Stephanie— and that I could draw on my unforgettable first love experience with Tracy Powell to make our moments together genuine. After all these years, I am proud I was able to bring so much of my personal experience—including enormous respect for a woman's agency to choose yes or no—into the work we did on *Forever*.

What I will always remember most about the *Forever* experience with John Korty, Stephanie Zimbalist, John Friedrich, Beth Raines, David Myers, and John Bailey is that it was a very loving and supportive environment to work in. I don't think I could have gotten a better first big experience in front of the camera. Reminiscing with me as I was writing this chapter, Stephanie told me without hesitation that "John Korty was one of the best directors I ever worked with." Coming from Stephanie, who has worked with many directors during her career, it was a powerful affirmation of my experience as well.

The "work" of making *Forever* was more special because it was my first big job. It took me from zero to sixty in 110 pages of screenplay. Before *Forever* I was a college student, going to class, doing college plays and musicals, working at KUOP, doing commercials and under-five parts (parts with five lines or less) on TV. I was having a good time at school going to parties, to games, and on dates. There wasn't any clear connection between being a college actor and a professional actor. What I was doing on campus was not an apprenticeship for a life in the industry. Making this movie was.

Other than my old Piedmont classmate Jim Kelly, none of my fellow UOP students wanted to have a professional career in movies and television. I knew one thing very clearly, and I decided it early: I knew I didn't want to hang out backstage smoking cigarettes, drinking black coffee, and arguing about Ibsen. I wasn't a "theater kid" in that sense, and I say that with no disrespect to Ibsen or those who love him. To be fair, I had never smoked a cigarette or sipped from a cup of coffee. My exposure to Ibsen was a play called *The Wild Duck* that I was assigned to read in an Introduction to Theater class when I was a freshman. Smoking cigarettes wasn't healthy, my father drank tea, and talking about Ibsen felt like a dead end. At the time, all of college felt like a dead end creatively.

I never took up smoking. I did end up moving to Los Angeles, rooming with my *Forever* co-star John Friedrich, and becoming part of a small community of professional actors who spent a lot of late nights at DuPar's Coffee Shop in Studio City. We sat in banquettes drinking coffee, eating stacks of pancakes, and talking about Marlon Brando, Robert De Niro, and Al Pacino. So, I traded the backstage of a college theater for DuPar's, tea for coffee and cream, cigarettes for pancakes, and debating Ibsen for conversation about the premier actors of our time. The biggest trade was the ambition that drove the conversation. When I first moved to L.A., I was thrilled at the prospect of working anywhere, but the people I was hanging out with at the time were focused on feature films. They aspired to play parts in the most prestigious scripts with the best directors and the biggest budgets. They lifted my sights.

There was so much I didn't know about acting as a craft while shooting *Forever*. While nobody can control the fate of when the job will come their way, in retrospect I wish I'd had more experience in some smaller parts before being in a position where my lack of craft was so easily detectable. I don't know if the television audience knew that I was totally raw. But industry professionals could tell, and that probably cost me some opportunities. On the flip side, an actor is never more appealing to the industry than when they are brand new with no credits, experience, or judgments against them. As with a newborn baby that everyone wants to hold, casting directors and producers want to meet an unknown actor because they are pure potential—and could become the next big thing overnight if they hit the screen with that certain something special. Every industry pro wants to discover the next big thing.

"Often in error, never in doubt." That's a family motto, as noted earlier, and it was me in a nutshell. When I was nineteen years old, with little life experience and virtually no real responsibility, I was incredibly certain of what I did and didn't need! In retrospect, not wanting to read Ibsen was a mistake. I could have stayed at UOP a little longer, done a few more student productions, and paid a bit more attention in class. After *Forever*, though, I had no interest in anything that wouldn't immediately advance my career and life aspirations. I wanted to be seen and heard. This movie of the week gave me a taste of what could be, and I wanted more.

Stephanie Zimbalist is still my friend. John Korty died on March 9, 2022. Sadly, I will never get another opportunity to tell him how special he was to me and to all of us. He was the first creative person of consequence who made it clear to me in action and words that I was both talented and worthy of acceptance just as I was.

John's faith in me (and mine in myself) would be tested many times in the years ahead.

CHAPTER 7

Wide-Eyed in Los Angeles

I GREW UP HATING LOS ANGELES. DISLIKE FOR OUR STATE'S LARGEST city is the one thing that unites the entire San Francisco Bay Area. It is often the only thing on which graduates of UC Berkeley and their archrivals at Stanford can heartily agree. In my 1960s and '70s boyhood, the Los Angeles Rams regularly thrashed my family's beloved San Francisco 49ers. I can't remember how many times I saw the Cal Golden Bears lose to the USC Trojans and UCLA Bruins. Sitting with my father and brother in Memorial Stadium, witnessing bitter and regular defeats, inculcated an early contempt for Los Angeles.

It wasn't just sports. My Aunty Dot, my grandmother's older sister, told me once she had visited Los Angeles in 1937. She had hated it, she said, and never went back. Other relatives described it as flashy, superficial, smog-ridden, and ugly. No one could possibly want to go there if it could be avoided. In the aftermath of *Forever*, I knew that if I wanted to "make it" as an actor, I couldn't avoid that place we all hated. It was wonderful to make a movie in the Bay Area with a Bay Area director, but such opportunities were rare. I had no choice but to pack up my yellow Volkswagen Beetle and start driving south.

This meant dropping out of college before my senior year. My father was adamant that I should finish at Pacific. Hollywood would wait, he told me. Dad had started college and never finished, and though he had been remarkably successful without it, he always regretted never getting that degree. Dad put all three of his children through college without any financial aid, but he never lost the chip on his own shoulder over having dropped out. What my father didn't understand was that I had a "film in the can," and that I needed to make my move now. Unlike other young actors, I'd be able to say I'd already starred in a movie—one that was coming out on a major network. That put an aura around me, a glow of mystique and untapped potential that is irresistible to the industry. That glow could launch me into stardom or leave me broken and disappointed, wondering what went wrong. I knew that I had to take the chance and take it now.

I was twenty-one. There was nothing Dad could say to make me change my mind. Yet.

The fastest way from the Bay Area to Los Angeles is on Interstate 5, which cuts through the vast hinterland of Central California. The San Joaquin Valley is famously hot, and on this August day it was blistering by 9 AM. The Beetle had no air-conditioning. I had to stop regularly for cold drinks. The trip took just over seven hours—the longest I'd ever driven in a single day.

I'll never forget going over the Grapevine for the first time. The Grapevine cuts through the Tehachapi Mountains that separate Los Angeles from the Central Valley. As I reached the crest of the Grapevine—just over four thousand feet high—I saw a massive wall of brown air in front of me. It was as dense as fog, but it wasn't the cool gray mist I knew so well in the Bay Area. This was smog: air pollution. Today, thanks to various environmental regulations, L.A. is much cleaner and clearer. In 1977, the City of Angels sweltered under a toxic brown blanket.

The minute I entered it, I could taste the air all around me. It was surreal. It was like this cloud was alive, and I had entered it. I could still see the sun above me, but the world looked completely different than it had just moments before.

As I came down the Grapevine into Santa Clarita and the northern suburbs of the city, I could make out the Magic Mountain Amusement Park, famous for its roller coasters, on my right. A girl I went to Pacific with, Melinda, worked at Magic Mountain as her summer job. It was a small thing, but I felt a little connection there. The famously dense Los Angeles traffic grew heavier, and if possible, the smog grew thicker. I stole glances at the AAA map on the passenger seat as I passed exits for the 14, 210, and 405 freeways before reaching my entrance to the 170. I was close now. Soon, the 170 became the 101. (I'm giving away that I'm an Angeleno: it's only in Los Angeles that we put the definite article before the freeway number. In the Bay Area, we talked about "taking 880"—in L.A., we speak of taking *the* 405 or *the* 710.)

I passed Universal Studios on the left and at last reached my exit: Barham Boulevard. Two more lefts, the crest of a hill, and I saw it on my right: the Oakwood Garden Apartments, right at the southern edge of Burbank. Oakwood was a furnished and unfurnished apartment complex where many actors chose to live when they first arrived in Los Angeles. Nearly fifty years later, it's still there today, under a different name. The complex was built into the hillside, blooming oleander bushes everywhere. Three or four large swimming pools for relaxation—and tanning through the smog. On the other side of the hill from these apartments was the HOLLYWOOD sign. I didn't know that then. You couldn't see the top of the hill through that filthy air.

The smog wasn't just ugly. It was a health threat. If you're a young actor in Los Angeles, you have got to look good. You need to be fit, not just for appearance but because at any moment, you might be cast as an athlete or a soldier. I was already a runner and relied on a daily three to four miles as my key to staying in shape. Living in Burbank, one of the challenges to outdoor exercise was the smog, which was so thick in the air that I had headaches and nausea after almost every workout. I have never been a cigarette smoker, but I'm sure my lungs looked as if I was getting through a pack of Marlboro Reds every day. I am so grateful that air quality has improved so significantly since.

John Friedrich had rented a two-bedroom apartment for us to share. I got my key from the office and let myself in. The apartment was completely empty, the bedrooms down the hall past the kitchen. John's room was straight ahead; mine on the left. After unpacking the Beetle, everything I had fit in one corner of the room.

A knock on the door. Standing there was a petite redhead, sprayed into her white blouse, jeans, and platform sandals. Other than the guy who had handed me my apartment keys, this was the first person I'd met in Los Angeles.

"Hi, I'm Valerie," she said as she strode in, not waiting for an invitation.

"How do you do? I'm Dean Butler," I replied, offering her a hand that she ignored.

"Sorry," she said, "I'm Valerie Landsberg. I'm a friend of John's." Within two seconds, Valerie was in the kitchen. Valerie was what my generation described as a "hot little package." She radiated sexual energy and confidence. Less than a minute after she'd knocked, I knew that she was a Beverly Hills native, an actress, a writer, and a singer. I had never met anyone like Valerie before. It hit me that if Hollywood was filled with women like her, I was in way over my head.

I *was* in way over my head.

In just a few short years, Valerie would become famous as Doris Schwartz, on TV's *Fame*. She and John had met while acting in an upcoming feature film called *Thank God It's Friday*, built around the L.A. disco scene. Valerie and John were part of a cast that included Jeff Goldblum and Debra Winger; the film would go on to win the Best Original Song Oscar for "Last Dance," sung in the movie by Donna Summer.

Valerie was the daughter of Alan Landsberg, a massively successful producer of docudramas and movies of the week. His current show on ABC was a weekly series exploring the paranormal called *In Search Of*, hosted by Leonard Nimoy.

My first Friday night in Los Angeles I folded my frame into the cramped space behind the bucket seats of Valerie's Alfa Romeo as she drove John and me to Westwood Village to see an opening night screening of *Looking for Mr. Goodbar*, starring Richard Gere. Westwood, just south of the UCLA campus, is not what it once was. In the 1970s, though, it was a ritual for industry people to go to the Village and Bruin theaters for Friday night openings of the biggest movies. The screens were huge, and the audio assaulted the ears.

I'd seen plenty of movies before, but watching *films* in Westwood was different. There was pride of ownership in the audience. The people who made these movies that would screen in theaters all over the world lived here; the most famous and respected of them very often resided within minutes of these theaters. You could feel the buzz at the ticket window, at the concession counter, and in the rush of people seeking out the best available seats before the lights went down. There was collective respect in the hush that fell over the audience when a movie began. I learned something vital about moviegoing that first Friday night in Westwood. At the end of the film, when the credits started to roll, nobody got up. Audiences in Westwood stayed in their seats and watched credits. On those Friday nights, you could be certain that many of those people whose names were on the screen were in the theater to experience the thrill of a paid audience watching their work for the first time.

I had an agent in San Francisco, but now I needed a representative in Los Angeles. I knew that getting the right agent would be made much easier because I had a "movie in the can," but I still needed to choose wisely. Because they knew *Forever* was coming out, I had agents courting me as soon as I arrived in town. I didn't know how to tell which ones I could trust. I was grateful that Stephanie Zimbalist offered to introduce me to her own agent, Ina Bernstein. Ina was the senior television agent at International Creative Management, or ICM. When Stephanie said the acronym, I looked blank. I had never heard of ICM, which only confirmed my status as an industry novice. As it turned out, I was in the best possible hands.

When I stepped into the elevator in the ICM building for the first time, I found myself standing next to Elliott Gould—then at the peak of his fame. It was just Elliott and me on a ride to the sixth floor. I didn't say a word during the short ride up, but I knew I was in a very good place if Elliott Gould was represented by ICM.

Ina Bernstein had started her career in New York working with Paul Newman, Anthony Perkins, and Joanne Woodward. When I met Ina, she was representing my friend Stephanie, her father Efrem Zimbalist Jr., Jane Alexander, Loretta Swit, Lee Remick, Maureen Stapleton, and Robert Mitchum—and many others as well. When I was shown into her enormous office, Ina was sitting behind a huge desk in a high-back chair facing wall-to-wall windows that looked out over West Hollywood, Sunset Boulevard, and the hills. Like Stephanie, there was nothing flashy about Ina. She radiated dignity, stability, and substance. Her hair was precisely styled to frame her face. She wore pearls and gold jewelry, and during our conversation Ina spoke to me warmly and kindly like a grandmother. She confirmed that *For-*

ever was going to be a very nice introduction for me into the Hollywood community, and that she would be happy to represent me. It would take me a long time to understand just how lucky I was. Agents like Ina rarely took on actors who had shown up in L.A. just days earlier, with a single "film in the can."

A few years later, Melissa Gilbert would tell an interviewer that I was the "hayseed type." She didn't mean Almanzo Wilder—she meant Dean Butler. She wasn't being cruel. Melissa was just explaining why I was Laura Ingalls' type but not hers. At the time, it stung a little, not because I wanted Melissa to be attracted to me, but because it made me feel like a naïve rube. The truth is, Melissa was on to something. When I first arrived in Los Angeles, I was wide-eyed and innocent. I had no idea what I was getting into in Los Angeles. Tinseltown was a shark tank, and I had been raised in a fishbowl within a close and stable family in a small town. I had attended a small private university located in Central California. I had lost my virginity at age nineteen, late by the standards of the day. I didn't drink much, I never smoked cigarettes, and I'd never taken a single hit of marijuana, much less tried any other illicit drug. I'd been surrounded by middle- and upper-middle-class white people all my life, and though I had been raised to be cordial to everyone, I had no real comprehension of diversity.

In those early years in L.A., I didn't understand how my sheltered life and limited experience colored how I was perceived. I didn't understand that in the entertainment business, casting directors and producers pride themselves on being able to make instant decisions. These are people who are trained to be incredibly perceptive. They are very hard to fool. Some of these people did think I was trying to fool them: I came across as so naïve, so innocent, so straitlaced with my "How do you do, I'm Dean Butler," that some industry professionals thought it was an act. What actor with the proverbial "film in the can" could possibly be this sheltered?

It was not an act. It was me. And apparently, that guilelessness didn't work in my favor. I didn't have enough life experience or confidence available to me to be in control of what I was doing in my auditions. I heard "No" and nothing but "No." Meanwhile, Stephanie was working nonstop, and John Friedrich seemed to get offered virtually everything he auditioned for. We had been peers on *Forever*, but outside of that environment Stephanie and John were completely different. They had a *craft*. I had, as Bill Wolak, my acting professor at Pacific told me, *facility*. I needed to get some street smarts—and I needed a craft.

John learned of a Santa Monica acting teacher, George Shdanoff. Shdanoff was seventy-two, a Russian émigré, and had coached the likes of Gregory Peck and Rex Harrison at Universal Studios. One of Shdanoff's most devoted Hollywood students, Leslie Caron, wrote that Shdanoff believed that acting was a craft that could be taught and ought to be learned. In other words, acting wasn't just a natural gift. John thought we should both audition for one of his classes. When I met Shdanoff at his Pico Boulevard studio, he was grimly serious. He wore a three-piece suit. He told me he wanted to "see and feel fire" in the audition. He didn't mean passion—he meant actual flames. It was a sense memory exercise. I had done very little sense memory work, but I tried to feel fire. I tried very, very hard to feel fire. Shdanoff saw that I was more willing than capable, but based on that willingness he accepted me.

During the ten-week class we did lots of sense memory exercises and some scene work from classic plays. It was the first of many Los Angeles acting classes that I would seek out and take during the next twenty years as I sought to acquire that elusive, precious *craft*.

Every summer the great acting teacher Stella Adler, most famous for her work with Marlon Brando, came out from New York to teach a series of classes. They were instant sellouts; the class I was able to get into was Script Analysis. The course was given over three nights, in a theater on Melrose Avenue in West Hollywood. It was packed with famous actors and others who were coming for the wisdom of a great teacher. All these years later, I remember only one of the plays she discussed: *Golden Boy*, by Clifford Odets. What I'll never forget was the way she held her audience spellbound for three hours. It was an amazing performance and very cleverly considered.

Stella had a table and two chairs set up center/center on the stage. On the table was the *Golden Boy* script and a vase filled with two dozen long-stemmed red roses. When she entered the theater from the rear of the house, there was a standing ovation. Stella, then in her mid-seventies, held the arm of her young male assistant and moved slowly, purposely, regally to the stage.

She turned to her rapturous audience, opened her arms as if to accept the love that was pouring over her. The applause seemed to go on for two or three minutes. She hadn't opened her mouth yet, but she had everyone under her spell. When she was ready to sit, the assistant held Stella's chair. Then he sat down immediately behind and to her right in clear view of the audience. Stella began to speak in a booming, dramatic voice. She addressed us all as "dahhling" as she welcomed us and acknowledged the presence of Karl Malden and Diana Ross in the audience. Then she introduced *Golden Boy* and spoke with intimate authority about Clifford Odets. Stella had an unusual affectation with her tongue as she spoke. It was as though when she talked, she was also licking imaginary stamps.

Stella would go on talking for nearly three hours with one twenty-minute intermission. As the evening went on, it became very clear to me that Stella's assistant, who maintained an adoring gaze on her throughout, served a singular purpose. His job was to help Stella keep the focus on her. If anyone in the audience got distracted or bored for a moment and looked away from Stella, the first thing they would see was her assistant, audience left, looking adoringly at the great teacher. It was simple, brilliant stagecraft, and it worked unfailingly well over the three nights of talks about great American plays peppered with wonderful anecdotes about "Marlon" and "Robert" (Brando and De Niro) and judgments about actors she disdained for their lack of "size" on the stage. She was a vivid example of her mantra for actors; "Don't be boring." Her lectures were performances filled with joy, rage, poignance, and even tears. When she reached the conclusion of her talks, she surveyed the audience and said, "Goodnight, dahhlings," before exiting the theater to thunderous applause on her assistant's arm. I'd never seen anything like Stella Adler before, and actors haven't seen anything like her since.

I still couldn't believe I was part of this world.

Living in Los Angeles was expensive. The money I'd made on *Forever* was going fast, no matter how careful I tried to be. I wasn't landing any paid acting work. I needed to get a survival job. Waiting tables or tending bar are the stereotypical survival jobs for actors, but I wasn't interested in those. I wanted a job where I could work with my hands, maybe work up a good sweat. I wanted to feel like I was creating something. I had always loved working with wood, so when I saw a job in a furniture store called The Barn, I applied. The Barn was, as its name implied, a rustic indoor/outdoor store in Van Nuys. They sold oak dining tables, chairs, rolltop desks, file cabinets, and bookcases. I liked the products. I got a job at The Barn and started working on weekends for $1.75 per hour. The learning curve was quick. It was honest physical work. I would sell tables and chairs and strap them onto the roofs of cars for people to take home. I made twenty-eight dollars my first weekend. The owners gave raises in increments of five cents per hour.

I had my survival job, I was taking class, I was auditioning, and I was getting to know the city of Los Angeles, which is all about learning the best ways to get from point A to point B at different times of day. With my *Thomas Guide* always in my lap, I figured out that my life in Los Angeles required me to understand the connectivity of a handful of freeways: the 5, 170, 134, 405, 10, and 110. There were many more, but those six were lifelines. Between 10 AM and 3 PM, those freeways could get me everywhere in the city I needed to go. I also learned very quickly that between seven and ten in the morning and three and seven in the evening I needed to stay off the freeways. They were parking lots.

On the *Tonight Show* many years ago, Johnny Carson asked Bette Davis, "What's the best way to get into Hollywood?" Johnny was asking a career question. Bette answered practically, "Take Fountain." She got a big laugh from Johnny's Los Angeles-based studio audience. She was right. Getting around Los Angeles and avoiding freeways is all about shortcuts. If you need to get into or through Hollywood, you take Fountain. If you want to get from the west side to downtown, take Olympic. From LAX to Hollywood, take La Cienega to Stocker to La Brea. From Hollywood to Burbank, take Highland to Cahuenga to Barham. Today, your phone can find the best route. In the 1970s, we needed to learn by trial and error.

Just as every Angeleno looks for shortcuts across town, young actors are always looking for shortcuts to success in the industry. We live in hope and expectation of finding the right agent, the right script, the right show, the right casting director, the right teacher, or the right look. The reality is that every actor who succeeds does so for one reason: they walked into an office and made an indelible impression on a person in a position to hire them. It's that simple, it's that hard, and it's that unpredictable.

I was astounded by the number of actors I met who were filled with total belief in themselves. They were certain about the parts they wanted to play, the projects they wanted to do, and the directors they wanted to work with. They made instant and savage assessments about their peers. My family says, "Often in error, never in doubt," but my family had nothing on young Hollywood.

In 1978, the community was abuzz about a script called *Ordinary People*, based on the 1976 bestseller by Judith Guest. *Ordinary People* was the directorial debut of Robert Redford. Young actors who saw themselves as film worthy speculated about who should be considered for the roles of Calvin, Beth, Conrad, and Dr. Berger. There was palpable outrage and vicious criticism of Redford when he cast Donald Sutherland, Mary Tyler Moore, Tim Hutton, and Judd Hirsch in these plum roles. Other than Donald Sutherland, who had a very successful film career, the others were dismissed as "television actors" who were incapable of bringing the depth of emotional life to what, in the hands of the right actors, would be a gripping theatrical film.

When *Ordinary People* premiered in theaters in 1980, it was a huge critical success. The two performances that most shocked the actors I knew were from Mary Tyler Moore and Tim Hutton, the two "television actors" whose casting was judged as certain to ruin the film. Both were extraordinary "ordinary people." Mary Tyler Moore revealed a desperate icy fragility that audiences had never seen in her television work, and Tim Hutton was amazing as Conrad, the family's troubled son. The lesson I took from my friends' shock was threefold: (1) prior experience is not always an indicator of future performances; (2) my friends, for all their talent, were not great judges of others' abilities; and (3) casting directors rarely make mistakes, even when we think they do.

As for me, I didn't sit in judgment about anyone's casting choices. I just wanted my next break. I got close. I was offered a pilot at Lorimar for a sitcom called *The Waverly Wonders* starring recently retired NFL great Joe Namath, but Ina Bernstein read it and insisted that I turn it down.

"I know you want to work, sweetheart, but it's not a good script," she told me.

I needed to work, and I needed the money that would come from doing a pilot. I tried to reason with Ina that even if the pilot didn't go to series, I would have the cachet of having done it. Ina wouldn't relent.

"You never want be attached to something that isn't good," was her final comment, and "we" turned it down. Ina was right: *Waverly Wonders* never got on ABC's fall schedule.

A few weeks after turning down *The Waverly Wonders*, I auditioned at Lorimar for *Dallas* to play one of Lucy Ewing's many boyfriends. One of Lorimar's casting directors, whose name I have erased from my memory, took me aside and coldly asked, "Who the hell do you think you are to turn down one of our pilots?"

If she had only known how much I didn't want to turn down one of their pilots! Now I had to wonder how much my decision about their pilot would affect my future.

There were other disappointments that stung just as much. I got deep into the casting process for *Friendly Fire*, a very big project at ABC starring Carol Burnett and Ned Beatty. I made it all the way to the mix-and-match sessions where groups of actors were put together with Carol and Ned to see which group looked most like a family. In the final readings I had been paired with Marc McClure, who audiences had seen recently as Jimmy Olson in *Superman*. Marc was terrific, easy, and relaxed in the way he worked, but I don't know how much we looked like brothers. The other pair of actors in the final mix to play brothers were Timothy Hutton and Dennis Erdman. We read for Carol Burnett, the director David Greene, the producer Philip Barry Jr., the writer/producer Fay Kanin, and the casting directors Mike Fenton and Jane Feinberg.

I think Tim and Dennis read first, while Marc and I were second. When we were finished, there was some quick conversation in the room. I'll never forget Philip Barry asking us, "Do you want to know who got it?"

Marc and I simultaneously said, "Yeah!"

Philip Barry smiled. "We'll call your agents in a few minutes."

Moments after I got back to my apartment, Ina Bernstein called. "I'm sorry, sweetheart, you didn't get it." I was devastated. If you're not going to be hired, what sadistic S.O.B. asks actors if they want to know who got it? It made no sense. Clearly Marc and I left the room as their first choice, and within minutes something changed their minds. Marc and I never found out what it was. That disappointment haunted me for a long, long time.

I knew intellectually that the entertainment business was often cruel, but to experience one disappointment after another took a toll. Maybe *Forever* had been a fluke. Maybe I could only get cast in things if I stayed in the Bay Area. Maybe it was time to go home.

I came home to Piedmont for Christmas 1978. It had been a hard six months in Los Angeles. It felt like ten years. Before the New Year, Dad and I had perhaps the most important conversation we would ever have. The short version of what he had to say went like this: "You're trying to succeed in Hollywood. It's a tough game, and there are no guarantees that it's going to work for you." He had no idea how tough it was, but he was right that there was no guarantee that I would succeed.

He was reading my mind. I nodded. Dad continued: "You've done three and half years of your undergraduate education. You need to finish at UOP. If you don't finish what you started and get your degree, you will regret it for the rest of your life."

Dad had flunked out of the University of New Mexico after his freshman year because he didn't go to class. His father cut him loose and told him he was on his own. Despite that early misstep, Dad had turned out well. The truth was that lots of people turned out well having not gone to college. Dad became very successful in the life insurance and financial services industry. He and my mother raised my brother, sister, and me in beautiful, stable homes. We had everything we ever needed and more. Despite his very real success, Dad felt that not having a college degree put him at a real disadvantage with his peers. It was a chip on his shoulder; it was a wound that wouldn't heal.

Neither of my parents had college degrees, even though each of my four grandparents had graduated from college. My mother never attempted to go past high school. She was the social one, while her younger sister, Alison, was the academic one. My aunt went to Vassar and later became one of the first women to earn a PhD in philosophy from Berkeley. My father's brother Thorne went to medical school and became a highly respected patholo-gist. My father's sister Jennifer had graduated from University of the Pacific.

"My education is always a question I can't answer," my father told me. "I don't want you to be in that same position. Every ap-plication I've ever filled out has asked about a college degree. I didn't finish what I started, so I can't answer that question." My dad very rarely got emotional, but I could hear his pain as he spoke.

"Please, Dean, I want you to be able to say that you finished what you started. I'm begging you. Finish school now so you'll never have to look back and have the regrets that I have every day of my life."

I heard his raw plea, and I know he felt my pride and my fear of failure. He was offering me the lifeline his father never of-fered him. And he was right. Whatever did or didn't happen in Hollywood, I needed to finish school. I needed to finish what I started. Acting could wait for another semester.

"Thank you, Dad, for giving me this chance to do what's right." I was thanking him in part because he was paying my tu-ition but thanking him far more for being so vulnerable with me. That was hard for him, and I wanted him to know I was grateful.

As I said, it was the most important talk I ever had with my dad. Looking back at my relationship with him, it wasn't a great relationship. From the time I was seven years old, I never felt emotionally safe with him, but I have no doubt that he loved me, that he wanted the best for me, and that he would've done anything for me. This was one of those moments when he shared his heart with me about something he believed was important for my life, and I'm forever grateful for the love that compelled him to help me help myself.

While that final semester back on campus at Pacific was a good thing for my life in the long term, and a welcome distraction from the career anxiety I was feeling at that time, it wasn't easy. Even though I was back in a familiar, beautiful place, surrounded by people I had worked and played with for five years, there were questions and comments like, "What are you doing back here? Are you a *has-been* already?" After such a disappointing year in Los Angeles, I was genuinely afraid I was indeed already a "has-been." I kept my head down for the next few months. As winter turned to spring, I swallowed the teasing and focused on doing as well as I possibly could. I would get my college degree by May, and I would bask in my parents' pride. I just didn't know what I would do next when I got back to Los Angeles.

I got my answer just weeks before graduation. I hadn't spoken to Ina Bernstein for more than a month, but on one afternoon in late March she left a message for me at my fraternity house. When I called her back her assistant connected us quickly.

"Sweetheart," she purred. "I have a meeting for you for *Little House on the Prairie*."

CHAPTER 8

My Journey to a Land of Long Ago

THE FIRST EPISODE OF *LITTLE HOUSE ON THE PRAIRIE* DEBUTED ON NBC on September 11, 1974. When Ina Bernstein called me to tell me I had a meeting for *Little House,* the show had been on the air for five hugely successful seasons. I had watched exactly zero episodes.

I knew almost nothing about the show. I'd seen lots of promos run on NBC, and I certainly knew who Michael Landon was. I'd grown up watching him play Little Joe on *Bonanza,* and I knew his Kodak commercials. I was totally aware that Michael was the star of *Little House,* but I didn't know anything about anyone else in the cast and wasn't in the show's target demographic. None of my acting friends watched the show. I had never read any of the Laura Ingalls Wilder books on which the series was based. All I had to go on was Ina Bernstein's excitement and enthusiasm.

"Michael Landon is so wonderful," Ina gushed over the phone. "Not only does he star in *Little House,* but he also writes it, he directs, and he's the executive producer! When Jack died, I cried my eyes out."

It would be some time before I learned that Jack was, in fact, a dog.

Ina continued. "Dean, if you get an offer to do *Little House*, you will do it."

That was a nice change. I was somewhat relieved Ina was encouraging me to come to Los Angeles to read for a show that she'd actually let me do. If, that is, I got an offer.

On a foggy spring morning in 1979, I flew down to Los Angeles to have a meeting at MGM Studios with Susan Sukman, the casting director for *Little House on the Prairie*. The show had just moved to the famous Culver City lot (now home of Sony Pictures) after spending its first five seasons at Paramount. I had never been to MGM before. I parked in the parking lot in front of the Irving Thalberg Building, walked to the main entrance, and was guided by the security guard to the first building on the left.

"*Little House* is on the second floor," he told me. "Go up the stairs, turn right. Susan Sukman's office is down the hall."

This was a different casting meeting from what I was used to. Susan's assistant, Darlene, greeted me with a warm, slightly mischievous smile. Usually, a casting director's assistant was businesslike at best, and frequently grim. It must be hard to see so many hopefuls showing up for so few parts. Except for Darlene, I was alone in the outer office. During my time in Los Angeles, I had grown accustomed to walking into castings and seeing half a dozen guys who looked a lot like me at every meeting. It raised my hopes to be the only actor there.

A moment later, the inner office door opened. There stood a woman with a big smile on her face and my picture in her hand. "Hi, I'm Susan Sukman. Come on in, Dean."

Another smile—and she had used my name too! Another thing that had rarely happened to me in a casting office.

Susan sat, and I sat. My eyes instantly went to the nearly foot-high stack of glossy photos on Susan's desk. This was the intimidating reality of being an actor in Los Angeles. There was a tremendous amount of "young leading man talent" in town. Good casting directors made it their business to know that talent.

Based on the stack of pictures in front of Susan, a lot of talent was being considered for this part.

This casting session I was stepping into with Susan was called a "meet and greet." It's the casting director's job to figure out not only if you can play the part, but if you will fit into the "family" of the show's cast and crew. Casting directors know they're dealing with actors who will be on their absolute best behavior, eager to please. It takes a highly perceptive professional to see through that carefully practiced façade.

There's a concept called the *7/11 rule*, and it has nothing to do with Big Gulps or Slurpees. In any business setting (and a casting session is certainly that), eleven judgments are made in the first seven seconds of meeting someone. We instinctively judge level of education, economic status, credibility, trustworthiness, sophistication, sexual orientation, level of financial success, political background, spirituality, ethnicity, and social desirability. We may turn out to be wrong about some or most of those, particularly if we're not trained casting directors—but we make the judgments anyway. You've also probably heard the saying "You don't get a second chance to make a first impression." That's especially true in casting sessions. A casting director is not only forming their own impression in seven seconds, but they are also assessing the first impression an actor, playing a particular character, will make on an audience of millions.

First impressions may or may not be accurate, but they are very hard to change. The best play you have with a professional casting director? Walk in as the most authentic version of yourself you have. I didn't have a plan to impress Susan Sukman. I just came into her office the way I always walked into castings: as the polite, well-behaved young man I was raised to be. I was clean, respectful, neatly dressed, and I spoke in complete, grammatically correct sentences. I did the same thing with a casting director that I did when I first met the parents of a young woman I was dating. I went with who I was, and that's who Susan saw that day.

I don't remember a lot about that first meeting, but Susan Sukman made a wonderful first impression on me. After just a few seconds, I felt like I was talking to someone with whom I could totally connect. The comfort of that first impression gave me the ease to be my best self with her. I had two more meetings with Susan for *Little House,* driving down from Stockton each time. On each visit, the stack of photos on her desk shrank. Twelve inches became six inches, then three. I knew I was in the hunt to play this young man whose name we always pronounced, incorrectly, as *AlmONzo.*

After a very warm third meeting in early April, I felt good about my chances—but then it got very quiet. I began to worry that the part was slipping away. I called Ina's office every other day asking for updates. There weren't any.

Back at Pacific, my friends were talking about the great jobs they'd lined up after graduation. I tried to avoid those conversations. All I could think was that if I didn't get *Little House,* I'd have nothing to show for my four years of college education, four years my father had paid for without a penny of scholarship or grant support. I could always go back to The Barn and sell oak tables and file cabinets, but for how long? Was that the best I could do? All I saw in my future was acting, but acting wasn't seeing me the way I hoped it would.

I was twenty-two. I felt on the verge of being a total failure.

And then one day in mid-April, Ina called. Michael Landon wanted me to read for him in two days. I was on a plane to Los Angeles the next morning. As soon as I got to the apartment, the phone rang. It was Ina Bernstein's office, with a message from Susan Sukman:

"Dean, when you go in to the read for Michael tomorrow, *whatever you do, don't act.*"

Don't act? I'm going in to read for *Michael Landon*, to *play a part* on his television series! What does this mean, "don't act"? I read and reread the pages of the script I'd been given. Almanzo needed to give Laura a pep talk after she'd had failed a test. The lines seemed straightforward enough, but the "Whatever you do, don't act" confused the hell out of me.

As I drove to MGM from Burbank the next morning, I ran the lines from the scene in my head while fending off a host of other worries. I was reading for Michael Landon, but I had not met Melissa Gilbert. The part was to play her future husband, the man with whom she'd fall in love. I knew from experience that casting love interests generally requires chemistry between the two actors. Would there be a mix-and-match session with Melissa after this reading with Michael Landon? And why hadn't I met anyone from NBC during this process? Would Michael Landon make the call on his own? Could NBC's head of casting, Joel Therm, veto Michael Landon's decision? Almanzo was a big part—and the casting would impact the appeal of the series moving forward. There was a lot at stake for me and the show. And I wasn't supposed to act.

All these thoughts rolled through my head as I drove to Culver City. After several visits to the *Little House* offices, I knew where to go. This time, though, I saw a green Ferrari parked in a spot that had been empty on my previous visits. Michael Landon was waiting for me. This was really happening. *Whatever you do, don't act.*

Darlene, Susan's assistant, greeted me warmly as I walked into the outer office. There was no one else in the room, but I could feel a buzz in the air. There were no other actors in the room, but I could almost feel my competition lurking. So many young actors would want this part. So many of them were very, very good. I sat down, took a deep breath.

I'd only sat for a single beat before Susan opened her office door, and invited me in.

"Michael, this is Dean Butler," she said with her now familiar warm and friendly voice.

"How you doin'?" he said, in a voice that I'd been hearing for what seemed like most of my life.

Michael did not get up. He sat on a couch across from Susan's desk on the far side of her office. His legs were crossed; one ankle resting on the opposite knee. If there had been a picture in the dictionary next to the definition of "Big 1970's Television Star," it would have been of Michael Landon as he was in this moment: snakeskin boots; sprayed-on jeans, tight chambray shirt unbuttoned nearly to the navel; gold Carrera sunglasses in the modestly lit room. A Star of David medal hung from the beefy gold chain around his neck. His face was framed by those famously casual-yet-studied curls. He had a cigarette clamped between his teeth. He was dazzling almost to the point of caricature.

If this hadn't been the biggest moment of my professional life, I might have asked, "Are you for real?"

Instead, I gave my standard, "How do you do?"

After a little small talk that elicited his unmistakable, infectiously good-natured giggle, we turned to the reading.

Don't act, don't act, don't act reverberated in my head as I turned to face Susan, who would be reading Laura's lines. Susan was a terrific reader. She didn't just cue lines but provided an emotional connection to the script. Somehow, I was able to focus on her and the sweet conversation between Almanzo and Laura. As we neared the end, out of the corner of my eye, I saw Michael lean forward and raise his hands to frame me.

It was a surreal and indelibly memorable moment. I kept not acting.

Michael didn't ask for any adjustments in the scene. He thanked me for coming in to meet him, and as I got up to leave, he asked me, "What are you doing the second week of May?"

"I'll be taking my finals at UOP and graduating on May 20," I told him.

He smiled up at me. "I think we can wait that long."

I thought instantly of Phillip Barry and that devastating meeting on *Friendly Fire*. Was Michael Landon offering me the job in the room—only to yank it back after I left?

I managed a polite "Thank you," and left the room, my mind whirling with emotion. I called Ina's office immediately and gave her a report. I don't remember the trip back to Northern California or getting back to school. All I can remember is how "I think we can wait that long" echoed and echoed in my head.

The waiting, however, was on me. It was mid-April. I still had a month of school left. Shooting on Season 6 of *Little House* was to start in mid-May—or a week later if Michael's statement to me had been authentic. As the days became a week, there was no news from Ina's office. At least with *Friendly Fire*, the heartbreak happened immediately. But now . . . a week became ten days, and still nothing. Hope and despair battled for the upper hand, and as the days dragged on, the latter began to win. The stakes were ridiculously high. Michael Landon was arguably the most singularly talented star, director, writer, and producer in television; *Little House* was one of television's highest-rated prime-time series.

I think we can wait that long. I didn't think *I* could.

Tuesday, May 1, 1979. Ina called at last. "They made an offer," she said.

Along with "You got it," "They made an offer" is the phrase every actor longs to hear. It means "they" want you—and they are opening the door to a negotiation of terms, most meaningfully on compensation.

I won't tell you the money that was offered, but it wasn't going to make me run out and buy a green Ferrari. There were twenty-two episodes ordered, and I would appear in thirteen of them. My credit would be at "producer's discretion." In some episodes I'd be billed as a guest star, and in others I would be listed as part of the ensemble in the end credits. Ina ran through the details of the offer, and I tried to listen, barely able to restrain myself from stopping her to say, "Whatever it is, I'll take it." Ina knew I wouldn't want to do much negotiating.

"Yes" was the only possible answer. It was official. It was real. I was now a member of the cast of *Little House on the Prairie*.

If this were our world today, I'd start texting my loved ones. Back then, though, I knew I'd get tied up on the landline with excited family if I started spreading the news. Before I called anyone, I walked over to the university's outdoor basketball courts and played full court for two hours. Afterwards, still hopped up on adrenaline and floating on air, I went on a five-mile run. Finally, I was calm enough to pick up the phone. I called Dad's office first. He was thrilled for me. With graduation just three weeks away, everything was working out better than either of us could've imagined. I told him, my voice filled with emotion, how grateful I was that he had insisted I finish my degree.

I had to make one more quick trip to Los Angeles before I walked across the stage to receive my diploma. I needed wardrobe fittings—and crucially, I had to meet with Michael Landon to decide on my hat. On a Thursday afternoon, I met with Michael in his office. With his long background in Westerns, Michael Landon took an intense interest in headgear. Hats, he told me, signaled the essence of a character. The *Little House* men's costumer, Mike Termini, had brought half a dozen hats for Michael to see me wear. Landon looked at the hats with almost childlike excitement, caressing them and holding them at various angles. At last, he zeroed in on a brown felt hat with a round top.

"What does this hat say about Almanzo?" I asked.

"This hat is like Dan Blocker's hat," he said softly. "Hoss was an uncomplicated man, and we need Almanzo to be an uncomplicated man." Dan Blocker had played Hoss on *Bonanza* and been Michael Landon's co-star for thirteen seasons. Blocker died at forty-three of a pulmonary embolism. I would later learn that for the rest of his career, whenever Michael needed to cry in a scene, he would think of his friend's unexpected passing and the tears would flow.

I had my marching orders. I was an uncomplicated man, joining an idyllic community that America loved. I graduated from UOP on May 20—my twenty-third birthday. Two days later, on May 22, 1979, I set out on the adventure that would shape the rest of my life.

Michael Landon had been true to his word. He *could* wait that long.

Almost everyone struggles with imposter syndrome at some point in their lives. It's the fear that somehow you've risen above your abilities, and you're about to be discovered as a fraud. I have friends who have been very successful in their chosen careers, and even after decades, they tell me they still expect to hear someone say, "Sorry, man, we made a mistake when we hired you. It was supposed to be someone else."

Imposter syndrome happens to actors too. There are plenty of moments in every successful career where you find yourself saying, "How the hell did I get here?" The difference between Hollywood and other industries is that we have casting directors. And as I've been told repeatedly, *casting directors don't make mistakes.* That's cold comfort to an actor who's missed out on a part they were sure was theirs, but it is powerful reassurance to an actor who has been cast in his first major role. Susan Sukman knew what she was doing. Michael Landon knew what he was doing. To indulge in too much imposter syndrome would be to denigrate their skill and their craft.

Michael Landon thought I could be Almanzo Wilder. It would be some time before I had a better understanding of *why* he picked me. It would also be a long time before I fully understood the parallels between my life and the character I'd just been hired to play.

When your acting career has been largely defined by one role, you spend a lot of time thinking about the ways in which you are—and aren't—like the character you played. I had other roles before Almanzo Wilder, and others after, but Almanzo is the reason you are reading this book. I was *Forever's* Michael Wagner, the *New Gidget's* Moondoggie, and *Buffy's* Hank Summers. Those roles will appear well down the page of my obituary if they appear at all. I am known for a role I was cast in at twenty-two, and which I last played at twenty-seven. I spent barely five years as Almanzo, but for millions, I am him and he is me.

Before I was asked to read for the part, I'd never heard the name "Almanzo" before. To my unpracticed eye and ear, it sounded Hispanic. In *Little Town on the Prairie* Laura Ingalls Wilder quotes her husband:

> *It was wished on me. My folks have got a notion there always has to be an Almanzo in the family, because 'way back in the time of the Crusades there was a Wilder went to them, and an Arab or somebody saved his life. El Manzoor, the name was.*

Some scholars doubt that origin, suggesting that Almanzo comes from German origin and means "precious man." Others have pointed out a similarity to the name "Alonso" which was a very popular man's name in mid-nineteenth-century America. My great-great-grandfather, the one who built my family's ranch, was born in 1842, fifteen years before Almanzo Wilder. His name was Albert *Alfonso* Moore. Though that name is certainly Hispanic, both DNA tests and family lore confirm I have zero Spanish ancestry. I've heard it suggested that names like Alonso and Alfonso were popular because they appeared in nineteenth-century romance novels. Perhaps that's the origin of Almanzo, too.

Like Almanzo Wilder, I am descended from pioneers. Albert Alfonso Moore, my great-great-grandfather, was the great-grand-son of a Captain James Moore. Originally a native of Maryland, Captain Moore served under General George Rogers Clark in the American Revolution. He was part of the daring raid that captured the British fort at Kaskaskia, Illinois, on the banks of the Mississippi River. That campaign opened a second front in the war and was a vital reason why the Yankee rebels would prove victorious. James Moore liked what he saw in the Illinois territory, and after the Revolution, was given a commission by the governor of Virginia to settle there and claim it for the commonwealth. My ancestor's original cabin still stands near Waterloo, Illinois.

In the introduction to this book, I quoted Albert Alfonso Moore's 1915 memoir, and his note that our family came "of sturdy stock." In that same book, my great-great-grandfather wrote:

> *Those dead of whom I write, abhorred with all mankind the notion of oblivion—being forgotten and as if they never lived. No doubt I would have pleased much any of those dead ancestors of whom I am to speak to have known in life (if possible) that in 1915 a descendant should write the name,—as, Enoch, or James, or John, Polly, or Betsy,—in kindly remembrance. One would rather be abused than forgotten. The longing for immortality on the earth, among kin and people—to be remembered and spoken and written of— is universal. There is a kind of immortality in "the recollec-*

tion one leaves in the memory of man." Myself, I gloom a
bit, in the tough that with brief lapse I will be as a "watch in
the night"—forgotten, and as if never born.

A.A. Moore doesn't cite the origin of those lines he quotes. After a little research, I found that they come from *The Memoirs of Napoleon,* by Louis Antoine Fauvelet de Bourrienne. Napoleon had little reason to fear not being remembered, but my ancestor did, and so do so many of us. I know this is one reason I'm writing this memoir.

A.A. Moore wanted to make sure his descendants remembered not only his life but the lives of his pioneer ancestors. I was raised in a family that was proud of its pioneer heritage; in addition to Captain James Moore, the Revolutionary hero, other family members crossed the plains in covered wagons and endured tremendous hardship and sacrifice. As we reassess our American past, I am especially proud of A.A. Moore's father-in-law, my great-great-great-grandfather Samuel Pike Hall. From his own father, Samuel Hall inherited a plantation and slaves in East Texas. An abolitionist, Hall freed his slaves in 1850, packed up his family, and moved to Central California. His daughter Jacqueline would later meet and marry A.A. The enslaving of our fellow humans was a stain on American history, and it is my "modest pride" that my ancestor quit that terrible practice long before the Civil War.

A.A. Moore was no Laura Ingalls Wilder, but they shared a deep desire to pay tribute to their forebears. They were both invested in ensuring that the struggles and triumphs of the past not be forgotten. Scholars have long debated the historical accuracy of the *Little House* books. Our television series took plenty of dramatic license. Though the "truth" was occasionally altered to meet the needs of network television, our show existed to make sure that Laura and Almanzo, their families and friends, remained a "recollection in the memory of man." For millions

This shot of a day on the ranch looks like a scene from *Little House*. It's actually the A.A. Moore Ranch circa 1906. This property has been in my family since 1885, the same time frame Laura wrote about in her later *Little House* books. *Source: A.A. Moore Family Archive.*

This picture of the Moore family convertible coach is one of the most treasured in our family, capturing our connection to rugged days gone by. The boy in the second row, A.A. Moore, would grow up to be my grandfather. His grandfather, also A.A. Moore, is sitting ahead of him in the driver's seat. This special carriage, once drawn by four horses, still exists and is on permanent display at the Oakland Museum of California in Oakland. *Source: A.A. Moore Family Archive.*

My parents are second cousins—nothing illegal. Peter Roeding Butler and Marianna Roeding Moore were engaged in 1955. *Source: Butler Family Photo.*

My life journey began when I was born in
Prince George, British Columbia, Canada
on May 20, 1956. I'm pictured here
with my mother, Marianna Moore Butler,
then twenty-one years old, in the apartment
my parents rented in Prince George
while Dad finished his service
in the United States Air Force.
Source: Butler Family Photo.

Christmas has always been my favorite
holiday. At the center of that holiday is
the special Christmas tree stand to the left
of my parents, Peter and Marianna Butler.
The original stand was created by
Henry Roeding for my grandmother and
her sister in 1910. This one was copied
for my mother and her sister in 1934.
Source: A.A. Moore Family Archive.

I was the firstborn of my generation of our family. My first Christmas was spent in Piedmont, California surrounded by three older generations of men whose influences shaped my life.
Standing: Maternal grandfather Arthur Moore. Seated, left to right: Great-grandfather Henry Roeding, me, and my father, Peter Roeding Butler. *Photo credit: Margaret Roeding Moore.*

I was no more than an infant when I was first held in a saddle. A few years later, I'm in the saddle on my own getting ready to go for an afternoon ride with my grandfather. You can see I've got the reins in my left hand (since I'm right-handed) and my heels are down in the stirrups. It was good training that would come in handy in the years ahead. *Photo Credit: Marianna Butler.*

When I was in the fourth grade, we went to the ranch on a winter weekend to get a saddle so I could do a horseback riding "show and tell" in my classroom the following week. The demonstration would be enhanced by my leather fringe jacket, most likely handed down to me from my cousin, Tom Bishop. My sister, Meg, is holding the bridle and Grandfather has the horse blanket. *Photo credit: Peter Roeding Butler.*

In the fall of 1973, I fell in love with sixteen-year-old Tracy Powell as I began my senior year at Piedmont High School. In so many ways, the love we shared helped define the man I would grow up to become. She remains a most treasured friend and an essential touchstone in my life. *Photo Credit: Piedmont High School Clan-o-log.*

Our family at home in Piedmont in the summer of 1975. *Photo Credit: Family Snapshot.*

The biggest break of my life happened in the summer of 1977, when I was cast opposite the lovely and talented Stephanie Zimbalist in a CBS Movie of the Week adaptation of Judy Blume's groundbreaking young adult novel, *Forever*. Photo Credit: *AGE FOTOSTOCK*

There was point between *Forever* and this moment on May 20, 1979 when I wondered
if I would ever graduate from college. My father threw me a lifeline, allowing me to finish
the undergraduate education I had started five years earlier. From left to right: my brother Scott,
Mom, sister Meg, and Dad surrounded me with love and congratulations.
I celebrated my twenty-third birthday, picked up my diploma, and left for Los Angeles
to start *Little House* two days later. *Photo Credit: Family Snapshot.*

When I got the opportunity to audition for casting director Susan Sukman McCray to play Almanzo Wilder on NBC's *Little House on the Prairie*, I had no idea that doing the show would change my life. My gratitude for the honor of stepping into the world of Laura Ingalls Wilder knows no bounds. This picture is the only non-production shot I have from my time on the series. Glad to share it here. *Photo Credit: Personal Snapshot.*

In 1985 I went from Manly to Moondoggie in *The New Gidget*. I loved working with the seventh Gidget, Caryn Richman, and one of our favorite directors, Roger Duchowny. *Photo Credit: Personal Snapshot.*

We did some fun, silly stuff on *The New Gidget*. In one episode I got to be a hippie.
Sorry, I don't have the picture where Caryn was Napoleon and I was Josephine. That would be a laugh.
Photo Credit: Personal Snapshot.

In my wildest imagination I never
dreamed I would get to Broadway.
I played Rapunzel's Prince for
320 performances in the
original company of *Into the Woods*.
Source: Personal Snapshot.

I first met Katherine Cannon
when she was auditioning for
Michael Landon's *Father Murphy*
fifteen years earlier.
When I met her again,
I knew quickly that she was
a woman with whom
I could build a wonderful life.
Photo Credit: Charles Butler.

In 2001, Katherine and I were married in a small ceremony at the Hotel Bel-Air in Los Angeles.
When I said "I do," I knew I was in for the rest of my life. Now it's been twenty-three years and counting.
She's my beautiful girl and she's made my life complete.
Source: Family Photo.

In 2008 I made a documentary called "Almanzo Wilder: Life Before Laura." It was a thrill to craft my own view of Laura Ingalls Wilder's Farmer Boy and produce it on location at the Almanzo Wilder Farm in Burke, NY.
Souce: Personal Snapshot.

On the occasion of *Little House on the Prairie*'s fortieth anniversary, members of our cast gathered in New York City to celebrate. During a shoot for *Entertainment Weekly*, I shot this selfie of Melissa Gilbert and me. Almanzo and Laura together again.
Source: Personal Snapshot.

In 2017 I traveled to
Frankenmuth, MI to spend
a weekend talking to
Little House fans of all ages.
Source: Personal Snapshot.

I think I was somehow destined
to play Almanzo Wilder in
Little House on the Prairie.
In this picture, taken by
Laura Ingalls Wilder scholar
William Anderson (you can see
half of Bill's head on the left side
of the frame), I'm standing in the
Wilders' Rocky Ridge Farm
living room in front of their
stone fireplace. This visit took place
in September, 2017.
Source: William Anderson.

Producing live television is
an incredible adrenaline rush.
Here I am in the producer's chair
for a Golf Channel broadcast
of *Feherty Live*.
Photo Credit: Personal Snapshot.

At the end of 2021, Katherine announced that she wanted a dog.
When Katherine wants something, I want it too. She researched
and decided on a Cavachon—a mix of Cavalier King Charles
Spaniel and Bichon Frise. We absolutely love this new member
of our little family. Our grandchildren named him Benny,
but for me he's the Booper. *Source: Personal Snapshot.*

Once Almanzo, always Almanzo. My life has been influenced not only by his Little House life but before that by my California-based, multi-generational family history. My early life couldn't help but prepare me for the experiences that followed through the years. *Photo Credit: Michael Roud.*

of viewers, ours was the main window they had into nineteenth-century American life. I am very proud of that *Little House* legacy.

Casting directors don't make mistakes. That doesn't mean they're omniscient. Neither Susan Sukman nor Michael Landon knew I had grown up steeped in my family's pioneer history. At the same time, the young man who walked so hopefully into that office at MGM was the product of a very specific upbringing, an upbringing that emphasized remembering the same pioneer virtues that animated Almanzo James Wilder. Over the decades, I have discovered more and more parallels between my life and that of the man whom I portrayed. I am convinced that some-how, Michael Landon sensed those parallels from the moment he met me.

Almanzo Wilder needed to be an uncomplicated man, and I was that. That did not, however, mean that my casting didn't bring complications—especially for the much-younger teen star who played the woman Almanzo was destined to marry.

CHAPTER 9

That Kiss

IT WAS TIME FOR THE FIRST KISS.

Melissa Gilbert and I were at the center of the penultimate scene in *Little House on the Prairie*'s most popular Season 6 episode, "Sweet Sixteen." For *Little House* series fans, "Sweet Sixteen" was a huge moment in the life of Laura Ingalls, to whom they had been devoted since she was an irrepressible, buck-toothed nine-year-old. Now, for the first time, they'd see her acknowledged as a woman by the man she had loved at first sight—a man who until that episode had viewed her only as "a nice young friend."

First kisses on television shows, as in real life, are a big deal. For most of us, those kisses happen in private places, between two people who dare to bring their lips together in a moment of urgently tentative affection and intimacy. Most of us remember these moments in our lives like they were yesterday because they are a rite of passage from which there is no turning back. The kiss in "Sweet Sixteen" represented two important firsts: the first television kiss between Laura Ingalls and Almanzo Wilder—and the first romantic kiss of Melissa Gilbert's life.

The moment played beautifully on screen for Laura and Almanzo, and audiences loved it, but underneath the romance of that moment, I can never forget that I, Dean Butler, was the last person Melissa would've chosen for this tender moment in her life. I didn't know then that I was a source of enormous discomfort for Melissa. More than the kiss itself—which audiences have loved for more than forty years—what I remember best was the unexpected off-camera disturbance that interrupted the set.

The scene was beautifully set up on the back porch of Nellie's Restaurant. Michael Landon, sitting quietly next to the camera, had just called "action." It was perfectly still on that cinematically perfect moonlit night. Almanzo was alone on the porch, lost in his thoughts, believing his ill temper had ruined his romance with Laura before it could even properly begin. But this was *Little House,* and suddenly, there she was in front of him. There was electricity and lemon verbena in the air. The words between them were charged with innocent yearning. Just as Laura and Almanzo's lips were about to touch in a kiss that fans had been impatiently anticipating, out of the darkness came a loud gasp followed by a very, very audible sob.

I heard Michael say, "Cut it." It wasn't a happy sound in his voice. My concentration was yanked out of the moment, and there we were on Stage 15 at MGM with nearly one hundred people gathered around us. Back behind the camera someone was crying. It was totally unexpected. This kind of outburst just didn't happen on our set.

After a second or two, I could see in Melissa's eyes that this interruption had come from a source all too familiar to her: her mother, Barbara Abeles. If I had known of Melissa's discomfort in advance, then her mother's outburst would've been easier to understand. As it was, from the beginning of my first season I had sensed that Barbara was not fully supportive of my presence in the show. Her unhappiness culminated, perhaps, in not being able to bear seeing me kiss her daughter. It was a protective displeasure; Barbara knew her daughter. I didn't, and in some sense, I'm glad. Had I known at the time how badly Melissa herself wanted this moment to be with almost anyone other than me, the kiss and so many other moments that audiences have loved for so long would've been much more difficult to create. For that reason, I'm grateful that I wasn't aware of the extent of Melissa's disdain—at least not during the early years we worked together.

Laura Ingalls Wilder had written what was happening that day on Stage 15 in her classic children's novel, *These Happy Golden Years*, published in 1943. But we weren't doing the moment the way Laura had written it, with Laura and Almanzo alone in a carriage on a moonlit night. I love that sequence in Laura's book, and it would've been wonderful to shoot it that way. For years people have asked me why that moment and so many others weren't captured as Laura wrote them. After all, Laura and her daughter, Rose, had developed into masters of simple descriptive prose. The simplest answer I can give is that Michael Landon didn't want to do the moment the way Laura wrote it. There were probably any number of reasons for the decision, not the least of which would've been the expense of a night shoot on location. I also believe that Michael was sensitive to the optics of having Laura alone on a moonlit night in a carriage with the much older Almanzo. Melissa and I were eight years apart in age, and fans weren't shy about pointing out the obvious differences in our physical maturity, which were considerable at that time. But hey—the real Laura and Almanzo were ten years apart, so we were historically in the ballpark.

Regardless of where the kiss took place, the result was going to be the same. Laura was going to marry Almanzo. There would be upsets and misunderstandings along the way, but the kiss we were about to shoot—if Melissa's mother's outbursts could be controlled—would make it a done deal.

Television is a fantasy world, but networks and studios have always had to be sensitive to the ways in which fantasy matches the values of contemporary society. Even as safe as *Little House* was for audiences, the challenge of making Laura's relationship with Almanzo acceptable was considerable, and I believe Michael's choice to cast me in that role was an acknowledgment that the line between what was palatable and not was very fine.

"Sweet Sixteen"—the name of the "kiss episode"—went into production less than seven months after I first met Melissa on the first day of shooting of Season 6 of *Little House*. I had learned I would be joining the cast of *Little House* barely three weeks before my twenty-third birthday on May 20, 1979. Melissa would turn fifteen just twelve days earlier on May 8. Today that eight-year difference between us is a tiny gap, but forty-five years ago, it was the Grand Canyon.

I was in the makeup chair, on location in Simi Valley, being prepared for my first day of shooting by makeup artist Whitey Snyder. Whitey was best known as the man who created the look that transformed Norma Jean Baker into screen goddess Marilyn Monroe. As Whitey gruffly made casual conversation and worked with his white sponge, into the trailer burst Melissa Gilbert. I had not met her before this moment, but here was Laura Ingalls in the flesh, dressed in one of her familiar prairie smocks, her auburn hair in those celebrated pigtails.

"Hi, I'm Melissa," she said with a confident smile.

"How do you do? I'm Dean Butler," I said while offering her my hand. My life training of good manners was in full effect.

My first thought was *Is she actually even fifteen years old?* It occurred to me that if she weren't who she was—the young female lead on an extraordinarily popular television show—she could have easily blended into any middle school hallway in America, more child than woman, albeit a very bright and engaging child with a big smile and that famously high-pitched voice. *She's the reason you're here*, I kept saying to myself as she spoke. *She's why you're on this show.* Casting directors don't make mistakes—and Susan Sukman (later Susan Sukman McCray) had chosen me to be the man Laura would fall in love with, and who'd fall in love with her. Based on how Melissa spoke and carried herself at the time, I thought it would take a season or two for our characters to plausibly embark on a romance. I was wrong.

The seeds of that romance were planted in our first on-screen interaction. In "Back to School" Part 1, the sweet and wonderfully talented Lucy Lee Flippen, playing Almanzo's sister Eliza Jane, introduced Laura to Almanzo.

> ELIZA JANE
> *Laura, this is my brother, Almanzo.*
> ALMANZO
> *Pleasure to meet you, Laura. My friends call me Manny.*
> LAURA
> *Pleasure to meet you, Manly.*

So much for three years to kindle plausible chemistry. The love between Laura and Almanzo would blossom in less than six months of screen time. (That we mispronounced Almanzo's name in that introduction—Al*monz*o instead of Al*manz*o—is a fact that Laura Ingalls Wilder aficionados didn't let us forget. It was an unforced error that we should've corrected, but now it's one of those fun tomato/tom*ah*to, potato/pot*ah*to conversations.)

Back on the set, with Barbara in a state of despair and Melissa and me trying to collect ourselves for another take, the question needed to be asked: was this kiss happening too soon? Was the age gap too vast for our audience to accept? Was it too big for even an accomplished and savvy fifteen-year-old? In hindsight, looking back through the lens of the huge cultural changes of the past few years, was there a way we could have played that kiss differently? In today's world I don't think the kiss could ever happen. Nothing like the casting of Melissa and me had happened before us, and I can't imagine it would happen today. In a world where Harvey Weinstein and Jeffrey Epstein have become notorious for abusing young and vulnerable women, even the most chaste on-screen kiss between a teen actress and a (young) adult man would be grounds for a lawsuit. The way Melissa tells it, she had no idea she was going to be paired with an actor who not only towered over her but was eight years her senior. No matter how poised, fifteen is invariably a very vulnerable age. Today, such a casting decision would be much more carefully considered. At the very least, today, Melissa would be in the room at some point to meet the actors under final consideration for the role of her future husband.

Personally, I'm very grateful Michael Landon put me there. Being a part of *Little House* has been one of the great gifts of my life, and I wouldn't trade it for anything. I don't think Melissa would either, but if she'd had a voice in my casting, I'm certain I would never have been hired. Thanks, Michael.

On-screen romance asks at least three things of an actor: to embrace the writer's words, surrender to the director's vision, and find in their fellow actor an attractiveness that allows the eyes to tell the truth. That "chemistry" between actors is perhaps the most important ingredient of all. Obviously, real chemistry doesn't always exist between the actors playing romantic relationships, but I think most actors would agree that it helps. That said, the shooting of romantic scenes can be more mechanical than intimate for actors because of the coverage—tight shots of intense looks, inviting mouths, grasping hands, torsos coming together, and on and on. When put together by a good editor and scored by a talented composer (we had both), those many shots can create a lot of on-screen energy. For the most part Michael didn't shoot that way, and given the nature of the show, I think he was very conscious of never heightening sexual chemistry between any characters on the show. It wasn't the *Prairie* way. We weren't making a steamy prime-time soap opera like *Dallas*. Michael would take his shirt off on occasion to show off his Malibu tan, and Karen would have her hair down at bedtime, thanks to an amazing wig, but there was never much coverage for editors to use to build urgency and passion in *Little House* scenes.

Fans with sharp memories might tell me I'm wrong, but I think the only time I had my shirt off alone in a room with Laura was when I was packed in ice playing the effects of a high fever. (The ice was real, by the way. I was freezing.) Bottom line: Michael wanted romantic scenes to play simply, honestly, and quickly, although David Rose's beautiful musical scores could have sustained and enhanced any amount of editorial magic used to build the emotional urgency of on-screen romance.

It's a point worth repeating: in "Sweet Sixteen," Laura would have her first "romantic" kiss. It would be Melissa's first in real life as well. For me, "Sweet Sixteen" was far from my first experience with intimacy, cinematic or otherwise. My first big on-screen romantic kisses were captured in *Forever*. My first real-life kiss happened when I was sixteen—at the end of a date with Penny Bloch at her front door after a dance at Piedmont High School. I'll never forget that Penny was my first kiss. I never went out with her again, but because it was the first kiss it was a memorable, slightly anxiety-provoking, wondrous moment.

I would spend much of my career as an actor playing a young man in love. *Forever* was the ideal preparation to play romantic roles. All the preparation in the world, however, could not make me into what Melissa Gilbert wanted for her first kiss.

I was not the only one who noticed that the age gap between Melissa and myself would be difficult to bridge if we were to present a convincing romance to *Little House*'s legion of devoted, protective fans. Not long after news of my casting broke, an August 1979 story in the Knight-Ridder newspaper chain began with this ominous prediction:

PRAIRIE MAN

*Dean Butler may have the trickiest role of the 1979–80
TV season. He has to convince viewers of that G-rated hit,
"Little House on the Prairie," that it's OK for a grown man
to fall in love with a pubescent girl.*

I was optimistic, and tactful, telling the reporter, "I think it's going to be handled very carefully." And the truth is, with the hindsight of forty-five years, I don't know that, given the circumstances, that we could have handled it any better than we did. On the series, as crafted by Michael Landon, Almanzo never pursued Laura. As audiences remember, it was she who schemed to win his heart from the moment she saw him.

As an aside, it was clear that the network knew we were venturing into risky territory. Not long after my introduction on the series in September 1979, our unit publicist, Bill Kiley, quietly sent me a clipping of a LETTER TO THE EDITOR from a Midwest newspaper. The letter was written by an upset mother of teenage girls, calling for our casting director (Susan Sukman) to be "burned at the stake" for pairing young Melissa Gilbert with "a grown man." How, she asked, would she be able to instill positive messages for her daughters about waiting for the right time with such "dating depravity" taking place on *Little House?* Bill attached a note to the clipping with a quick word of encouragement. "You can't please all the people all the time. Keep your head up. BK."

As careful as Michael was, it was impossible to prevent all harm—and it's clear to me now that Melissa was genuinely uncomfortable with the way the screen romance between us was dealt with. I had the job of convincing viewers that it was acceptable for a man in his twenties to fall in love with a girl in her mid-teens, and with a great deal of help, I did that as best I could. What I couldn't do, and what nobody in our *Little House* family could do, is alleviate Melissa's discomfort with me.

In her own memoir, *Prairie Tale*, Melissa devotes a chapter to that first season working with me. It's titled evocatively enough, "Oh Shit, They Got a Real Man."

In that chapter, which she generously sent to me before the book was published to make sure I would be OK, she wrote about meeting me and being hit by a perfect storm of disappointment, fear, anger, and even nausea.

She and I have talked about our first meeting many times over the years. "How was I going to do this?" she recalled during a recent phone call. "You were a man, a grown-up man with a car and an apartment. I was a really young teenager. I wasn't allowed to wear heels. I was still wearing Mary Janes. I couldn't pierce my ears. I wasn't allowed to shave my legs, and I'd never even been on a date."

The thing that surprised me most in all of this was discovering that Melissa hadn't been given any advance awareness of who Michael was casting.

"They told me that the character of Almanzo was coming, and that the relationship was coming. And that was kind of it."

Melissa was one of the biggest young stars on television at that point, with an army of agents, managers, and publicists. I would've thought, on her behalf, that they would've demanded she be told everything about the actor who was going to play Almanzo.

"It was just, okay, that's him, and in two years you're going to be married. And then shortly after that you're giving birth, and I'm only going to be seventeen. Help. How do I do that?"

"The biggest problem I had during all of that," Melissa told me, "was the physical space thing. I just wasn't ready to have that kind of physical contact with anybody. When it came to sex and physicality and all that, I was basically being raised by a Puritan."

That was funny to me. "Your mother who'd been married four times was a Puritan?"

"She was a total Puritan in talking to me about sex and intimacy. I would try and have these conversations with her, and it would just inevitably boil down to, 'Good girls don't.'"

120

Melissa wrote about how "inconvenient and disappointing" this had to be for me.

Having known Melissa for decades, seeing her in her relationships and in her public life, it's hard for me to imagine that she ever would've thought of herself as a disappointment to anyone, but this was a bizarre situation for her to handle. Frankly, it was a little bizarre for both of us.

During my early days on the series, I asked Michael if he could suggest books, historical or fiction, that would help me be in sync with his vision for the series. His response was clear: "The only thing you need to read is what I write." There could be no doubt that Michael's vision for the show was rock solid and affirmed by ratings success.

When it came time to introduce Almanzo, Michael was certainly mindful of the standards of the late 1970s. This wasn't the nineteenth century anymore. Underage girls didn't date men in their twenties—and certainly weren't supposed to marry them. Even as the empowerment of women was growing in the culture, Michael had considered the critical and audience reaction that would have come if he'd written Almanzo as actively pursuing Laura. Critics would have eaten us alive. Instead, Almanzo was presented as an unattainable object of innocent desire. My job was clear: I had to look good on camera and stay out of trouble off camera. I had the genetic talent to do the former (you'll see pictures of my parents later in the book), and I was raised by them to do the latter. I was a perfect benign object.

I've long believed that much of the affection that has come my way over the years was the result of the audience's deep devotion to Melissa's Laura. She was America's young TV sweetheart. If audiences honestly believed that Laura loved Almanzo, then they would too. But with Melissa's off-camera aversion to me so well documented in publications like *TV Guide*, it's a wonder I wasn't heckled on the street in the same way fans hissed at Alison Arngrim, who was *Little House*'s "nasty Nellie." I'll never forget what Melissa told one national magazine: "Laura may love Almanzo, but I'm not attracted to the hayseed type." What could I say? I was raised with hayseeds all around me.

Despite those kinds of comments in national publications, the audience seemed to like me. I'd like to think I had something to do with that, but it was mostly the result of Melissa's sweet, yearning portrayal. She played it wonderfully—even though she wasn't the slightest bit into it—a reality that became increasingly clear off camera. She was doing her job. And my job, despite the petulance and indifference that came my way nearly every day, was to be the man who loved Laura.

I want to push back on one thing Melissa says in her memoir. She writes that she thought that the age gap between us was "inconvenient and disappointing" to me. It was neither. Unlike other situations I was in through the years, from the beginning I had no expectation of a personal relationship with Melissa, and that was as it should've been. It wasn't an inconvenience as much as it was a challenge. I wasn't disappointed that we didn't have instant chemistry: I just knew I had to do the best I could to build rapport with her and serve Michael Landon to give our audience the sweetest, most storybook romance possible. In the end, as the actor, it didn't matter what Melissa or I were feeling; it's what the audience felt, saw, and believed that mattered. By that standard I think we succeeded.

I don't recall Michael saying much to either Melissa or me before or during the filming of the "Sweet Sixteen" kiss. My memories of my own first kiss made me certain that this moment would be huge for the audience. They loved Laura, and they were eager to be flies on the wall for the most meaningful romantic moment of her young life. Knowing now how much Melissa was dreading it personally, I have to say that she never betrayed a hint of unease. As she has repeated many times through the years, she was "just being the Laura she was supposed to be." For me the task was to be "the man who loved Laura." Nobody could've predicted Barbara's outbursts, which were repeated twice before we got the kiss that made the final cut. I don't think Michael wanted to add any additional pressure for either Melissa or me, so he kept it light. Looking back, his ease with the moment was a real gift.

As our lips came together on four different takes, Melissa never gave the slightest sense that she was uncomfortable. Perhaps she wanted to shrink into the stage floor thanks to her mother's sobbing, but she gave no sign of it—even though our crew teased her incessantly in the weeks building up to the scene.

"Hey, Half Pint, how do you feel about your big kiss?" Melissa retorted that she would rather have kissed Scott Baio or Shaun Cassidy, teen idols of the era much closer to her age. In her book she said she didn't want to kiss anyone with stubble!

In a conversation we had, Melissa remembered the day of the *kiss*. "I knew the 'Sweet Sixteen' kiss was a big deal, because my mom was coming, which didn't happen very often and that made me nervous. And then the way Michael staged it, it wasn't just a kiss; it was very technical, actually. We looked, we leaned. For me, as a dancer, it felt like a dance more than anything. So that actually made it kind of okay, until I heard my mother sob and then all I wanted to do was get out of there."

Yet again and again, Melissa closed her eyes and we kissed. As soon as Michael yelled "cut" for the final time, she scurried away to the craft table "to get rid of any cooties."

As for the playing of the moment, I decided that if Almanzo was confident, *prairie suave,* and sure of himself, it wouldn't work. Instead Almanzo was gentle, naïve, and in a state of genuine wonder. Every time I've watched that scene since, I've been grateful I made that decision. I was eight years older than Melissa, but I think I came across as younger than she was. The Dean

Butler who unnerved Melissa was a grown man who shaved and had his own apartment, but Almanzo Wilder was just a painfully shy young man in love.

The #MeToo movement has changed so much of how we think about women, men, and consent. #MeToo has brought about a major reassessment in Hollywood as well, and it's provided a new and sometimes uncomfortable lens through which to view the work that was created years ago. To name one example, Molly Ringwald—the iconic star of so many 1980s teen coming-of-age movies—has written that in retrospect, she's deeply troubled by the sexual politics of films like *Sixteen Candles*.

My wife, Katherine Cannon, who came into the industry at nineteen, faced many uncomfortable situations as a young actress with men in Hollywood. It's not surprising. Men have pursued the women they desired throughout human history, frequently under conditions where the imbalance of power made it hard for women to set boundaries to stop unwanted attention. In the twenty-first century we, the human *we* of men and women alike, are reevaluating the rules for how we interact with each other. It's time. We're seeing old choices through new eyes, and I think that's a very good thing.

The week the episode aired, in February 1980, Melissa gave a slightly different story to the *National Enquirer*, attributing her anxiety to her own lack of experience: "I was nervous because I thought, 'He's twenty-three and when I kiss him, he's going to think 'what is she doing?'" She went on to remark that "Dean was as nervous as I was. So, between the two of us, we calmed each other down." I'm not sure if Melissa believed that at the time, or if that was something NBC's public relations department, worried about the age gap, suggested. Looking at the *Enquirer* story through a contemporary lens, it's a clever trick to describe us as equally anxious. It flattens the distinction between our levels of experience, and perhaps was meant to make the gulf between twenty-three and fifteen (the *Enquirer* inexplicably made me a year older) seem less problematic.

As for me, I was raised to have an almost reverential respect for women's boundaries. In my family, we were taught that a gentleman never makes a woman feel uncomfortable, and I took that very much to heart. I'm proud of how I worked with Melissa, despite our age gap, and glad that she doesn't attribute any malice or lecherousness to me (although she didn't appreciate that I crooned "Strangers in the Night" to her during one of our first post-marriage bedroom scenes). I still trust that I was the right person to play Almanzo. I couldn't help my age or my appearance.

I leave it to you, the reader, to judge whether I was the right actor for the role. I'll say that in hindsight, the only thing I'd change about that scene would be to get that ridiculous curl of hair off my forehead. I looked like even more of a geek than usual, but it doesn't matter what I think. Fans of the show loved that kiss. The way we filmed that moment honored the arc and purpose of an iconic show. What could have been an uncomfortable moment for millions of parents and kids watching together at home became instead something charming and tender, timeless and sweet.

Pundits will continue to reassess the art of the past, holding this show or that movie up for critical scrutiny. On balance I remain proud of my work, proud of what we all did together. And though I may not have been Melissa's or her mother's choice for her first kiss, for my legacy with the show I'm proud that I was her Almanzo, and I am so glad we told that story so gently, so tenderly, and so well.

CHAPTER 10

"Home Is the Nicest Word There Is"

I F YOU SEARCH ONLINE FOR LAURA INGALLS WILDER QUOTES, THIS IS one of the most popular you'll find. Except you won't find it in any of the *Little House* books. It was written for the premiere of our show, an episode titled "Harvest of Friends," and delivered by Laura (Melissa Gilbert). The script for that first show is credited to writers John Hawkins and William Putman, but that line is unmistakably Michael Landon. I'd be willing to bet my old buckboard that Michael wrote it and inserted it into the "Harvest of Friends" teleplay.

Michael rewrote, polished, and edited every *Little House* script. As much as any line of dialogue ever written in any of our episodes, "home is the nicest word there is" defined Michael's deepest wish. More than anything, what animated his creative vision was the desire for family, warmth, and the safety of home. He wanted it for himself, for his children, for his television family, and for your family too. In an all-too-short life, Michael worked tirelessly to deliver this single, comforting idea.

In a recent conversation with me, Melissa Gilbert quoted

Michael from memory: "Nothing's more important than home and family; no success, no career, no achievements, no accomplishments, nothing's more important than loving the people you love and contributing to a community."

You do not need to know Michael Landon's story to guess that his deep devotion to family was born of his own bitter and painful experience. He was born Eugene Maurice Orowitz in Collingswood, New Jersey. The second of two children, Eugene grew up in a very unhappy family. As Michael's longtime friend and collaborator, producer Kent McCray, told the story, Michael's parents, Eli Orowitz and Peggy O'Neill, were more than simply unhappy. They were in a textbook dysfunctional marriage, unable to speak to each other. Eugene was the designated go-between so his parents could avoid directly speaking to each other. Kent said, "His mother would say to Eugene, 'Tell your father dinner is ready,' and his father would reply, 'Tell your mother I'm not hungry.'"

The lore about Michael, as told by himself and others, is that as a boy, Eugene found refuge from his unhappy home by retreating into his fertile imagination. He developed a keen and disarming sense of humor and later channeled his energy into sports. Eugene excelled in track and field; his senior year of high school, he was ranked the nation's top javelin thrower. That earned him a scholarship to the University of Southern California (USC). Los Angeles was a long way from Collingswood, and that appealed to a boy desperate to escape his parents' dysfunction. Eugene came to Los Angeles with a simple plan: get his education, graduate, join the service, and win a gold medal at the Olympics.

When young people discover *Little House* for the first time, they often ask, "What's with Pa's hair?" Michael Landon's abundant locks were an obvious anachronism on a show that worked hard to be faithful to the look and feel of the Wilder books. Some people think it was a 1970s hairstyle that Michael thought flattering, but Michael's devotion to his curls dated back to his boyhood. It was, he told me, the secret to his success.

One day, in between shots on Stage 15, Michael told me the truth about his distinctive hair. I was still the new guy in the cast, and a few minutes alone with Michael was an opportunity I relished. Michael told me that in the early 1950s, decades before long hair was popular or acceptable on young men, young Eugene began to believe that like Samson in the Bible, his strength was derived from his hair. "My hair is how I threw the javelin 193 feet when I only weighed 125 pounds," he told me.

Eugene was convinced his hair was the secret behind the ability that won him that athletic scholarship to USC. Once on campus, however, his hairstyle stood out as weird. Several football players, who often wore their hair so short that it was like peach fuzz, teased him relentlessly. One day, they held Eugene down and shaved his head. Without his long hair, Eugene believed his strength was gone. Desperate, he began throwing harder to compensate, and soon tore the ligaments in his shoulder, permanently ending his career as a javelin thrower. USC revoked his scholarship, and Eugene dropped out of college.

That's as much of the story as I got before it was time for the next shot. A brief synopsis of what happened next for the boy from Collingswood.

Unwilling to go back to New Jersey, Eugene took a series of survival jobs. While working at a warehouse, he befriended a fellow employee, an aspiring actor. One day, that warehouse friend needed a scene partner for a last-minute studio audition. He pleaded with Eugene to play the part of an emotional Jewish soldier in a powerful scene from the Arthur Laurents play *Home of the Brave*. Eugene went in prepared only to do a favor for a friend, but when the pages called for the soldier to cry, he did. As Michael would say years later, "I suddenly realized that acting was a great release for me. I could cry when I was someone else and get a lot of things out of my system that I couldn't get out on my own."

I've never met an actor who could cry on cue so easily and so well. I don't know if Eugene's actor friend from the warehouse got the part. Eugene, however, had found his calling.

There are at least two versions of how Eugene Orowitz became Michael Landon. Both versions explain that Eugene found the name for which he is famous after mixing and matching first and last names from the telephone book. Michael found an agent and was just twenty when he got his first big break: the title role in 1957's *I Was a Teenage Werewolf.* The film got mixed reviews, but *Variety* praised Michael's "first-class characterization as the high school boy constantly in trouble." Two years later, he was cast in *Bonanza* as Little Joe Cartwright, and the role made him an international star.

Over his fourteen years on *Bonanza,* Michael polished his acting skills and had the time to hone his ease and natural charm in front of the camera. Those years also became a writing-and-directing master class that would equip him to be the extraordinary showrunner he would become on *Little House.* In the series television business, the term *showrunner* is used to describe the top-level creative decision-maker on the show. From the start, Michael had a crystal-clear understanding of the show he wanted to make and of his audience appeal; he instinctively avoided doing anything on screen to disappoint or upset his legions of fans. You could argue that getting his head shaved was a lucky break in disguise; you could argue that meeting a warehouse co-worker who was an actor was a stroke of good fortune. Luck is important, but Michael's towering success was the consequence of exceptional self-awareness, talent, tremendous internal drive, and extraordinary instincts about what audiences wanted and needed to see.

Michael often said he was completely disinterested in a big-screen career; instead, he devoted his professional life to creating family-friendly television. He devoted his private life to creating the real family of which he had been deprived as a boy. He married young, at twenty, and went on to have two more wives and nine children. He was not a perfect husband or father, but there is no question that he did his absolute best to create something beautiful, stable, and abundant for those he loved. Michael poured his yearning for loving, committed parenting into the character of Charles Ingalls, where he was able to model for audiences the kind of family communication and closeness he wished he'd had during his own unhappy childhood.

I am often asked what Michael Landon was "really like." Indeed, it's one of the two or three most common questions I get about *Little House*. I understand why people ask. There's this standard cultural assumption that most actors are nothing like the characters they play. Tabloids and tell-all memoirs have fed our collective appetite for salacious gossip. At the same time, especially with something as beloved as *Little House*, fans have a deep-rooted hope that their favorite actors really were like the roles they played. My friend and co-star Alison Arngrim, who played Nellie Oleson, is often asked if she is as nasty in real life as she was on the show. I'll tell you the truth: Alison is one of the most outwardly happy and optimistic people I've ever met, far from the "prairie bitch" image that she has tirelessly cultivated for half a century. Her glass is always half full, and she sees the absolute best in everyone. I'm not sure I can say the same thing about myself, but I always try to put my best foot forward.

I can tell you about the Michael I knew. It's important to phrase it that way because the Michael that Dean Butler knew was not the same Michael that Melissa Gilbert knew. Melissa's Michael was not Karen Grassle's Michael, or Merlin Olsen's Michael. My Michael was not the Michael his children knew. Leslie Landon, Michael's daughter, is devoted to her father's legacy. Mike Jr. had a different, more nuanced perspective about his father. (The 1999 CBS television movie *Michael Landon, the Father I Knew* captured Mike Jr.'s unique relationship with his dad.) Each of us had our own experiences with Michael, and we each filtered those experiences through the lens of our own personalities.

I have written of my own complex relationship with my father. I know very well that my siblings experienced our dad very differently. My Peter Butler was not my sister's Peter Butler, and if she were to write a memoir, she would tell different stories about our father. That doesn't mean one of us is being dishonest or has a better memory! We simply saw different things and experienced the same things differently. Families are intricate systems, and the *Little House* family was no exception. You can read the wonderful autobiographies written by the women of our show; they share their own memories of Michael. Nothing I say is meant to devalue or discredit what they saw and shared.

My wife, Katherine, also knew Michael, as she had been in the cast of *Father Murphy*, a show that Michael created, produced, and directed. Though she did not work with Michael as closely or for as long as I did, she has her own indelible memories of him. Over many years, Katherine and I have shared countless recollections, and as we have grown older, she has helped me clarify my own memories and understand them better. I was in my early twenties when I started on *Little House*, and in my late twenties when we filmed our final episode. One of the benefits of writing this book all these years later is that I have the emotional awareness to put my experience with Michael (and everyone else) in better context.

The twinkle in Michael's eyes was real. So was the steel in his voice when you'd upset him. In the first chapter, I recounted how Michael reacted so generously when I nearly drove a wagon team into a tree—and how, just a short time later, he responded icily when it appeared I questioned his judgment. Another revealing "Michael" moment I've never forgotten came during a rare scene. Michael deployed physical violence very rarely on camera, so when scenes called for stage fighting it was special. I'd studied stage combat, and I enjoyed the physicality of that aspect of our craft. I was excited to film this scene. A farmer had cut off water to Almanzo's fields, and in a rage, I was to attack him. Michael would pull me off.

In the first take, I was caught up in the excitement. When Michael grabbed me from behind, I struggled with him. He called "cut," and calmly asked me to go limp when he grabbed me. I understood what he told me, but on the next take, still excited, I struggled again. Again, he called "cut." Michael's voice had only the faintest hint of an edge as he repeated the instruction.

"Go limp."

"Yes, sorry," I replied.

I will never understand why, on that third take, I couldn't go limp. I kept struggling. Without calling "cut," Michael yelled, "I said go limp!" In one single move, he lifted me off my feet and threw me across the barn. I flew through the air like a rag doll. I was at least three inches taller than Michael, and I weighed 190 pounds. It didn't matter. His strength was overwhelming. Maybe he wasn't kidding about the power in that hair.

There were audible gasps from the crew, and a few snickers from those who had been working with Michael a long time. I tumbled and rolled in the dirt and straw on the floor of the barn, and I remember saying something like, "What the hell?" I wish I could have said something light and clever to fix the moment, but my mind was blank. Michael didn't say a word. We went straight into the fourth take, and this time, I was limp as a dishrag in Michael's hands.

"Cut. Print," Michael said. He never mentioned the scene again.

Our producer, Kent McCray, had been friends with Michael

Landon since they were both making *Bonanza*. Kent's long history with Michael meant that he understood our director, showrunner, and star better than anyone else. One afternoon, just a few weeks into my time on *Little House*, I sat in Kent's MGM office and sought some reassurance. I'd already felt Michael's bite, and I'd seen how curt and aloof he could be. I'd also seen his incredible warmth and humor. He was the sun, and the rest of us were orbiting around him, trying to figure out how to get closer without getting burned. I already knew millions of Americans saw him as a member of their family, but he was my future on-camera father-in-law. I was in awe of him.

Sitting in Kent's office, I went fishing for help. "Michael is a pretty complicated guy," I offered. I expected Kent to agree with the obvious, and perhaps share an insight about how to better understand this charismatic, impenetrable man.

"No, he isn't," Kent replied, looking me straight in the eye. "Michael is very simple."

Kent wasn't joking. He and Michael had been friends for decades; Michael often remarked that Kent was the brother he never had. I don't know if Kent saw a side of Michael none of the rest of us did, or if Kent had simply figured out Michael's rhythms, discerning a pattern and a predictability that the rest of us could not.

I never knew Michael the way Kent did. He never became simple to understand, at least not for me. We all watched him run the production with exquisite sensitivity—and then become bored and belligerent later in the day, after an afternoon of sipping vodka from a white Styrofoam cup. Michael was invariably wonderful in quiet moments with actors, but he could also test the dignity of women in our company as he told some of the most misogynistic jokes I have ever heard in my life. Everybody would laugh because the jokes were funny, but they were also filthy—and by today's standards, wildly inappropriate.

I would venture to say that forty years ago there wouldn't have been a single set in Hollywood that would've met today's more evolved standards of behavior. It was a different time, even on shows as outwardly squeaky clean as *Little House*. Anytime you put men and women close together for extended periods of time, people are going to say and do things that perhaps they wouldn't otherwise. That said, the *Little House* set wasn't a target-rich environment for any kind of questionable behavior on my part. I was too old to have anything but the most arm's-length relationships with the kids, and I felt too young for the more senior cast and crew who for many years worked and played hard together. I had a lot of fun experiences during my time on *Little House*. I asked out a number of our attractive guest stars, but I never dated any of our regular cast members or our crew.

With Michael gone, Melissa Gilbert rightly sits in the center of the *Little House* television legacy. As a practical matter, it is our "Nellie Oleson," Alison Arngrim, who is the heart and soul of our cast, and is *Little House*'s most active and durable advocate. Alison embraces *Little House* like no one else, and fans of the series adore her.

When we were working together all those years ago, when she wasn't in curls and flouncy dresses, Alison was a punk rocker who could frequently be seen wearing sleeveless T-shirts, ripped jeans, and black Converse high-tops. Her makeup was mostly severe black eye shadow, and she drove an old black and white Ford Ranchero. She looked like a bad girl, but you could tell she was always having fun with her image. Years later, who would've imagined that "Nasty Nellie" could be so beloved?

I've been doing *Little House* events with Alison for decades. Alison's portrayal of Nellie is adored by *Little House* fans because she gets the joke that Nellie is an archetype of (sometimes benign) evil in pin curls and lace. As fans sneer, boo, and laugh at Nellie, they get to consider their own darker impulses and the karmic cost of the consequences Nellie always faces in the end.

There are a lot of people in American public life who should be taken down a peg, just as Nellie is in episode after episode. Nellie gives us the pleasure of seeing swift and certain consequences for bad behavior. She's a tonic for the soul.

Alison, who is incredibly bright, saw the potential gift of this character the first time she read the script. "There's something not right about this girl," Alison told her father, Thor Arngrim, who was also her manager and publicist. After hearing his daughter read the scene out loud, as only she could, he told her, "don't change a thing." She's been Nellie ever since. In "Country Girls," her speech in which she declared with cold, snobby certainty that Nellie's house was the best in Walnut Grove perfectly established who the character was—and the love-hate relationship that has connected Alison to fans forever had begun.

In her book, *Confessions of a Prairie Bitch*, Alison shares many funny stories and observations from the set, the challenging reality of her childhood, and the grown-up advocacy work she's done for children and the HIV community, all with her unique humor and fundamental goodness.

To give audiences an in-person dive into her life and career, she's created the *Confessions of a Prairie Bitch* one-woman show that she performs all over the United States and in France (in French!). I saw the show for the first time several years ago in De Smet, South Dakota, and the audience of all ages absolutely loved it.

Through the many years of doing appearances together, in Q&A sessions Alison always talks about "everybody's favorite" *Little House* episode, which—according to Alison—is "Bunny." In that episode's penultimate moment, Nellie, who is faking paralysis to guilt Laura and get out of chores and homework, is shoved by Laura down a steep hill in her wheelchair. As the wheelchair plummets downward, bouncing and rattling, Nellie screams in terror, and we watch in delight as she is flipped head over heels into the mill pond. Nellie's fakery is revealed to everyone when she stands up, blubbering pathetically. Audiences always roar with laughter as she tells the story.

At that point, I indignantly jump in and insist that "everybody's favorite" *Little House* episode is actually "Sweet Sixteen," but (predictably) my stories about shooting Laura's first kiss aren't as funny as Alison's story about "Bunny." She's the comedian, and I'm the sincere guy. Romantic characters are never as much fun as the comic antagonists. Alison has been our comic antagonist, our jester, and our welcome wagon for nearly fifty years. More than any of us, Alison deserves the credit for keeping our *Little House* cast connected to each other and present for fans who love staying connected to the show.

Side by side with Nellie on *Little House*'s "love to hate" list is Katherine MacGregor as Harriet Oleson. I saw Katherine for the last time in summer 2018 at the Motion Picture Television Fund Retirement Home in Calabasas. At that time, she was in a serious decline, and I wasn't surprised that the clues that had helped her remember me during previous visits didn't work. Katherine MacGregor died just a few months after I last saw her. Thirty-nine years earlier, when I met Katherine on a beautiful May morning on the set of *Little House*, she became an instant favorite. Her commitment and her power were magnetic. As Mrs. Oleson, Katherine MacGregor could be charming, funny, and shocking all in the same breath. She was a force of nature, and she brought the fullness of her bigger than life personality to every moment she played.

Little House fans always ask me if Katherine was like her character. I've always said that for me she was exactly like Mrs. Oleson. I say that because I found Katherine, both as herself and as Harriet, to be completely irresistible. I loved being around her in or out of costume because she was always fun, and she was always present. I loved her because she was passionate about her ideas, generous with her talent, and totally engaged in her life.

Her favorite subject, on or off the set, was acting. That love of her work and her appetite to get everything out of every moment defined her for me. She was totally vested in every gesture, expression, and calculated intention. She was a walking, talking master class, and I adored her. Yes, I did follow her around, as Alison Arngrim once suggested, "like a puppy dog," but I found comfort, safety, and endless humor in her energy.

In many ways, Katherine's energy and singular focus reminded me of my great-aunt Margaret. In reading this, any members of my family old enough to have known Aunt Margaret will have an instant, vivid image of Katherine. For much of my youth, Aunt Margaret, my maternal grandfather's aunt, was the senior indomitable matriarch of my family. Her singular focus on her interests and needs dominated my family's attention in person and from a distance for as long as she lived. Her life force was enormous. She was one of those people who drew attention and respect whenever she entered a room.

Katherine MacGregor's similarities to my aunt Margaret were familiar and comforting to me, and I was drawn to her as I entered my new *Little House* life. She was smart, generous, highly opinionated, and passionate about her work as an actress. Katherine prided herself on being very well trained. She was a devoted student of the late Sanford Meisner, whom she studied with in New York City, alongside the likes of Dustin Hoffman and Robert Duvall. She always affectionately referred to them as Dusty and Bobby.

Katherine loved talking about the transformation of Mrs. Oleson through the years. When the show began, she was rather cold and unapproachable behind the counter of the Mercantile, but as the show became more successful, she began to think about the appeal and longevity of the character and began injecting humor into her performances with the goal of transforming her haughty, unapproachable shopkeeper from fearsome to foolish. This was Katherine's craft and talent at work. I was fascinated how that specific change took the hostility off her scheming and judgment and made Mrs. Oleson increasingly fun for audiences to root against. Over time, she grew from Walnut Grove's frightening antagonist into a character that audiences loved to hate, and she had a wonderful time doing it. Michael and the other writers took notice of what she was doing and began writing for Katherine to accentuate the humor, which she did with fearless confidence.

While she loved the work and had a huge impact on the evolution of the series, I always sensed that Katherine was hurt over not being paid what she was worth to the show. All you had to do was look at the call sheet to understand why. On any show the names at the top of the call sheet are invariably the highest paid.

Until *The New Beginning* in Season 9, the first five names of every *Little House* call sheet were permanently typed in: Michael Landon, Karen Grassle, Melissa Gilbert, Melissa Sue Anderson, and Lindsey-Sidney Greenbush. The names of fifteen to eighteen more actors could be entered by hand on individual episode call sheets, numbered from six to twenty-three as reoccurring or guest characters. None of those handwritten actors were paid as much as those whose names were typed in at the top. This is the way the Hollywood system works. Since Katherine MacGregor, Richard Bull, and Alison Arngrim were always down the list of characters, they were never going to be paid as much as members of the Ingalls family, even though their contributions to the life of the series were essential to the dramatic appeal and impact of the Ingalls family.

Katherine's agent tried for years to renegotiate her contract, but that effort was always thwarted by the reality of her number on the call sheet. One way that could've been solved in the third or fourth year would've been to give her billing at the end of the main title, something like "and Katherine MacGregor as Harriet Oleson." Of course, that might well have led to understandable tension with Richard Bull and Alison Arngrim, so in the interest of collegiality, it was best to leave the title alone. Regardless, by the end she was so hurt by the way she was treated that she refused to appear in the final three *Little House* movies. The public story was that she was on a religious pilgrimage to India. The unhappy truth is she walked away because the people who truly understood her value to the show could have paid her accordingly—but refused.

Katherine always had an edge to her. She was feisty, funny, and opinionated, so in one sense, her upset about being underpaid was just part of who she was. Having stayed friends with her for decades after our show ended, I can say that the pain of that rejection was always right on the surface, and I know she carried it with her for the rest of her life.

Though my relationships with the adult cast members were much more significant, I note that on the whole, I thought the kids on our set were amazing. There were good parents and guardians around to keep them in line, and we had two great set teachers, Marion Fife and Helen Minear, running the on-set school. On the surface, there's a lot of glamour in being a child actor, especially for kids with big parts in movies and television shows, but it's a lot of pressure to be good on the set and in the classroom, and that was expected of all the kids. They were all bright, so they handled the challenges of being in and out of the classroom very well. Alison Arngrim is one of the smartest people I've ever known. She told me that her on-set school was more like a study hall than an intense academic environment, but she still had to do the reading and pass the tests in her school to graduate, and she did. To my knowledge, all the kids did.

A lot has been written through the years about the siblings working on our set: Melissa Gilbert and her younger brother, Jonathan; Matthew and Patrick Labyorteaux as Albert Ingalls and Andy Garvey; Robin and Rachel Greenbush as Carrie Ingalls; Brenda and Wendy Turnbaugh as Grace Ingalls; Jennifer and Sarah Coleman—and later Michelle and Jennifer Steffin—as Rose.

Melissa and Jonathan Gilbert approached their work very differently. Melissa made it her business to know everybody's lines, she could follow everyone's conversations, and she was a straight A student in school. Jonathan only wanted to know his own lines, so he could be surprised by what was happening in his scenes, and according to Alison Arngrim he deliberately underperformed in the classroom to keep expectations low. In that respect, he was very much the character he played.

Matt and Pat Labyorteaux were very different kids, but they were both wonderful on camera. The three sets of infant twins were essentially extras and went uncredited on the show. All these years later, Wendi Lou Lee, one half of the Grace twins, and Jennifer Donati, one half of the first Rose twins, have reconnected with their *Little House* family, and it's been a fantastic experience for all of us. They are now both beautiful grown women, married with children of their own. They have few tangible memories of their time on the set, other than what they've been told by their parents, and what they can see for themselves as they watch the show on television and look at still photos. Candidly, I wasn't sure how fans would react to them, but in fact it's been a lovefest for everyone. In the years ahead, barring unforeseen events, Wendi and Jennifer will inevitably become the oldest surviving members of our cast, and I know they will represent the *Little House* legacy very well.

Shannen Doherty was not a twin. When we were working with Shannen, she played Almanzo's niece, Jenny Wilder. She was just beginning what was going to become a colorful career. My wife, Katherine, had worked with Shannen on *Father Murphy* before she joined the cast of *Little House: A New Beginning*.

"Even at ten or eleven years old Shannen knew she wanted to

be a star," Katherine recalled. "She wanted the cars and the furs and the fame. You couldn't miss it."

I had the same reaction to Shannen; she was talented, she had an appetite for the work, and it was crystal-clear that she wanted to be a star.

In talking about Shannen's drive to succeed, Katherine mused about a conversation she had with the late Jimmy Stewart in 1970 on the Wheeling, West Virginia, set of *Fool's Parade*. Katherine was nineteen and just starting her career. She and Jimmy were talking about becoming and maintaining a movie star career. My girl was on top of the world being in that movie with Jimmy Stewart, George Kennedy, Strother Martin, Kurt Russell, and William Windom.

When Katherine casually shared with Mr. Stewart that what was most important to her was being a solid working actress and added, "I don't care about being a star," Jimmy replied as only he could, "Then . . . then you won't be a star. It doesn't happen if you don't want it."

"I'm not sure I want you to write that," my wife told me as she recalled her exchange with one of America's all-time great movie stars. "I was so fortunate to be there. Should I have wanted it more?" she wondered.

"You were being honest," I replied. "So was Mr. Stewart. I don't think you ever really wanted any part of that life."

Shannen got a good taste of the stardom she sought, but today our former castmate is in a fight against terminal brain cancer and I wish her peace and comfort.

Jason Bateman and Melissa (then Missy) Francis joined the cast of *Little House* in a Season 8 two-part episode called "The Lost Ones." I had never seen Jason before. Missy had been working in the industry since she was two years old. They were both instantly amazing on camera, and they've both had wonderful careers. Jason's career, in particular, is off the charts remarkable and closely resembles Michael Landon's unique multi-threat strengths as an actor, director, and producer. I note that Jason's screen persona has evolved tremendously from childhood to the present. As a kid, Jason was all smiles and snarky charm, but as he's grown older, he has become much more restrained and world-weary. Today, Jason plays survivors: he's always hanging on for dear life to get through the impossible messes his characters are placed in, and watching him do it is both uncomfortable and great fun at the same time.

Melissa transitioned from acting to a career in news and had great success for a time as an anchor on Fox Business. She's written two books, *Diaries of a Stage Mother's Daughter* and *Lessons from the Prairie*, in which she used her *Little House* life to help explain the events of her adulthood.

As a cast, we've had no connection that I'm aware of with either Melissa or Jason since they appeared on the series. Maybe that will change in 2024.

In 2014, as we marked the fortieth anniversary of the debut of *Little House*, I joined many of our cast members for a press junket in New York City. While on a bus from one event to another, I had a long talk with Karen Grassle, who played Caroline Ingalls. I had never known Karen well but had always been in awe of her gifts. I had watched—as we all had—as she took the brunt of Michael's off-color humor and sarcasm. As we rode on the bus that day, Karen told me she was thinking of writing a memoir. I remember wondering what she would say about her relationship with the man that so many fans viewed as a near-perfect human being. As it turned out, *Bright Lights, Prairie Dust: Reflections on Life, Loss, and Love from Little House's Ma* is quite a straightforward account.

I watched as Karen worked incredibly hard to do the best work she could every time she stepped in front of the camera. She has been frequently named as one of television's most beloved mothers. Melissa Gilbert once said Karen was the most beautiful woman she had ever seen. For all she did on camera to be a steady, loving wife and mother she endured a level of disrespect on our set that I've never forgotten. I'm floored that she delivered such consistently wonderful performances despite it all.

Underneath the surface of Karen's outward beauty and gentleness is a level of intensity and strength that defines a commitment to integrity and excellence that has sustained her throughout her life. When Katherine and I read Karen's memoir, we were impressed by her nuanced look at her life before, during, and after the show. Melissa described Karen to me recently as "one of the most active feminists I've ever known." (If you know Melissa's formidable political career, that's saying something.) Reading her book reminded me that the few awkward moments I had with Michael were nothing compared to the challenges she faced. Karen persevered and always stood up for herself in an atmosphere that at times could be both crude and belittling. She rose above it and delivered consistently grounded, loving performances that are a credit to the series.

Michael played America's favorite father on TV. Off camera, he was a father figure to a great many young actors. He loved them, and they adored him. With adults, Michael could be alternately charming and cold. With the kids, he was consistently safe, warm, and endlessly encouraging. That made his affair with a crew member even more destabilizing to the *Little House* family—and absolutely shattering to Melissa Gilbert.

I don't know exactly when Michael's affair with Cindy Clerico began. I do know I was one of the last of the adults to realize what was happening. I was still, in many ways, a naïve young man. I do remember the day when I finally saw it with my own eyes. The company was shooting on Stage 15, which had something like twenty standing sets on it. When you came to work, you looked for the lights to know which set we'd be shooting on that day. This particular day we were in the church, filming one of the Sunday sermon scenes. The whole cast was needed; Reverend Alden was preaching, and we were to sing a hymn.

At one point in between shots, I turned around and saw Michael and Cindy (who was Melissa Sue Anderson's stand-in), just a few feet off the set, playing backgammon. They cuddled together like a flirtatious high school couple. Even in my comparative innocence, there was no mistaking what I was seeing. I turned to one of my castmates and whispered, "Wow, they're pretty friendly." I got an exasperated glare that made it clear that I shouldn't say another word.

I do not exaggerate when I say that our company was quietly devastated. We put up a unified front of denial because we had no other conceivable choice. That silence made it even more painful for everyone, particularly for the kids on the show and their parents, who viewed Michael not only as a special friend but also as a father figure. In her memoir, Melissa recounts that she was devastated by the affair. She adored Michael's family, and "Aunty Lynn" (Michael's wife) was one of her mother's closest friends. The adult actors knew affairs were common enough, but it was harder to take with Michael. He embodied family values on camera, and in many ways, off it as well.

This wasn't a typical lecherous producer bedding a young starlet. This was everyone's dad, cheating on mom. Even the most world-weary and experienced among our cast were unsettled.

It got much worse when the tabloids found out.

From 1980 to 1982, I traveled almost every weekend doing promotion for *Little House*. I would get on an airplane on Friday afternoon and travel to media markets all over the country. I'd talk to local press, ride in parades, and go to dinners, lunches, and breakfasts with affiliates and their advertising clients. I loved this part of the job. I met television professionals all over America and got to connect with our most fervent fans. I'd return to Los Angeles on Sunday night and be on set first thing

Monday morning. I was proud that I could help both the show and NBC and have fun while doing it.

One late summer weekend in Atlantic City, I came face to face with the reality that Michael's affair with Cindy was public knowledge. I was at an event with a group of NBC personalities, including the late anchor Jessica Savitch and a childhood hero of mine, the former San Francisco 49ers quarterback John Brodie, now a commentator. When it was my turn in front of the press, the first question was about Michael.

"Can you confirm that Michael Landon is having an affair with a stand-in?"

I was utterly unprepared for that. I had never gotten a question like that from a reporter. I realized later the timing of the question was no accident. *Entertainment Tonight*, now the longest running daily syndicated entertainment news show in television history, would premiere on that following Monday night, September 14, 1981. They were looking for a juicy sound bite with which to launch the program. (I would get to know a lot about *Entertainment Tonight* on a very personal level relatively soon.)

"I don't know anything about that," I said awkwardly.

The reporter repeated the question, and I replied, "We have nothing to talk about."

I wish I'd come back with something glib and clever. *What about all my affairs?* That would have been a cool and deft response, but I didn't think of it until the plane ride home. When the presser was over, an NBC representative apologized for not preparing me for the possibility of that question. She assured me that I had handled it well, but I felt unsettled. The innocence that I had brought with me to *Little House* was fast slipping away. I wasn't as devastated by Michael's affair as Melissa was, but it was hard to reconcile what I was seeing with his "perfect husband and father" image. More to the point, I disliked that I now had to deflect questions about Michael's personal life. In a strange way, it made me feel complicit. To say "I don't know anything" when I did? It was not a position I'd been in before, and I didn't like it.

I want to be fair. While Michael's affair was jarring for all of us, it was a very small part of the overall experience I had on *Little House*. And even as our illusions about him as some sort of perfect man fell away, we remained collectively and individually in awe of his skill as a writer, director, producer, and actor. As immensely talented and creative as my castmates were in their own right, on that set we were all just extensions of Michael Landon's imagination and his enormous craft. Everybody in our cast and crew would have walked through fire to deliver for him. And deliver we did.

I wouldn't have been cast as Almanzo if I hadn't been innocent. Yet in hindsight, I wish that I had had a stronger acting craft, a better sense of myself, and more confidence before I came on the show. I had no idea how little I knew about acting until I saw the cast at work. I willed myself not to be intimidated by Michael, but I don't think anyone close at hand could've missed that I was. For years after the show was over, you might be surprised to learn that I had *Little House* dreams that put me back on the set with Michael. Every once in a while, I'll still dream I'm with Michael in Walnut Grove, and we're working, trying to get it right. Sometimes, in these dreams, I do get it exactly "right," and I see his broad grin. Other times, I am falling short, and I can sense his impatience as I'm struggling to deliver what he wants. There is no one outside my own family whom I have dreamt about so often.

These dreams are an affirmation of the enormous respect I had for Michael Landon, and the gratitude I will always feel for having been invited into his world.

I will be asked about Michael for the rest of my life. I don't mind that. I do wish that I had better answers to give. I wish I could have known him better, found a way past that grin and those sunglasses and gotten into his confidence. Like so many of us, I wish I could have seen the simplicity that Kent saw. When Michael was a young star on *Bonanza*, he had the courage to ask the show's producer and lead writer, David Dortort, to teach him the craft. I didn't have that same courage, and to be fair, very few people did. David Dortort was, by all accounts, a gentle and accessible man. For me Michael Landon was a force of nature; a brilliant writer, director, and actor. He always appeared to be too busy for me to engage him as a mentor.

I did write something for him once during the first season. It was a story for Eliza Jane Wilder in which she'd get her heart broken by a mysterious stranger. When I handed Michael the treatment, he gave me a grin and said, "I'm always looking for stuff like this." I hoped he would read it and talk to me about it, but he never mentioned it again and I couldn't bring myself to ask about it. I never asked him if what I had given him inspired any part of his script for one of my favorite episodes, "Laura Ingalls Wilder." That two-part episode featured Laura's wedding to Almanzo—and included a heartbreaking story for Eliza Jane. Eliza falls in love with a friend of Almanzo's from the city, Harve Miller. Harve jilts "my" sister in a plot line often described by *Little House* fans as among the show's saddest and most moving. (Harve was played by the wonderful James Cromwell, early in his stellar career.) It's absolutely possible that Michael came up with that on his own—a love interest for Eliza Jane made sense— but still, what we filmed was very close to my treatment. It would've felt good to know that I'd had even a small impact on Michael's creative vision for the show.

Though Michael and I did not know each other as well as I would have liked, he did see my broken heart once. In 1982, I fell in love with Mary Hart—the host of *Entertainment Tonight*. Things turned serious, and we got engaged. Mary came with me to Simi Valley one day to visit Walnut Grove, which was located at the Big Sky Movie Ranch. She was at ease wherever she went, and she and Michael hit it off instantly. These were two people at the absolute apex of their respective crafts. Michael asked if their conversation was off the record; Mary laughed and assured him that this was entirely a personal visit. Watching the effortless banter between my fiancée and the man who had created the entire world I inhabited was remarkable.

Little House: A New Beginning came to an end after our first season. Nobody expected it. Michael had planted several plot seeds during Season 9, including the arrival of Robert Casper as Mr. Montague, and Willie Oleson falling in love and getting married. Perhaps we should have seen it coming. Our ratings weren't horrible, but they certainly weren't as strong as they had been.

It was tough to put my finger on, but there was a trend of death and disconnected plots during that ninth season, starting with the departure on the Ingalls family in the season premiere. In that same episode my visiting brother, Royal (Nicholas Pryor), comes for a visit with his daughter Jenny (Shannen Doherty). Royal dies, and then Jenny tries to commit suicide.

Later, Billy Barty was our guest star in an episode called "Little Lou." His wife dies, leaving him alone with an infant child. Even though Laura says that he stays in Walnut Grove, we never see Billy or the child again. The same thing happens in "The Wild Boy," in which Mr. Edwards adopts a troubled child, but we only see him twice more after his first appearance.

In "Marvin's Gardens" we meet Dr. Marvin Haynes, who, we're told, has been practicing in Walnut Grove for years, but his failing eyesight is forcing him to retire. We'd never met Dr. Haynes before that one and only appearance—odd in such a small town. In "Child with No Name," the deaths continue with Laura and Almanzo losing an infant son.

In "For the Love of Blanche," Mr. Edwards meets a dying man whose last wish is to have Isaiah take care of Blanche, a three-year-old orangutan. This for me was one of the most bizarre episodes we ever did. Victor French could play off of anyone or anything, but viewers had good reason to wonder *Where are they going with all this?* Later, in "May I Have This Dance," Laura inherits money from a friend we've never met, we move into a huge place that becomes a boarding house, and along comes Mr. Montague, who knows everything about everything.

Michael was still firmly in charge of what we were doing, and the actual production continued to run like a Swiss watch, so nobody in the cast questioned the tone of our stories as we made them. When they aired, though, the episodes lacked the kind of emotional center that had grounded the show for so many years. It looked like we were grasping at straws, and as it turned out, NBC saw that too.

Michael called all of us personally after the season ended with the news that *Little House: A New Beginning* had been cancelled. The reality is that every show eventually gets cancelled. For those who had been there from the beginning, for whom twenty-two-episode pickups had become the norm, hearing that it was over was a shock. No matter how much success the show had achieved, it was hard not to feel that this cancellation made us all losers. In our business, where people are always quietly rooting for the failure of their competitors, we could all feel it in the air.

However, we got a reprieve several weeks later when Michael called again to tell us that NBC had green-lit three two-hour movies that would allow him to properly bring the series to an end. Those three scripts, *Look Back to Yesterday*, *Bless All the Dear Children*, and *The Last Farewell* put us all back in business again for about six weeks of production.

In *Look Back to Yesterday*, Michael and Matt Labyorteaux take center stage when Charles brings Albert home to Walnut Grove for a visit, but it's clear immediately that Albert is very ill. All the signs point to Albert dying at the end, but it's not clear based on Laura's closing voice-over that that's what happens. Fans have debated Michael's cleverly unclear ending for years.

In *Bless All the Dear Children*, Laura, Almanzo, and Mr. Edwards are in a chase to find Baby Rose, who has been kidnapped by a woman distraught over the death of her infant child. We find Rose on Christmas Eve and agree to adopt a delightful young boy named Samuel, who helped us find her. It's a hopeful ending. Victor directed that script, and I think that, with his help, I delivered my best overall performance in five years.

The Last Farewell, in which we all decide to blow up Walnut Grove, was the story that put the final ending on the series. I never agreed with the "if we can't have it, you can't either" theme that shaped the plot, but there was no doubt that as we all walked out of the demolished town that *Little House* was well and truly over. I think we all understood that Michael had no desire to revisit the *Little House* world in the coming years, and blowing it all up was a visually stunning way to achieve that end. Now it was over, and there was no going back. We all did our best, but Michael was a superstar and none of us could replace the power of his presence for the audience.

Would it have been nice to do another year or two? Purely in financial terms it would've been incredible. Creatively, however, I think we had taken *Little House* as far as it could go. Season 9 exhausted the Laura Ingalls Wilder source material and without Michael's compelling on-screen persona the show lacked heart and gravitas.

Not long after those final movies were completed, Mary Hart broke off our engagement. It was the worst one-two gut punch of my life, and there's no other way to put it; I was completely devastated. I fell off a cliff into an abyss of heartbreak and despair. It was awful.

I saw Michael a year later. I walked into Gold's Gym in Venice for a workout. He was there, filming an episode of *Highway to*

Heaven's first season. In all candor he was the last person I wanted to see, but there he was. I walked up to him to shake hands and say hello. It was odd, but I knew what he was going to ask before the words came out of his mouth.

"Did you get married?"

The question was like a dagger because I was not over the breakup yet. I'd had multiple fender benders and was completely lost in auditions. What made it worse is that I was also totally vulnerable to Michael, because, well, he was Michael.

Melissa has often remarked about the power of looking into his eyes. "If he cried, I cried. If I laughed, he laughed." Patrick Labyorteaux (Andy Garvey) always talks about how Michael had the ability to let people into his eyes. If he wanted to connect on a personal level, he could, and he was genuinely connecting with me in that moment.

I did not want to get emotional in the lobby of Gold's Gym. I held myself together just long enough to say a hoarse, "It didn't work out, Michael."

Gratefully, he didn't bust me. "You'll be OK," he said kindly. "Stay strong."

I shook his hand and turned away because I wasn't strong, and I didn't know what else to do. I never saw him in person again.

In the spring of 1991, when Michael announced that he was terminally ill with pancreatic cancer, it was an enormous shock. He was only fifty-four. It seemed impossible that a man so vital, powerful, and willfully independent could be struck down at such a young age. To no one's surprise, Michael handled the time between the announcement of his diagnosis and his death with grace, dignity, and characteristic courage. I wrote him a letter to offer support and my gratitude and sent it through Kent. I wanted Michael to know I was thinking of him, but I know he was deluged with cards, letters, and calls. I do not know if Michael read my letter. Either way, I am glad I wrote to thank him one more time for the opportunity that had changed my life. I meant every word.

Michael's funeral was at Hillside Memorial Park in Culver City, not far from MGM. It was deeply moving to me that Michael's family invited his "*Little House* family" to sit with them in the front rows at the service. Other mourners included countless celebrities, crew members, and two of Michael's most famous fans: the former president and first lady, Ronald and Nancy Reagan. Melissa delivered a powerful eulogy, and not for the first time, I was enormously impressed by her strength and composure.

"We'll all be together again." That was Michael's emotional promise to the *Little House* cast and crew after we wrapped *The Last Farewell.* I knew deep down inside that I'd never work with him again. I was sad about that, but I believed that I had gotten whatever I was going to get from the *Little House* experience. Time has shown me differently. The truth was that I had only just begun to receive the full measure of gifts that *Little House* would give me over the decades to come. Michael has been gone a long time, and I am much older now than he was when he died—but I am still learning from him.

Even now, I'll remember something he said or did and I'll say to myself, "*Now,* I get it." And I am so grateful.

CHAPTER 11

From Manly to Moondoggie

THAT ON-CAMERA KISS WITH MELISSA GILBERT WAS A DEFINING moment of my time on *Little House*, and indeed of my career. By a strange coincidence, another kiss landed me my first post-*Little House* gig. This next smooch, however, couldn't have been more different from the one Almanzo planted on Laura.

My first venture into prime-time comedy—and my first real work after *Little House*—came with a 1984 guest slot on *Who's the Boss?*. The Tony Danza/Judith Light show would be a hit on ABC, running for eight seasons. I was cast for an episode called "Mona Gets Pinned," the fourth installment in the show's first season. My character would be Jason, the college-aged love interest for Katherine Helmond, who played Mona. Helmond was fifty-five, and the setup was that she'd have a brief fling with a guy young enough to be her son.

Melissa never met me before I was cast to play her future husband. The producers of *Who's the Boss?* took a very different approach. At the final callback, each of the aspiring Jasons was asked to meet Katherine—and sweep her into his arms with a passionate, juicy kiss. The producers said it was about finding someone with whom Katherine, an older married woman, could be comfortable. As had happened so often before, my upbringing and respect for women proved an important asset. The kiss I planted on Katherine Helmond got me the job, and I spent a week filming that fun episode.

Traditional multicamera sitcoms are very different from single camera shows like *Little House*. Working on a sitcom is like doing a little play each week. Day 1 starts with a table reading, and then you go straight into blocking and run-throughs. The script is continually rewritten as the writers and producers sharpen the humor based on what is and isn't working. By the fourth day you're working on the actual set with cameras, and on the last day there are final run-throughs, last tweaks of dialogue, and then two recorded performances in front of a live audience.

Katherine was wonderful, and very respectful of my inexperience in sitcoms. The cast and crew were a great group in rehearsal and on the stage. And yes, Katherine Helmond and I did have a few "after work meetings" to work on our scene together. Though the age gap was significant (Katherine was five years older than my mother), I was completely at ease. As Melissa Gilbert could attest, the discomfort of age-gap kissing scenes has less to do with the age of the older person than the age (and experience) of the younger!

My next job was a movie of the week called *Gidget's Summer Reunion*, the latest revival of a franchise that had begun with the 1959 Sandra Dee movie and evolved into the famous Sally Field TV series.

Gidget had begun as a series of books written by a Jewish war refugee, Frederick Kohner. Kohner based Gidget (a blending of "girl" and "midget") on his own daughter Kathy; the other characters and storylines were inspired by Kathy's friends. Kohner had been struck by his daughter's determination to succeed in the male-dominated Southern California surfing world. His stories centered around a young woman's pluck, resilience, and spirit. Audiences in turn found it irresistible to read about and watch this irrepressibly determined teenage pixie challenge the boys. All the actresses who played Gidget were very cute, but they never led with their sexuality. The books and the subsequent films established a powerful, popular example for young girls who wanted to break barriers and succeed in a man's world. While neither the books nor the filmed adaptations have proved as enduring as the *Little House* books and series, *Gidget* remains an influential and beloved part of American pop culture.

I was cast as Jeff "Moondoggie" Griffin, Gidget's husband. Caryn Richman was cast in the title role. Once again, I'd be the supportive romantic partner to the proto-feminist young heroine of an adaptation of an iconic series of books. Once again, I'd be playing another incarnation of myself, just as I had in *Forever* and on *Little House*. Dean Butler was very much part of Michael Wagner, "Manly" Wilder, and Moondoggie, and casting directors could see it. As I've said, for better or worse, casting directors rarely make mistakes.

Gidget's Summer Reunion was light and breezy, uncomplicated, and populated by attractive people who you wouldn't mind hanging out with for a couple of hours during an evening. There were no complex social issues being explored. The biggest challenge of our little movie was whether Gidget would be able to get Jeff's old friends together for a surprise birthday party—and whether Moondoggie could resist the come-ons of his older female boss. The settings were beautiful, as were the bikini bodies, and Gidget and Moondoggie were together and still in love at the end. A perfect, uncomplicated trifle.

Caryn Richman was the ideal Gidget, and from my perspective we hit it off right away. She had my undivided attention from the day we met. Rom-coms are all about chemistry between the leads, and Caryn and I had great chemistry. As always, it's much easier (and certainly more fun) if the sizzle of attraction is mutual and real. It is not news that production sets populated by attractive people working long hours together have become launching pads for relationships off camera. Filming this movie, Caryn and I were doing a great many romantic scenes—while wearing next to nothing. It was an ideal situation for blurring the lines between professional and personal, and I was delighted when that began to happen. I had wanted it to happen with Stephanie Zimbalist, but she had kept a firm, if friendly, boundary in place. With Melissa, there was great respect—and thanks to our age gap, zero possibility of chemistry. With the lovely Caryn, I had a romance that clicked on screen and off.

And then there was Mary Frann. In our movie, Mary played Ann Bedford, Moondoggie's older and seductive boss. Mary was already famous for her wonderful role on *Newhart*. She and I once had dinner together after wrapping for the day. One thing led to another, and Mary and I ended up on the beach, in the moonlight, horizontal in the sand for several hours. Perhaps Mary was doing fantasy research for the scenes where I would reject her later, but honestly, I didn't care. When the beach got too cold, we continued our research in the comfort of Mary's beautiful car. The things we do to get the work right are all-consuming! Eventually, I realized that I had to be on set in a few hours, ready for more fun with Gidget. Very reluctantly, I crawled out of Mary's car and went home for an hour's sleep.

In my most famous role, I was paired with an actress widely considered to have been too young for me. Let me note again that it is ironic that time and again, in real life, I have had many of my most intense relationships with older women. Mary was thirteen years older than I was, but that didn't matter in the least to either of us. Mary had been a beauty queen, a former Miss Missouri, and like other beauty queens I've known in my life, her glamorous style was forever shaped by that early pageant experience.

A few years later, I briefly ran into Mary again, backstage after a show I'd done on Broadway. We had an all-too-brief but very warm reunion. A lovely person and an immensely talented actress, Mary died in her sleep in 1998, at just fifty-five. I was shocked and very sad. "Remember me with smiles and laughter, for that is how I will remember all [of] you. If you can only remember me with tears, then don't remember me at all." That's a Michael Landon line, often misattributed to Laura Ingalls Wilder. My lasting memory of Mary Frann will always be of her smiles and laughter, punctuating an unexpectedly passionate night on a Malibu beach. I think she'd like to be remembered that way.

Most of *Gidget's Summer Reunion* was shot in Southern California, but we finished the movie on Oahu. My father had grown up in Hawaii, and I had inherited from him a deep love of the islands. Perhaps it was because I was far from Los Angeles and my normal routine, or perhaps it was the spectacular hotel suite overlooking Waikiki Beach, or perhaps it was Caryn's dancing eyes, but on our first afternoon in Hawaii, I smoked pot for the first time. I was twenty-nine, and until I took that joint from Caryn, I had never taken a toke of marijuana in my life. I'm not going to say precisely what happened next, but there was something, something, and something more, followed by a long, wonderful sleep. It was awesome.

Gidget's Summer Reunion got good ratings. Conversation quickly turned to making it into a series. In 1985, there were several syndicated reboots in the works: *What's Happening, The Monkees*, and *Charles in Charge*. A Gidget show fit right into those plans, and we had the ideal producer to make that happen. Harry Ackerman was known as "the Dean of Television Comedy." He had already created many of the most beloved sitcoms of the 1950s and 1960s: *Father Knows Best, Dennis the Menace, Leave It to Beaver, The Farmer's Daughter, Hazel, Bewitched, The Flying Nun*, and of course the original Sally Field *Gidget*. At one point seven of

157

Harry's shows were on the air at the same time, a distinction no other producer achieved.

Harry was a gracious gentleman: thoughtful, softspoken, and kind-hearted. He would always answer, "Harry Ackerman here," when I called him on the phone. There was a bright and cheerful formality in Harry's style that was helpful in keeping everyone moving in the right direction, particularly as *Gidget's Summer Reunion* evolved from a movie of the week into a backdoor pilot for *The New Gidget* series. Harry got his star on the Walk of Fame not long after he shepherded our movie into a full-fledged series. Caryn and I were there in Hollywood the day they gave Harry his immensely deserved honor. Harry died in 1991, but his influence on American television endures.

As happy as Caryn and I were that we now had a series, I realized that there'd be no break from the diet and the working out. They say the camera adds ten pounds, and in my case, it's more like fifteen. I tend to carry weight in my face and neck, and if I'm not on top of what I'm eating, there's no hiding the consequences. On *Little House*, of course, I was almost always in long-sleeve shirts. I had to mind my fitness, but I didn't need abs. Our syndicated series—christened *The New Gidget*—needed a Moondoggie who looked like a surfer. A washboard stomach was a professional necessity.

I lifted weights in the morning at Gold's Gym. In the afternoon, Caryn and I took aerobics classes together. We sweated gallons a day. Exercise alone wasn't enough to get me swimsuit ready. I needed to get my sloppy diet under control. I ate according to the then-popular *Fit for Life* strategy, which was based on food combining. Fruits and vegetables were at the center of every meal, and they were combined with either carbohydrates or proteins, but never proteins and carbs together. I was living on meals of chicken and broccoli or baked potato and broccoli, but never chicken and baked potato together.

No ice cream, no cookies. I told my sweet tooth to shut up for a while; I had work to do. By the first day of filming for the series, I was down to 172 pounds on my 6' 1" frame. I have never come close to being so fit again.

When I was cast in *Forever*, John Korty had given me the choice of being filmed playing tennis, basketball, or swimming. Swimming was my best sport, but my very pale skin would not look good on camera. I had chosen basketball. With *Gidget*, I was playing a surfer. I'd spend most of my time with my shirt off. I could get a beach body by hitting the gym and laying off my beloved Rocky Road, but I couldn't discipline myself into a tan. Too much time in the sun, and I'd be "Lobsterdoggie." (As a boy, envious of the tans that my father, brother, and sister got so easily, I spent much too much time in the California sun. I don't know how many layers of skin I burned off. In later years, I've had to cope with various skin cancers, including melanoma. I get myself checked religiously by the dermatologist, and if you're old enough to remember watching me on television, you should too.)

The only solution was body makeup. Every day, week after week, our makeup artist would roll his eyes, sigh, and break out a big sponge, a bucket of warm water, and Ben Nye pancake makeup. Like sponge painting a kitchen wall, he'd apply a tan from my neck to my feet. It's a wonder I didn't destroy my shower drain washing off that thick brown layer every night.

Just as my stand-in drove the horse team on *Little House*, I would never have to catch an actual wave on camera. And with a lot of self-restraint in the kitchen and hard work in the gym— and that Ben Nye pancake—I *looked* like a surfer. What's more, I had a co-star I adored, and we had twenty-two episodes ordered. As far as my friends and family were concerned, I'd proved I could have a career after *Little House*. I'd gone from the prairie to the beach—or, in Los Angeles terms, from Simi Valley to Malibu, and from Culver City to Burbank. What mattered was that I was working, and I knew enough to know how lucky I was.

That transition from prairie to beach was also a transition to comedy. *Summer Reunion* had been a romantic comedy with equal parts romance and comedy; *The New Gidget* would be a more straightforward comedy. Just as I needed to get my body into shape, I needed to tone my funny bone. To do that, I chose to study with The Groundlings— Hollywood's legendary improv comedy troupe. Looking back, it remains one of the best decisions I ever made. I was never going to be a Robin Williams or a John Ritter, but the opportunity to laugh and play in a supportive environment with thirty talented people was an amazing gift to my spirit and confidence. For four hours a day, three days a week, for ten weeks before production, I turned off judgment, got loose, and laughed.

Our teacher, the wonderfully funny Randy Bennett, taught The Groundlings improv method. Randy taught us the central rule: Never Deny. Whatever was said by one actor in a scene had to be accepted as a fact and then built on with the next lines by the other actors.

Here's a simple example. If someone started with, "I love it when the sky is green in the morning," the follow-up had to build on that premise in some way. The next line could be something like, "Yes, but it's the purple clouds that I love most." The actors accept that the sky is green, and the clouds are purple. No one says, "I think the sky is yellow and the clouds are violet." That would be a denial, and denials kill the comedy. They could continue with, "It's springtime, and the trees are going to be full of cows soon."

As the actors look up, imagining this strange combination of colors and livestock above them, their minds are whirling on what to say next. Perhaps the next line is, "Don't you hate going under the trees in the springtime?" Improv is the complete commitment to trusting yourself and the actors you're on stage with. It is as much team sport as theater.

I developed my own characters at The Groundlings, two of

which were very well received. There was "Big Bob," a loud, bombastic redneck based on my Oklahoma-born brother-in-law, Noell Michaels. (I have great admiration and respect for my sister's husband and have for more than forty years. He is not always loud and bombastic.) The second was "Aunt Maggie," drawn from my many years watching (and doing the bidding of) my unforgettably imperious great-aunt, Margaret McClure. After a little liquid encouragement I can still do Big Bob and Aunt Maggie.

I met my longtime friend Rick Livingston at The Groundlings. Rick had twenty-seven fully realized characters after the first week of class, and he could do them all on request. If anyone in our group had potential to move on to a big career in comedy, I thought it was Rick. Over the years, Rick has done a lot of stage and on-camera work, and he's written some hilariously clever scripts. While he never got to *Saturday Night Live*, where I think he would've flourished, he did a wonderful job guest-starring on an episode of *The New Gidget*. (Rick is in one of the funniest commercials I've ever seen in my life, a spot called "Swear Jar" for Bud Light. Look for it on YouTube.)

After ten weeks at The Groundlings, I was as loose and relaxed on stage as I've ever been, and as ready as I could be for my first steps into broad youth-culture comedy. What I wasn't ready for was the horrifying thud of disappointment I felt when I read the first *New Gidget* scripts. They not only weren't funny, but I couldn't follow them as stories that had a beginning, a middle, and an end. How could so much un-funny be packed into a 22-minute script?

On *Little House*, Michael Landon polished every last syllable until it was perfect. I knew I had been spoiled by Michael's showrunning, of course, but I had no idea that professional screenwriting could be this sloppy. They could put laugh tracks on every line, but the shows weren't funny—and no one would be able to follow them. Our risk of colossal failure was multiplied by the reality that the studio planned to shoot five shows at a time on a fifteen-day schedule.

It was a strategy born of making the best use of time and money and giving us maximum beach exposure. Since we were just months away from air, this was—in theory—a brilliant idea. We would go to the beach for three or four days and jump from show to show shooting all the beach scenes for five episodes one after the other. After that we'd move back to Warner Brothers and shoot all the interior house scenes, then to the backlot for the exteriors and so on. It was a very smart and efficient use of resources, but this approach also required our writers to have five scripts at a time polished and ready to go. These scripts were not only *not* polished, but they were also almost indecipherable.

Caryn and I reminisced recently about our mutual horror about the lines we had to say. She told me: "I had to let that go, otherwise I would've lost my mind. After a while, I just knew I was changing my bathing suit, getting my body makeup touched up, and I was going to smile and deliver these lines as real as I possibly could with the Gidget spirit." For the record, Caryn was absolutely right. There was nothing she or any of us could do but go in and do the work.

I wish I had had my co-star's perspective. As crazy as it sounds, I felt nearly suicidal after the first few table reads. I felt this unfunny writing would mark me for years. As actors, Caryn and I would be the faces of this disaster, and we would be blamed for this awfulness. It wasn't fair, but that's how it worked. Michael Landon had promised me he'd never let me look bad, and he kept his word. There was no way for these scripts not to make us all look terrible, and I was panicked.

I phoned Harry Ackerman. He wasn't happy to get my call, but he listened. "Send me your suggestions, and we'll consider them," he said. Before we hung up, Harry added, "Dean, you can never ask for this again."

I wasn't a writer. I'd never written actual dialogue, only a treatment. I was desperate, and I tried my hand at it. The problem was that it wasn't just the dialogue that needed fixing. These scripts needed down to the foundations reworking, and there just wasn't time. Shooting was beginning in a day or two. I sent Harry my suggestions. The scripts didn't change much, but I had voiced my concerns and offered fixes. In doing so, I had crossed a line that most actors don't.

I never offered a single creative suggestion on *Little House,* other than that one story idea I mentioned. Michael established the ground rules early. He wasn't going to entertain questions or anxious requests for approval. His rules were strict, but the comfort zone of professionalism that he created around all his actors was rock solid. All any of us had to do was show up, play, and go home. Everything else was done. The more experienced cast members who had been on other shows could fully appreciate what Michael was doing. Some of us didn't realize how "spoiled" we were to work under his level of writing and direction.

Somehow, we made those first episodes of *Gidget* work. And for all that was wrong with how this show was being run, nothing could ruin the magic of having a starring role on a new series.

Caryn told me recently of her vivid memory of our first day of shooting in the studio. "I was driving to Warner Brothers over the hill from Hollywood to Burbank, it was about six in the morning, and I came around that curve on Barham with tears streaming down my face."

"Good morning, Ms. Richman," was her greeting from the guard at the gate. Caryn was the star, the number one on the call sheet. She was playing the title character. It made an indelible impression on her.

I felt the same way. I loved driving up to the studio gate, seeing my face on a billboard overhead, and having the security guard greet me by name and wave me onto the lot so I could drive to the stage where I was going to work that day. The scripts may have been awful, but there is something wonderful about being welcomed and wanted. Sometimes, being recognized in public by fans can be delightful; other times it is awkward. To be seen, recognized, and welcomed with a smile by the gate guard who always seems delighted to see you? That's a heady experience.

Different from most sitcoms that were shot with multiple cameras in front of a live audience, *The New Gidget* was going to be a one-camera show shot on film like a drama and then sweetened with a laugh track in post-production. That wasn't the problem. The problem was that the first round of production was absolute chaos. The set was loud and disorganized. You couldn't hear yourself think between shots—and the shots themselves were awful. It was horrible to realize that the production was just as haphazard as the scripts.

One of the first establishing shots I saw was set against the back of the same Paradise Cove restaurant where I'd had dinner with Mary Frann. You couldn't see the beach in the shot. The sun was too bright, and the most notable feature of the restaurant on film was the air-conditioning unit on the roof. Why even bother shooting on location if it looked this bad? As we watched the dailies, co-executive producer Ralph Riskin—who had been one of the producers of *The Dukes of Hazzard*—leaned over and asked me, "Why did you let them shoot that shot?" He was half teasing, half serious. *Why had I?* He was right there when it happened! Why had *he* let them shoot that shot? Ralph, Caryn, and I weren't the only ones shaken by those early rounds of dailies. We were in a lot of trouble. Studio executives were watching as well, and they could no longer ignore that something had to be done and done quickly.

The studio's rescue plan came in the form of a bright young producer named Larry Mollin. We never saw Larry or knew he was working with us until after our first five shows were shot. As Larry told me recently, the studio brought him in to "do post"

(post-production work) on our first episode. They liked his "rescue plan" and gave him the next four episodes to fix. Larry had written pilots and had experience developing shows. He had also been on staff for two successful NBC series, *CHiPs* and *Knight Rider*, so he knew how to "feed the beast" that is series television.

Larry saw in the first edits of the shows what had been obvious to everyone. "The shows didn't really track. So, we needed a way to make them track," Larry told me. Being the inventive producer that he was, Larry suggested that the shows could be made more understandable with vignettes that he called "Gidget-Overs." It was a clever idea. Larry had himself been an improvisational actor, so he understood how to make something work on the fly. Gidget-Overs would be written for the top of the show, for act breaks, and for the end of each episode. Caryn would be found in some comedic scenario consistent with the theme of the episode and she could explain to viewers what they were going to see and what they had seen in four Gidget-Overs of thirty seconds each. Larry's Gidget-Overs saved those first five episodes and gave the show its creative signature.

"The studio said, we want the show younger. Let's make it more about the youth culture," Larry told me. The tone of the series was reimagined, and under Larry's capable guidance, much of the cast was replaced with an eye to skewing toward a teen audience. When I'd been on *Little House*, I'd been positioned as a teen heartthrob; now, at twenty-nine, I was going to give up screen time to real teenagers. I struggled with the idea that Caryn and I would likely have a diminished presence in this more youthful approach, but considering that our time periods were weeknights in prime access with reruns on Saturday mornings, something had to give.

Larry made our show bigger, broader, and sillier. He was far and away a better writer than our first showrunner. He was funny and had a smart and clever take on youth culture. The

studio loved what he was doing. The studio did product place-
ment deals with youth lifestyle companies like Ocean Pacific
and QuickSilver, and suddenly I was wearing tank tops and
bright red trunks. Caryn's bikinis got brighter and smaller. I remember it flipped her out having to stand next to Sydney
Penny, who played Gidget's niece Dani. Caryn half-jokingly described Sydney as having a "twelve-inch waist." Sydney was a bud-
ding beauty, to be sure, but Caryn was a beautiful woman. She
had nothing to worry about. Boys of all ages would get Caryn. I
certainly did.

Once Larry Mollin began to run the show, a lot of things got
better quickly. Our second round of scripts were hugely improved over the first, and our new director of photography, Jim
Swain, brought in a much more cohesive camera crew. Yes, our
stories were wackier, but they *worked*. As silly as the storylines
were, they made sense—and trusting in Larry, we all threw ourselves into the work without hesitation. We ended up having
three directors whom we all liked through the run of the show.
Thirty-seven of our forty-four episodes were directed by just
three men: Doug Rogers, Roger Duchowny, and Ted Lange.
(Lange had been one of the stars and directors of ABC's popular prime-time series, *The Love Boat*.) All three of these directors
understood what we were being asked to do, which, as Roger
Duchowny put it, was to make "pink fluff and cotton candy."

One of our favorite episodes was 1987's "Gilligidge Island,"
which was the premiere episode of our second season. As the
title suggested, this was a spoof on the classic Sherwood Schwartz
comedy. Bob Denver and Alan Hale Jr. themselves guest-starred
in their famous roles as Gilligan and the Skipper. The two of
them led our little family on a "three-hour tour" that led, inevitably, to a shipwreck on a tropical island. It was a treat to work
alongside actors I'd grown up watching—especially when they
reprised the original roles I loved.

Another favorite episode was a musical called "Drag City." Larry Mollin wrote the lyrics to the songs and his brother Fred, our music director, wrote the music. We had the opportunity to pre-record songs and then sing them on camera as we sped around in a Bucket T dragster. It was totally silly but a real challenge. Caryn had done a lot of singing at that point. I had done much less, but I was willing. In the wacky, fun-loving spirit of the show, being willing to step up and play was what mattered most.

In talking to Caryn, I found out that we agreed that our all-time favorite episode was titled "The Christmas Curl," directed by our production manager, Ken Koch. In our story Gidget becomes a little Scrooged out while directing a community theater production of the Charles Dickens holiday classic, *A Christmas Carol*, and on Christmas Eve is visited by three ghosts who help her rediscover the real meaning of Christmas. I was *Jacob Knarly*.

I don't know what possessed me, but to prepare myself for our dive into Dickens, I watched the 1938 *Christmas Carol* film that starred Reginald Owen as Scrooge. The performance of his ghostly deceased business partner, Jacob Marley, was dark and screechy, and that's what I brought in and delivered on camera. At the time, I thought it was pretty good, but once I saw what our other ghosts were doing—very "Gidgety" spins on the Dickens ghosts—I realized I made a huge mistake. This is where film and stage are so different. In a stage production what I did would've been part of a rehearsal process and thrown out. When working on film, actors need to come to the set with their performance well considered. It's not finished until the director says, "Cut. Print," but there isn't time in most TV series schedules for experimentation. With my Knarly Marley performance I knew I'd screwed up, and I went to Ken and groveled for a second chance. After beating me up for a minute or two, he agreed. I think this was the only time I had ever asked for a redo on anything. Fortunately, I asked for it before the setup had changed, so it didn't take a ton of time to go again. Ken was a wonderful unit manager. On that day, I appreciated him for his flexibility as a director.

The New Gidget ran for forty-four episodes, at which point Columbia Pictures Television decided it wanted to get out of the syndication business. The show stopped abruptly. *Little House* had had its famous goodbye, and America had watched our beloved town blown dramatically to smithereens. As I would learn, that kind of farewell episode is rare in American television. It's more common for the plug to be pulled without any formal conclusion. With only forty-four episodes plus the two-hour backdoor pilot, there were not enough titles to create a good package of shows for syndicated runs on independent stations. The business has changed, and in today's streaming environment forty-eight episodes would be great—except for the matter of the music. Just as with *Forever*, the reuse cost of *The New Gidget* soundtrack was too much. (Our music for the pilot included a re-recorded version of the Beach Boys' "Little Surfer Girl," which featured Dean Torrence of Jan & Dean singing backing vocals. I met Torrence at that recording session, and we bonded over sharing a relatively uncommon first name and discovered that we lived only a few doors away from each other on Rodgerton Drive in the Hollywood Hills.)

As a result of the licensing issues, you can't find *The New Gidget* on television. Even if you could, it would not be the cultural treasure that was *Little House on the Prairie*. Still, I am proud of the work we did to make this fluffy confection of a show and participate in the revival of a classic American character. Caryn Richman and I remain great friends, and on occasion, we still sing together in public.

As it turned out, singing was about to become a much, much more important part of my career.

CHAPTER 12
Broadway

WHATEVER ELSE I'VE DONE AS AN ACTOR AND PRODUCER, MUSIC always finds its way back into my life. It has been part of my life as a performer since I first stepped on stage. For a few years after *The New Gidget*, music became not just a passion, it became a good part of my living.

My early attempts at singing were more enthusiastic than promising.

In high school, I sang a Cat Stevens song in the talent show and was pelted by pennies and nickels. (These were not tips.) At Pacific, I absolutely destroyed Cole Porter's "All through the Night" in every performance of *Anything Goes*. The local theater critic remarked: "Dean Butler is so charming you forget about his voice." It was a fitting backhanded compliment.

Little House brought more opportunities to sing, and I seized them with the questionable reasoning that if I was good enough to be on this huge TV series, I was good enough to sing in public. The first and only time I sang on the show (other than in church with the rest of the cast), was in a Season 7 episode called "Divorce Walnut Grove Style." The song was called "My Only Love," written in the episode by a character named Brenda

Sue Longworth, played by the beautiful and talented Wendy Schaal. "My Only Love" was a simple little song with music by our *Little House* composer, David Rose. (David is, in my view, nearly as important as Michael Landon and Kent McCray to *Little House*'s lasting success.)

Before we shot the episode, I worked on the song with David Rose at his house in Sherman Oaks. While playing his tiny up-right piano, David taught me the song. I practiced singing it in a soft, romantic way. I felt confident I sounded good, and David liked my approach. A few days later, when Michael heard me singing the song on set to the pre-recorded guitar track, he stopped me right away. "No, no," he said, "I want you to sing it bad."

"Bad?" I asked, hoping I hadn't heard him correctly.

"Bad," he repeated, "BAAAD!" That was the last thing I wanted. I had been bad plenty of times without meaning to be, and now I could be good—but had to be bad on purpose? It didn't make sense. Besides, what was it Michael had promised about never letting me look bad? But when I saw the episode, I had no complaints. The corny way I sang it to resolve Almanzo's first big spat with Laura worked well enough. (I still think it wouldn't have hurt to let me sing the song nicely.)

I did much more singing away from the *Little House* set. In late 1981, our cast participated in a holiday special for NBC called *An NBC Family Christmas.* All the casts of NBC's prime-time shows gathered on stage in downtown Burbank to share some holiday cheer. There was a point where the actors from different series were supposed to sing lines from a holiday song that would be put together in post. We needed to appear as one big happy NBC family. I don't remember the song, but when the music came over the studio public address system, for Melissa and me to sing, I had a hard time hearing it. We did three takes, and I was convinced I was off pitch. I was in a bad mood, enough to annoy Melissa.

"What's wrong with you?" she asked.

"I can't hear the music." My co-star's expression suggested that next time, I should avoid making it her problem too.

The control room could see that I was getting upset. After the show, a pleasant man about my age approached me with a warm smile and introduced himself.

"Hi, Dean," he said, "I'm Sam Haskell and I'm with the William Morris Agency. I could see during your song that you were worried about your pitch. I'm going to be in the editing room when the song is put together, and I promise you that if your pitch is off we'll get you into a studio and have you sing it again."

I was both relieved and disarmed by his genuine kindness. "That's very nice of you."

As we shook hands, Sam said, "Dean, I want you to know that my wife Mary and I love *Little House*. We never miss it."

I thanked him. A few days later the phone rang, and I was surprised to hear Sam's warm Mississippi accent on the other end. "Hi, Dean, I'm in the editing room and I'm listening to you, and your pitch on the song is just fine. We don't need to do anything. You have nothing to worry about."

Hollywood is a town where a lot of people promise things they have no intention of delivering upon. I was frankly shocked that this guy had done what he had said he was going to do. This was someone I wanted to know better. "It's very kind of you, Sam, to let me know. I really appreciate it."

That exchange was the beginning of one of my longest and most treasured friendships. Sam Haskell, a son of Amory, Mississippi, is simply one of the finest people I've ever known. Sam was in my first wedding, he has represented me, we've judged pageants together, I've produced for him, and we share a deep love of Christmas traditions. More than forty years after we met for the first time, Sam is the same good, honorable man he has always been. For many years, Sam was one of the most successful packaging agents in the business. Following his agency career, he became a philanthropist and an Emmy-winning producer. I can't count the number of times through the years that I've called him for help, and he's always been there for me. I would do anything for him, and it all began with the line of a song in *An NBC Family Christmas.*

Buoyed by having survived that initial experience, I began to sing more at promotional events. My manager, Jon Feltheimer, introduced me to songwriter and arranger, Jay Asher. Jay was a great aficionado of Top 40 music from the 1950s to the early 1980s. As we drank coffee and talked, he played on his piano and sang hit after hit with an infectious sense of fun, while encouraging me to sing along so he could get a sense of my range and skill. To be honest, there was very little actual skill, but I made up for my lack of skill with enthusiasm. We ended up deciding on the Dion classic, "The Wanderer," a medley of *Young Rascals* tunes, and an arrangement of the Muppet hit, "The Rainbow Connection." Jay wrote up charts for me to follow, and I was ready to perform with my small but reliable repertoire.

For several years in the early 1980s, I sang at NBC promotions and charity events. Perhaps the most memorable of the latter came when the March of Dimes invited me to appear at the Grand Ole Opry in Nashville. I sang the massive Kenny Rogers hit "The Gambler" to an audience of five thousand devoted country music fans. I got a great *Little House* intro, stepped on stage, and quipped to the audience that if I forgot the lyrics, they'd be sure to help me out. When I walked off stage, I was greeted by country legend Roy Acuff; he slapped me on the back and told me, "Get back out there, boy, and give 'em an encore." When I came out the stage door, I was rushed by a sea of young women who nearly ripped my shirt off. What twenty-five-year-old guy wouldn't be in heaven after affirmation like that?

I don't know what possessed me to think that I could sing at the cathedral of country music, but somehow, that confidence came. For me, performing was all about stepping up and working big. Forget phrasing or tone or pitch; when the music started, I was like a fire hose aimed at the audience. I had had great fun at the Opry, but I knew I wanted to get better.

I got a new singing teacher: Nathan Lam. Nathan had coached the likes of Rod Stewart, Lionel Ritchie, and Don Felder of the Eagles. A funny, high-energy man, Nate focused on helping me create a smooth transition between my chest and my "head voice." At the end of every lesson Nate would let me sing songs, either with his accompanist, Joan, or on his very cool karaoke audio system. When he told me that I sang "Hotel California" better than his student who helped write it, I was walking on air.

After *Little House* and *Gidget* ended, I didn't just need to improve my skills. I needed to work. Nate suggested I start auditioning for musicals. I knew I had improved, but I didn't feel ready to sing at the Pantages. Nate nudged me toward a smaller venue, and I landed my first gig, back at The Groundlings. I was cast as an understudy, playing Nick in *Casual Sex*, a comedy musical about two women who go to a Club Med-like resort in search of wild and crazy times. The show was raunchy, silly good fun. I worked with Jon Lovitz and Kathy Griffin and saw each of them developing the personas that would later lead them to great fame.

A month or two after *Casual Sex* closed, one of my agents, David Westberg, called with news: I had an audition to play Tony in a New York-based production of *West Side Story* that was going to tour in Japan. *General Hospital* star Jack Wagner had to drop out of the show and the producers were looking for a replacement. *Casual Sex* to *West Side Story* was a huge leap; this was the music of Leonard Bernstein and the lyrics of Stephen Sondheim! This was the choreography of Jerome Robbins! This was one of the most important shows in the history of American musical theater, inspired by William Shakespeare's *Romeo and Juliet*! It doesn't get any more loaded than that.

Before I committed to the audition, I called Nate. I knew *West*

Side Story: Tony's biggest song, "Maria," is a beautiful ballad with a towering B flat at the crescendo of the melody. Nate convinced me I could land it: "It will be work, Dean, but you absolutely can do this." With Nate's reassurance, I told David Westberg I'd audition. I wasn't afraid to not get the job. I was afraid to show up to the audition and embarrass myself.

The director, Alan Johnson, was a member of *West Side Story*'s original Broadway company and one of two directors sanctioned by Jerome Robbins to direct productions of the show. Alan agreed to come to David Westberg's house in West Hollywood to audition me privately. He was a kind, soft-spoken, thoughtful man. Alan could not have been a nicer person to meet before a terrifying experience. When I played Tevye at Piedmont High, I'd dreamed of Broadway—but the general consensus was that I didn't have what it took. Now, I was auditioning for a Broadway legend who had devoted much of his life to this one iconic show. Somehow, I held my nerve—and a day after the audition, they offered me the part.

West Side Story centers on the romance between Tony and Maria. Not long before we left for Tokyo, I met "my" Maria, Lauri Landry. Lauri was a brown-eyed beauty, a powerful soprano with big Broadway dreams. Unlike me, she had been focused on musical theater from the start of her career. With her confidence and talent, I had no doubt she was going to be a massive star. I was also coming to the end of my romantic relationship with Caryn Richman. Caryn and I would stay good friends, but we were both ready to move on.

Once in Japan, Lauri and I moved quickly from one promotional press event to another between breakfasts, lunches, and dinners in beautiful restaurants. I was smitten. Lauri didn't seem to feel the same way, but I thought that perhaps that might change. One afternoon, Lauri came to my room. She wanted an aspirin for a headache. On impulse, I reached for her and tried to kiss her. Lauri pushed me away firmly and ran out of the room.

I had never done anything like this before, and I've never done anything like it since. The whole event played out in less than ten seconds nearly forty years ago, but I have carried the guilt of that unwanted advance around inside me ever since. That behavior was completely inconsistent with who I was and am. Having done such a stupid and wrong thing, the only good choice I had was to do the next right thing: never try to approach Lauri again. I apologized again and again, but the chill endured. She couldn't or wouldn't forgive me. And as someone who had always thought of himself as a "good guy," this was a sobering, cautionary experience. It was a painful lesson.

Neither of us could walk away from that uncomfortable moment. We both had to live with it through the rest of the promotional trip and ten weeks of performances. Eight shows a week, we played out our beautiful Romeo and Juliet love affair in front of packed houses; eight shows a week, I played opposite a woman I knew wanted to be as far away from me as possible. It wasn't fun.

Apart from my wrecked relationship with Lauri, I had good relationships with other members of the cast. I enjoyed getting to know my understudy, Steve Blanchard. Steve was a big, tall, strapping guy with a major-league voice. Every sound that came out of him was amazing. I knew from day one that I would never be able to come up to Steve's level vocally. That was tough to process, but it was my issue alone. It wasn't because of Steve. He was positive and supportive and never made me feel less than. After listening to Steve's beautiful voice day after day, I knew I was never going to miss a show. There was no way I was going to let people hear Steve and wonder if this production of *West Side Story* would be better if he were singing Tony every day.

I probably should have let Steve have a show or two. I had

never sung eight shows a week, so my voice was failing, most no-
ticeably on the B flat in "Maria." The note blew apart at least
once during final rehearsals and in one of our opening weekend performances. There was nothing I could do to finesse that
note. I had to go for it whether it was there or not, and on several occasions it was not.

I'm grateful that no one judged me, at least not in a way I noticed. Anyone who knew the show knew the song was hard to
sing. If I were a tenor, none of this would've been hard, but
Tony is almost always sung by baritones—perhaps because it's
more exciting when those top notes are a reach for the actor
playing the part. The first seventeen minutes of *West Side Story*
are brutal: "Something's Coming," "Maria," and "Tonight" right
on top of each other. While I struggled in the beginning of the
run, I did recover and get stronger once we got on a normal
schedule. We had a few costume malfunctions, including a
breezy night at the end of the Dream Ballet where I found myself standing downstage center with my Levi's completely unbuttoned.

One of the fascinating aspects of performing in Japan was
that our audiences were completely silent during our performances. You could feel their energy beyond the footlights, but
out of respect for what we were doing there was no clapping
after any songs. Even at intermission there was nothing. You
could've heard a pin drop in the house until the curtain call,
when we received generous, appreciative applause.

Another unexpected treat of working in Japan was their tradition of gift giving. In the American theater audience members
will sometimes bring flowers to actors and actresses—in Japan
this tradition was expanded to include expensive gifts. I was
given everything from gorgeous collections of paper to elabo-
rate photo albums, food, paintings, porcelain collectibles, hand-
crafted boxes, pearls, and even watches. I shipped boxes of
beautiful gifts home from Japan to Los Angeles. The kindness,

generosity, and appreciation I received, particularly from so many lovely Japanese women, was overwhelming.

Little House on the Prairie was very popular on Japanese television, and I have little doubt that my association with *Little House* was a significant factor in the choice to cast me as Tony. The Japanese love affair with *Little House* had begun decades earlier. With Japan defeated and in ruins at the end of World War II, the U.S. State Department had ordered Laura Ingalls Wilder's novel *The Long Winter* translated into Japanese and widely distributed around the country. MacArthur reasoned that reading Laura's story of survival from the deprivation and hardship of a harsh winter would resonate for the Japanese people as they worked to recover from the horrors of war and rebuild their country. Our TV series, with its emphasis on family and community, built on the values offered in Laura's books, and I could see that appreciation in the faces of thousands of people who came to see our show and greet me afterwards.

Among those who came to see the show were my newly divorced parents. I will always be grateful that my father bought his ex-wife a plane ticket to come and see her son in Japan. It was great to have them there.

After stands in Tokyo, Nagoya, and Osaka our tour ended in Fukuoka, on Japan's southernmost island. Our tour sponsor, Asahi TV, created a wonderful send-off for our company. As the streamers fell to the stage in Fukuoka on our closing night, there were hugs and good wishes all around. Much to my surprise and gratitude, I got a quick but genuine hug from Lauri. What I had done couldn't be forgotten, but perhaps it was forgiven. And then it was over. Within months, the specifics of blocking, choreography, dialogue slipped away, replaced by an overarching sense that *West Side Story* would live as a defining moment for the rest of my life.

Once I was home, I had no idea what was going to happen next. That's the life of an actor. I went back to Nate and kept singing. My singing was much stronger after Japan, so when David Westberg called with another audition for a current Broadway show I was far more ready than I had been before.

The show was *Into the Woods*, the second successful collaboration of composer Stephen Sondheim and writer/director James Lapine that had begun with *Sunday in the Park with George.*

For the *Into the Woods* audition, Caryn Richman recommended that I do a few sessions with a hugely talented but then largely unknown performer named Cortes Alexander. There were two songs for the audition. I met with Cortes a couple of times and focused on performance. It has long been said that Stephen Sondheim's songs give performers everything they need to succeed. I was struck by the language in both songs that clearly and cleverly told the stories of these characters. At the end of my second session with Cortes he turned to me and said with no hesitation, "You're going to get this part."

As a result of all that reassurance, I felt relaxed and ready heading into the audition at the Los Angeles Music Center on a late summer day in 1988. Five people, including writer/director James Lapine and Stephen Sondheim himself, sat at a table. I was looking at Broadway royalty, and I was amazed I wasn't more intimidated.

"Hello, I'm Dean Butler," I said, and after a second, added, "I haven't done a lot of this kind of audition, so I'm not sure what to do next."

Sondheim smiled. "The first thing you're going to do is hand your music to the accompanist and then you'll come right back here, and when you're ready, you'll sing for us." He was warm and welcoming and put me completely at ease. It made me think back to my experience as a tiger trainer on NBC's *Circus of the Stars*. The safest you'll ever be in a cage full of tigers is the first time you step in. After that, it's only a matter of time until they try to kill you. Then again, the tigers hadn't killed me.

I handed off the music, came back to center, and sang parts of

"Agony" and then "Hello, Little Girl." It seemed easy; I don't recall them asking for any adjustments on either song. Then we
read a short scene between the princes, we talked for a minute
or two, they thanked me for coming, I thanked them for seeing
me, and I walked out and went home. Two hours later, they
called David Westberg and offered me the part. I think David
was as dumbstruck as I was. After one meeting and singing two
songs, I was going to Broadway. I would be there for most of the
next year.

When I got to New York, I stayed first in the wonderfully atmospheric Chelsea Hotel while I looked for an apartment and
got my bearings. When I wasn't looking for a place to live, I
spent my days rehearsing and doing costume fittings—and my
nights at the Martin Beck Theatre watching *Into the Woods* from
the back of the house. The show blew me away. It was beautiful,
funny, and emotionally gripping. The cast was wonderful to
watch. I couldn't wait to meet all of them and be a part of the
company. After a few nights of watching from the house, I began
to shadow Chuck Wagner, the actor I'd be replacing. Chuck had
been Rapunzel's Prince but was heading out on the show's national tour as Cinderella's Prince.

I found a great two-story apartment on West 86th Street, a
block from Riverside Park.

The first time I rode the subway from my apartment down to
the theater district, the reality of life in New York came into
sharp focus. It was a Sunday morning. At a Midtown stop, a
highly agitated woman, stark naked, burst into the subway car,
screaming at the top of her lungs that she was Jesus Christ. As
other passengers rushed to adjacent cars, she wrapped herself
around the guy sitting across from me. Stunned, I watched him
fend her off with his guitar case. Twenty seconds later, she
slumped over—passed out cold. It was an unforgettable introduction to the New York subway system.

Many people fall in love with New York. I did too, but it was a temporary infatuation. I am a sixth-generation Californian to my core, and so I never considered moving there permanently. Bizarre incidents on the subway aside, I did love my time in the Big Apple. I experienced the four seasons for the first time in my life. I walked as much as I could; it was thirty-one blocks from my apartment to the Martin Beck Theatre on 45th Street, and I made a point to do the walk multiple times a week. On the way, I loved to walk past Zabar's at 80th and Broadway and smell fresh roasted coffee beans floating on the crisp morning air. I loved walking by 30 Rock to see ice skaters during the Christmas season. The first burst of green in the spring brings the city to life, and the sweltering heat of the summer had me dripping with sweat the moment I walked out the door of my apartment. I ran almost every morning in Riverside Park and worked out at the Paris Health Club on 96th Street.

Not everything in New York was enchanting. One afternoon, I came home from the health club to find my apartment had been broken into. The thieves took my brand-new television, my LaserDisc player, my ten-speed bike that I'd shipped from California, and two expensive leather coats. What they took was worth at least $3,500 in 1988. I called the police. When the officers came and took a report, I asked them if I'd ever see any of this stuff again. The officers laughed—respectfully—and said, "Your property was sold for drug money in ten minutes. You'd have a better chance of seeing Raquel Welch naked than ever seeing your stuff again."

By coincidence, I'd seen a barely clothed Raquel Welch working out just minutes earlier at the club. Anything is possible in New York, apparently, and dreams do indeed come true. As it turned out, seeing a half-naked screen siren was a good deal more likely than recovering stolen property.

In a Broadway theater, dreams come true eight shows a week. A team of dedicated, talented creatives must come together perfectly for the show to successfully deliver its entertaining message and justify the considerable ticket price. That's the commitment of Broadway; execution on the highest level every time the curtain goes up. Every person working in every Broadway theater lives by that commitment. Each has unique tasks they must execute, both on stage and off, to enthrall and inspire the most discerning and demanding theater audiences in the world. There's a lot on the line for anyone.

On Tuesday, September 20, 1988, I did the show for the first time. When I arrived at the theater that afternoon, I saw my name on the cast list. In the lobby there was a large picture, taken a few days earlier, of Robert Westenberg (Cinderella's Prince) and me singing "Agony." After an afternoon "put-in rehearsal" (like a dress rehearsal, but with no orchestra or costumes), I was as ready as I was ever going to be for that night's performance.

Two days earlier, I'd watched as Chuck Wagner had packed up his corner of our surprisingly basic fourth-floor dressing room. The faded semigloss beige paint on the walls was chipped and peeling, and there was very little room to maneuver. It didn't matter. It was Broadway.

"The RP [Rapunzel's Prince] is all yours now," Chuck told me. I could hear the emotion in his voice as we gave each other a hug. He was passing the baton. I felt the weight of what it meant to take on this role, and to bring the Sondheim/Lapine vision for this role to life.

Now, this was my dressing room—or rather, half of it was mine: I shared it with Phil Hoffman, the original "Steward" in the cast. My makeup kit was open, and the appropriate pancake, sponges, and pencils were neatly set out on a clean white hand towel, along with a bag of lemon Ricola lozenges and a bottle of water. I had taped congratulatory telegrams that I had received onto the wall next to the long mirror Phil and I shared. My brand-new, custom-fitted costume hung behind me on a hook. My beautiful new boots—so like Almanzo's boots in *Little House*—sat waiting on the floor. It was showtime.

Before making my first entrance, I sat next to the great Meryl Louise, who was playing Little Red Riding Hood's grandmother. Meryl was in her sixties then, and a beloved Broadway baby. Chuck had told me that visiting with Meryl before going on to sing "Agony" had been a favorite part of the whole experience. Meryl was a delight, just as I had been promised. When the horns sounded, signaling the arrival of the two princes, I bounded onstage to meet Robert Westenberg for our scene and song. On cue the music began, and following Robert's opening verse I sang my first words on a Broadway stage,

High in a tower, she sits by the hour maintaining her hair.

As I walked off stage after that first song, I passed Chip Zien who was playing the Baker. He teased me, deadpan and straight: "Is *that* the way you're going to do it?" For a split second I panicked, and then I saw his grin. Yes, that was the way I was going to do it. I would do it exactly 319 times more over the next eleven months.

My direction was to do exactly what Chuck Wagner had done. Initially, I did just that, but it didn't take long for me to discover that performing the role the way Chuck had done meant leaving a lot of laughs unlaughed. I began to deliver the lines more intentionally, in a way that would reliably trigger an audience response. It didn't take long to come into conflict with James Lapine over my "improvements" to the delivery of dialogue. James didn't care about laughs for the sake of laughs. If laughter happened, that was fine, and if it didn't, that was fine too—his was a sophisticated approach. My take was to give the audience a fun experience, and I reasoned that if I was saying the dialogue as written, which I was, ensuring laughs was a good thing. James and I met often during the first few months of my run. Our meetings were always a struggle. He could never tell me what he wanted, but he could always say what he hated. As a result, whatever target I tried to hit, he made it clear I was missing.

After one mutually frustrating session, James said that he wanted to release me from my contract. I was devastated. My first call was to Stephen Sondheim. I left him a message and he called back within an hour.

"What's up?" he asked.

"James wants to release me from my contract," I told him.

Stephen was surprised and assured me he didn't know anything about it. Then I asked what to me was a vital question. "Am I ruining the show?"

"I think you're doing a very good job," he told me. "Don't worry about James." Stephen added that Joanna Gleason, who had won the Tony for Best Actress in a Musical, told him that she loved what I was doing in the show. Unlike James, Stephen could tell an actor exactly what he wanted them to do and why it would work. While he was famously unkempt and disheveled in his personal appearance, he was unfailingly articulate and crystal clear about his songs and how he wanted them sung.

Feeling a little better after talking to Stephen, I approached Robert Westenberg in the theater, told him what James had said and asked him, "Am I ruining the show?"

Robert responded, "Honestly, Dean, the scenes have never worked better. That's just James being James."

I decided to tell James I wouldn't accept a release, but if he wanted to pay off my contract in full, I would leave. It was a gamble, but I suspected that the economics of the show made a payoff impractical. James told me I could stay, adding, "But I'll never talk to you again."

Well, okay then! Talk about a blessing in disguise! While I didn't enjoy being at odds with anyone, I realized I could never make him happy. If I could do my work and be left alone, it was the best possible outcome to a difficult situation.

My castmates were wonderful. Robert Westenberg, Chip Zien, Joanna Gleason, Pamela Winslow, and the late Marin Mazzie were all incredibly gifted. I loved to watch them work, and I learned from them. They were magnificent colleagues, and they made me feel like I belonged with them on Broadway. I've followed their careers for years, and I'm proud I shared this season of my life with them.

I did not miss a single performance as Tony in *West Side Story*. I did deliberately miss one Sunday show in my eleven months with *Into the Woods*. In January 1989, my beloved San Francisco 49ers made it into Super Bowl XXIII against the Cincinnati Bengals. As soon as the 49ers won the NFC championship, I knew I would call out on the day of the big game. My good friend Chris Schueler—a rabid Bengal fan—would be in town that weekend. Watching the Super Bowl with him would be an extra treat.

You don't normally get to call out of a Broadway show for a football game. Fortunately, I had a semi-legitimate excuse. I'd been dealing with knee pain for weeks, and I'd received physical therapy for it. The show's staff all knew about the condition. The cold winter weather made the pain worse. I never let myself limp—at least not until the Saturday night before the Super Bowl. It wasn't distracting to the audience, but it was noticeable enough that after the curtain, our stage manager Frank Hartenstein approached me to ask if I was OK. I told him I was in pain, and that I would let him know in the morning if I was going to be able to go for the next day's matinee. Frank immediately alerted my understudy, Jonathan Dokuchitz, to give him time to prepare. I called Frank early Sunday morning; Jonathan went on as Rapunzel's Prince and did a great job.

As for me, my aching knee did not stop me from exploding

off the couch in excitement when Joe Montana hit John Taylor for Super Bowl XXIII's game-winning touchdown with 0:34 left on the clock. The 49ers had won four Super Bowls in the 1980s, a decade that was good to them—and to me. The next time my favorite team would win another championship, Joe Montana would be retired—and I'd be in a very different (and much more difficult) place in my life.

CHAPTER 13
My Season of Struggle

MICHAEL LANDON OFTEN SAID, "THERE WILL ALWAYS BE WORK."
He didn't say that the work would be what I wanted or expected.

One job that came along unexpectedly was the Samuel Goldwyn Studios production of Donna Deitch's *Desert Hearts*. In 1985, there were very few LGBTQ films made for mainstream exhibition. *Desert Hearts*—based on Jane Rule's 1964 novel—is the story of a professor's wife (played by Helen Shaver in the movie) who comes to Reno in the late 1950s to get a quick divorce. She reluctantly finds herself drawn into an intense affair with an emotionally and sexually fearless younger woman, played by Patricia Charbonneau.

I'll never forget that audition. There was no script to read in advance of the meeting, so I went in totally blind. There was still a glow of *Little House* around me, so people had a perception of who I was going to be when they met me. At least that's what I believed, and it translated as confidence. I was excited to be going in for a feature film, even if it was going to be a niche production. I hadn't done a theatrical film before, nor had I heard of Donna Deitch. I had been told that she directed documentaries, and that this was going to be her first feature film.

Donna was warm, sassy, and likable, so I was immediately at ease sitting down across from her. When we started talking about her script, it was clear that she was passionate about this story. It was equally clear that the subject matter, a lesbian love story, was completely outside the boundaries of the commercial themes that had dominated my career.

I listened for a few minutes, and then I interrupted Donna with a question. "Who wants to see a movie about a couple of lesbians?" I don't know what possessed me to ask this question. In retrospect it was tactless (if not outright offensive), but that's what came out. She could've ended the meeting right there, but instead Donna grinned.

"That's perfect. Read."

As it turned out, the role of Darrell represented mainstream resistance to homosexuality, so my question was exactly the point of view she was looking for. I read the scenes, and she offered me the part the next day.

That kind of candor didn't always lead to the same result. I remember going in to meet Don Bellisario, one of TV's most prolific and successful showrunners. He was casting *Air Wolf*, which ended up starring Jan Michael Vincent and Ernest Borgnine. In my infinite wisdom, I asked Don, "How many shows can you make about a helicopter?"

After a very brief pause, he answered, "I have a few ideas. Thanks for coming in."

He ended the meeting before I read a single word. Live by the sword, die by the sword.

Desert Hearts was shot on location in and around Reno, Nevada. The cast and crew stayed in a little motel, the Grand Motor Lodge; it reminded me very much of the unpretentious Sonora Motel, where we always stayed when *Little House* went on location in the Sierra foothills. The film had a tiny budget, but Donna worked miracles with the cast and crew she had. Both in front of and behind the camera, my colleagues were extraordinary professionals, and many went on to great things.

The film received critical acclaim on its release and over the years has become still more admired as an iconic work of LGBTQ cinema. I did not realize at the time that this would be the only feature film on my acting resume, but in retrospect, I'm very proud it is. It's an important movie. Few people today would say what I blurted out in my audition; the world has changed, and perhaps our movie played a small part in creating that change. As for me, as the guy who always got the girl, it was an interesting twist to be the guy who lost the girl to the girl! Once again, though, the through line of my career was unmistakable: my job in *Desert Hearts* was the same as it was in *Forever, Little House,* and *The New Gidget*: to support a young actress who was the center of the story.

There's a funny bookend to my *Desert Hearts* story. After the film was released and had a little buzz around it, I got a call from my agent telling me that Madonna wanted to meet me. My agent didn't know why, but that's not an invitation you turn down. So, one night in early 1986, I drove to Burbank to the studio where Madonna was mixing her latest record. When I came into the studio, "Papa Don't Preach" was pounding on the speakers. I was taken to a small seating area in the back of the studio. After a few minutes, Madonna walked in, introduced herself, and sat down next to me. She looked nothing like the boy toy that her hugely popular MTV videos presented her to be. She was wearing jeans, a white shirt, and a nicely tailored jacket.

After a moment of conversation, it became clear that Madonna was uncomfortable. She excused herself and quickly left the room. When she came back a moment or two later, she was with her video director, Jamie Foley. They both sat down and stared at me. Now I was sitting with two uncomfortable people. I was confused. *What the hell was this?*

"I'm sorry," she said, "I think we've made a mistake. You're in *Desert Hearts*, right?"

I assured her I was. "When we saw Dean Butler in the opening credits, we just assumed that he was the guy who worked at the dude ranch."

Oh.

"No," I said, "I'm the guy who owns the casino."

"Yes, I see that," she said very nicely. "We wanted to meet the guy who works at the dude ranch for our *Papa Don't Preach* video."

"Ah," I said. "You want to meet Alex MacArthur. He played Walter, who worked at the dude ranch."

"Yes," she said. "You were good in the film, but I guess we want Alex MacArthur, if he's the one who worked at the dude ranch." The queen of '80s pop repeated "dude ranch" with emphasis.

"Well, if there isn't another part in your video, I'll be going home. Sorry for the confusion."

Madonna smiled. "Thank you for coming all the way over here, and I'm sorry for thinking Dean Butler was the one at the dude ranch."

Madonna's people quickly found Alex MacArthur. He was perfect for the part as the baby daddy in *Papa Don't Preach*. It would have been fun to have been in one of the most famous music videos of the decade, but in retrospect, it's become one of my favorite stories of rejection.

The rejections were rarely so amusing. When I came back to L.A. after my year on Broadway, the rejections began to pile up. The bookings began to vanish. Increasingly, I felt like I wasn't what casting directors wanted. Ina Bernstein, who had opened so many doors for me at ICM, had retired some years earlier. My friend Sam Haskell—whom I'd first met on the *NBC Family Christmas* special—was now representing me at the William Morris Agency. He would invite me to come to his office and work with him on my auditions. Sam was one of the busiest and most successful agents in town. I'd been represented by some good people after Ina, but no one had ever volunteered to coach me for auditions.

Sam and I reconnected recently to talk about those times. "You were frustrated because you didn't think you should have to read for parts," Sam remembered. "But more importantly, you were losing touch with yourself."

He was right, and there is nothing worse for an actor than going into a room having lost touch with that essential something that makes them unique. When you're coming in the door trying to be what *you think someone wants* rather than *who you are,* it never works.

"There was probably some desperation too," Sam offered gently.

"There was a lot of desperation," I replied.

By the early 1990s, I was in trouble. I had been very smart with the money I made on *Little House,* setting aside as much as I could for a future rainy day. The rainy days came, and they did not stop. I went through my savings, bleeding out cash and IRAs at a dizzying rate. I reasoned that working would stop the bleeding, but my desperation clung to me like a stink. I wore that stench into every meeting. Casting directors could smell it, and as I wrote earlier, casting directors don't make mistakes. They saw me for exactly who I was at that point in time. I was becoming like a drug addict who needed a fix. It wasn't an attractive energy. For an actor like me, attractive energy was my product, but I could no longer access that innocence and optimism. My auditions got worse and worse.

Acting is always a crapshoot. When I was young and beating the odds, it didn't feel like much of a gamble. When you're on a lucky streak, you think it will last forever. Now, as I approached my late thirties—a time when my peers were coming into their own—I felt lost. It didn't matter that I had been a television star a decade earlier. All I knew was that I wasn't working, I wasn't making a living, and comparing my yesterdays to my today was crushing me.

I needed to change directions. I just didn't know how to do it, or where to go. I showed up to auditions, grimly hoping for a door to open. And then one did—and not where or how I expected. Some of my earliest work had been commercials. Now, in the early 1990s, commercials were the only work I could get. I was happy to take what I could get. It was on the set of one of those commercials that the door into my next life swung open.

Wilford Brimley was a wonderful character actor, famous for *The Natural, Cocoon,* and more recently the NBC series *Our House,* in which he starred with soap diva Diedre Hall and Shannen Doherty. He was also a credible pitchman, and on the day I met him he was pitching Quaker Oats. Wilford and his family were having a happy breakfast together, and I was playing one of those relations at the table. It was a simple thirty-second spot.

Or not so simple. For a director of photography (DP), shooting eating scenes always presents challenges. Filming a table of ten people interacting with each other offers many opportunities to get it wrong. I was familiar with the process from many episodes of *Little House.* For actors who have been involved in eating scenes the shooting requires matching everything you do with food, utensils, and looks, beginning with a master shot. Over time, doing these scenes becomes second nature, even if the technical necessity of all the matching isn't fully understood or appreciated. I did my best on *Little House* to pay attention to the technique of shooting these scenes.

For the oatmeal ad, the establishing master shot of the family eating breakfast was set up over Wilford Brimley's left shoulder. This would establish the axis upon which all the other coverage, including Brimley's critical close-ups, would be shot. After shooting this master, the director wanted to shoot the close-up right away so all the critical dialogue would be out of the way while the star was still fresh.

To save time, the DP wanted to *cheat the reverse* so he wouldn't have to flip the camera and the lighting 180 degrees on the set. This did mean that the table and the cast had to be completely reset, but Polaroid pictures had been taken of everything, so moving all the tableware wasn't a big deal. Cheating the reverse is a timesaver for the camera and lighting crew, but it can create screen direction problems if it isn't shot correctly.

While the table was being redressed, I could see there was some tension between the DP and the script supervisor about where the camera should be placed for the cheated reverse on Wilford Brimley. The script supervisor was respectfully insisting that the camera position was incorrect, and the DP was insisting that he was right. There was not only a technical side to this story, but a sociological one as well.

As I recounted all this to my wife, Katherine—who has plenty of her own script supervisor experience on commercials—interrupted. "Was the script supervisor a woman?"

She already knew the answer.

"Yes," I answered, with a dawning awareness of exactly where this was going. Over her many years of her career in front of and behind the camera, Katherine had witnessed countless men dismissing women on film sets.

A script supervisor's job is continuity. Until this commercial shoot, I had never seen a script supervisor, male or female, dismissed out of hand on matters of continuity. Continuity is their job. I had watched Michael Landon and our DPs, Ted Voigtlander and Haskell "Buzzy" Boggs, work out these POV tricks with script supervisors Erika Wernher, Charlotte Yerke, and Duane Toler on *Little House.* I had always paid attention.

I wasn't attuned to see the conflict between the male DP and female script supervisor in sexist terms. However, what was very clear to me was that this male DP wasn't going to be told by a female script supervisor where to put the camera. Having seen many cheated reverses, it was also clear to me that the script supervisor was right, and the DP was wrong. I had no stature on this set. I was little more than an extra hired to eat breakfast with Wilford Brimley, but I knew this DP was about to make an unnecessary and potentially expensive mistake. It was an error that would be difficult to fix in post without reshooting the scene or flipping the negative (a fix of last resort).

Unless we're trying to confuse or disorient the audience, establishing and maintaining the correct screen direction is always a priority. We want the audience to accept what they're seeing as logical and accurate.

As I considered what to do, I remembered my grandfather calling me "a fount of misinformation." I had been a know-it-all as a child. I didn't want to step out of place. At the same time, I hope that if I were about to make a huge mistake, someone who knows better might offer me helpful guidance. On this occasion, as a professional, I knew I had information that could help this man. I had to balance that sense against the fact that our business was (and remains) highly unionized. Speaking out of turn to another professional in a manner that could be construed as disrespectful or disruptive can be cause for grievance.

I decided the best strategy was to first find a piece of paper and draw a diagram of the table and camera positions that showed "the axis line" and the necessary position of the camera for a cheated reverse. I quietly took it to the DP, introduced myself to him, told him briefly about my *Little House* background, and showed him on paper why the shot he was about to make would "cross the line" and be a mistake.

He looked soberly at my drawing. I could tell he was uncomfortable as he realized his camera was very much in the wrong position. He shook his head before whispering to me, "I've never understood the line." That was quite an admission from one of the two people on the set whose job it was to have knowledge of camera direction.

This DP, who was likely making north of ten thousand dollars a day in the early nineties, could've barked, "Who the hell are you to tell me my job?" Instead, after looking at my diagram once more, he thanked me, shook my hand, and stepped away to collect himself. Within a minute or two, the camera was quietly moved to the correct position and the gaffer readjusted Wilford's key light. The delay added fifteen minutes to the day. Nothing further was said. I don't know if the DP apologized to the script supervisor, though he certainly should have. When the commercial ran on television, all the geography was correct.

That experience on a Quaker Oats commercial came at a time when my career was struggling. It also came as I grew increasingly curious about what it would be like to work behind the camera. I remember watching the Ken Burns documentary series *The Civil War* when it debuted on PBS. It was told with old black-and-white photographs, single camera interviews, haunting atmospheric music, readings of historical letters, and compelling narration. I was gripped. Somehow, I wanted to find a way to tell stories like that.

My first chance to tell a story from behind the camera came from an unexpected source: my grandmother. One late summer morning in 1991, I got a phone call; my mother's mother, the matriarch of our family, was getting married again, twenty-two years after the death of my grandfather. The wedding would be the following Saturday. Her fiancé was a stranger to me, but not to my grandmother. She had been engaged to this man, Allen Lawrence Chickering Jr., more than sixty years earlier. They had been students at UC Berkeley together—and then, in 1929, he broke off the engagement. (Allen would admit to me that he broke things off because my grandmother wouldn't sleep with him before they were married. He called it the greatest mistake of his life.)

My grandmother married Allen's fraternity brother, Arthur Moore. Allen married as well—twice. By the time he was widowed for the second time in 1991, Allen and my grandmother each had had children, grandchildren, and great-grandchildren. Over the decades, they only spoke a handful of times. A few months after his second wife died, Allen invited my grandmother up to his country place in Oregon for a weekend of trout fishing and conversation. At the end of her visit, Allen proposed marriage a second time. My grandmother said yes.

One week after she got back from Oregon, my grandmother—Margaret Roeding Moore—married Allen Chickering at our family ranch. They were both octogenarians, had had numerous health scares, and saw no reason to wait. Besides, in one sense they had already been waiting—for sixty-two very long years. To see the matriarch of our clan giggling like a schoolgirl was a shock to all of us, but no one could deny how very, very happy they were together.

I loved their love story. Learning more about my new step-grandfather and his remarkable professional life, I became convinced theirs was a story I could tell on film. It wouldn't be for PBS, only for the family. Since Allen had long wanted to do a biography of his life, he agreed to finance the project for eight thousand dollars. He gave me total creative control, and I set about to tell this story with zero prior experience producing, writing, or directing anything since I was at Piedmont High. I started collecting family pictures and home movies from Allen while also acquiring historical video and photo assets that would allow me to carry Allen's life from childhood to the second time he asked my grandmother to marry him.

I needed a workspace and a small team who could help me put it all together. On the Internet, a brand-new source of information for me at that point, I found B&W Digital Post in Studio City. After I told them Allen's story and admitted I had no budget, the owners agreed to give me unlimited access to a brand-new Avid nonlinear editing system and an apprentice editor for ten dollars an hour. I accepted their extraordinarily generous offer instantly.

I was familiar with tape-to-tape editing, because a few friends and I had owned a resume production company called Custom's Last Stand years earlier. We pioneered producing video resume tapes for actors. We did the editing on industrial Sony U-Matic tape machines.

When I started cutting at B&W, I knew nothing about nonlinear editing. I was introduced to B&W's apprentice editor, Alex Gittinger. Alex had an acting and filmmaking background, and he was learning the Avid editing system as we started the project. Alex's capacity to teach himself this new technology and then use it effectively was exceptional. The concept of ingesting video tapes into a computer and then being able to edit and manipulate footage without damaging or degrading the original source material was revolutionary and fascinating. The worst mistake you could make, I soon found out, was failing to save your work as you did it. The biggest catastrophes were power and hard drive failures.

I basically moved into B&W Digital Post, set up tables, and organized assets from books, photo albums, and videotapes. I wrote the script and recorded temporary voice-overs, and then cut the documentary based on a simple outline Alex and I created together. The long hours we were spending demanded stamina, creativity, and the willingness to make decisions that could keep the process moving forward.

It was the most thrilling, absorbing work I had ever done. I was making the decisions, and I loved it.

During this time, I was still getting called for auditions. I couldn't have been less interested in pulling myself away from

my edit sessions to learn generally uninteresting scenes for a series guest-star role. It was hard to motivate myself to drive across
town to deliver lines for casting directors who were running
twenty-five guys who looked just like me through their office
every two hours.

The producing work, in contrast, was a completely different
experience. In that editing room I could lose myself in a story
I loved and whose development I could control. Producing
documentaries in an editing room is a lot like doing a jigsaw
puzzle, but instead of a picture on the cover and all the exact
pieces in the box, you only have a concept of what it should
look like when it's done, and a huge range of possibilities, based
on the interviews, B-roll, still images, music, and graphics that
you have available. As an actor, I'd sometimes winced at how I
looked on screen. I remembered Michael Landon's promise to
never let me look bad, but a few times, I winced at the choices
his editors made. Now, at last, I had the power to choose what
audiences saw.

During those long days in a dark room, I could forget about
my collapsing acting career and let go of my desperate need to
succeed in my auditions.

After several months, working round the clock, writing, and
editing, Alex and I had an hour-long film. We called the documentary *Absolute Integrity*. When I played the film for our "premiere" screening at a restaurant in Carmel Valley, Allen and my
grandmother were very happy. Admittedly it was a very friendly
audience, but seeing such joy on the faces of my family gave me
the push to walk through an opening door into the next chapter
of my life.

I submitted *Absolute Integrity* for Telly Award consideration in
the "Documentary" category and received their highest prize
my first time up at bat. The Telly Awards is not a competition
where there is just one winner per category. At the Tellys, work
is judged by a standard of professional quality. The top 7 to 10

percent of judged work is granted Winner status with the top 18 to 25 percent of the work receiving a Finalist award. *Absolute Integrity* was a Winner. I ordered silver trophies for me, for B&W Digital Post, and for Alex. I don't remember what I ended up paying Alex for the work he did for me, but it was a fraction of what it was worth.

Not long after we finished *Absolute Integrity*, I was asked to be a co-host of the Leukemia Society's national telethon. I approached Jim Zrake, the producer of the show, and asked if he would let me create several video packages that would roll into the show. After watching a few minutes of *Absolute Integrity*, Jim agreed to let me produce several packages for that telethon. The one that I remember best told the story of Michelle Carew, the daughter of baseball great Rod Carew. It was a beautiful, inspiring story of family love and hope, and Alex did a wonderful job cutting it. We started at B&W Digital Post and finished the piece at a Burbank post house that was owned and operated by two brothers, Greg and Wayne Gears.

The Gears brothers were heavily into motor sports with Toyota and Honda. (They sure had the right name for it.) They had a coverage contract with Toyota Racing Development to shoot and produce an annual highlight film covering Toyota's participation in several elite racing series. I saw an opening. Before long, the Gears were sending me to races all over the country as their representative to shoot interviews and racing footage with members of Toyota-sponsored teams. At the end of my first season shooting for the Gears, they invited me to write Toyota's 1998 season highlight film. I was ecstatic to get to express myself in this kind of high-energy project. I titled the film *The Heart of Racing*. The Gears brothers had never used a narrator before, but I knew it was essential for the story. I hired Jefferson Kaye, one of the great voices in the business and a veteran of NFL films, to do our voice-over. We created a compelling, watchable highlight film.

I had done my first real documentary for someone other than my family. This wasn't just a side gig. This was becoming my future.

During that auto racing season, I met Champ Car's vice-president of television, Keith Allo. We've worked together for twenty-five years now. He hired me as field producer for Championship Auto Racing's weekly highlight series, *Inside CART* on ESPN. That led to working as the lead producer of Olympic Hall of Fame induction packages for the United States Olympic Committee's 2002 and 2004 induction ceremonies. Those shows later aired on USA Network and NBC. The packages were snapshots of great Olympic careers told using original interviews supported by archival footage of extraordinary Olympic accomplishments.

As a teen, I'd fallen in love with sports documentaries while watching highlights of Mark Spitz's triumphs in the pool at the 1972 Munich Olympics. Thirty years later, I was creating the same sort of story packages that had inspired me as a boy.

While I have never left the sports world, I did spend several years producing, directing, and shooting a series of military-themed documentaries. Working with my friend Rick Okie, in the mid-aughts I went to Vietnam, Iwo Jima, Seoul, and the Philippines to capture stories for *Goin' Back*, a limited series Rick was producing for Discovery Military Channel. It was profoundly moving to tell the stories of different generations of American fighting men as they returned to the battlefields where they had fought for their country, lost their friends, and shed their own blood. Some of the veterans were stoic; others broke down in floods of raw emotion. As respectfully and reverently as we could, we told their extraordinary stories.

There will always be work, said Michael Landon. And just as *Desert Hearts* is my one feature film credit as an actor, my turbulent transition period in the 1990s brought me my single career writing credit. I had first met Robin Bernheim on the set of *For-*

ever, she was—and is—Stephanie Zimbalist's best friend. After writing several episodes for Stephanie Zimbalist's series, *Remington Steele,* Robin became an in-demand writer-producer of shows in a variety of genres.

In the mid-1990s, Robin was doing a show with William Shatner. Called *TekWar,* it was a science fiction production based on Shatner's own novels. I got the opportunity because of Robin—and my Canadian birth certificate. *TekWar* was produced in Toronto, and as with all television shows produced in Canada, rules stipulate that 55 percent of those who create, write, produce, or act in those shows must be Canadian. The producers wanted to hire an American director for a specific episode, so the tradeoff was to hire a Canadian writer to meet their Canadian content requirements. Although I hadn't lived in Canada since I was six months old, my birth certificate made me the right guy for the job.

They asked me to come in and pitch a few ideas. My successful one-line pitch: "From her grave who will Natalie Simpson identify as her killer and what will she do to stop him? Next time on *TekWar.*"

They bought the log line. With Robin and other members of staff, we proceeded to break the story into acts and scenes. I had five days to write the script, and I worked round the clock. It was rewritten extensively, which I think was part of the plan, but I got the credit, got paid, and had a great time doing it. I was hoping to play a part in the episode as well, but my audition for William Shatner was one of the strangest of my career. Shatner feigned confusion that I didn't understand his directions, and I didn't get the part. Shatner has had a reputation for being tough on other actors, so this wasn't a total surprise. I remain a total fan.

And then came *Buffy, the Vampire Slayer.*

I don't remember my audition to play Hank Summers, Buffy's dad. As I've said, I wasn't in a good place in terms of my acting, and by 1997 I was doing all I could to transition to producing documentaries. I still read for parts, but without much optimism. To my surprise, they gave me the role. (Actor Anson Williams—famous as "Potsie" on *Happy Days*—told me later that he was in the room when I read, and he pushed them to hire me as Hank. I wish I could say I remember seeing his face, but it was all a blur.)

The *Buffy, The Vampire Slayer* movie struck me as silly, but Joss Whedon, the film's writer, obviously saw more potential in the Buffy character than the movie enabled him to explore.

Five years later, Whedon reintroduced his *Slayer* for television, this time with the darker, smarter tone that the studio had exorcised from the movie. According to Whedon he was possessed, "by the idea of some woman who seems to be completely insignificant who turns out to be extraordinary." The series combined the teen angst of *My So-Called Life* with the "monster of the week" sensibility of *The X-Files*. Audiences got to see Buffy and her friends face deadly threats with a quirky gallows humor, trusting that this new kind of heroine—one with a ditzy name and superpower skills—was there to keep them safe.

Hank was never going to be a big part of Buffy's life in the series, which was focused on her being raised in a single parent home by her mother—and supported at school by the man who had taken Hank's place: Buffy's father figure, Rupert Giles. As played by Sarah Michelle Gellar, Buffy was a reluctant hero in training. Slaying demons hadn't been her choice—but it was her calling, and she accepted it. Reading the early scripts, it wasn't hard to see that this was going to be a very cool show. And in hindsight, *Buffy, the Vampire Slayer* represented still another opportunity for me to support a compelling female character, this time not as a love interest but as—in Buffy's own words—her "shiftless and absentee" father.

I did not work closely with Joss Whedon. At the time, he was well on his way to becoming an enormously influential showrunner. Since the #MeToo movement, there have been credible accusations of misconduct aimed at Whedon, including from some of the young women who appeared on *Buffy*. I never saw anything untoward on set, but I believe my fellow cast members. Michael Landon was far from perfect, but he was a safe, loving, and adored father figure to the youngest actors on *Little House*. He set a standard for me of what a showrunner should be, especially one who works closely with young people. Joss Whedon, for all his gifts, apparently did not meet that standard.

By the time I was cast on *Buffy*, nearly twenty years had elapsed since I made my debut on *Little House*. Instead of warm nostalgia, *Buffy* offered viewers a clever, nuanced, and complex fantasy world—a world that was under constant threat. I appreciated the chance to play a slightly darker character. If nothing else, I was certainly no longer an "innocent," as Michael Landon had described me, and in my few appearances as Hank, I was able to offer a maturity and complexity I'd never had in a television role.

In real life and on screen, there are many ways a man can impact the women around him—both for better and worse. For the first and only time in my career, *Buffy* gave me a chance to play a man who brought pain rather than comfort to a show's lead actress. In my first episode, "Nightmares," Hank Summers tells Buffy that she's a huge disappointment. Hank blames Buffy for his divorce from Buffy's mother. It's a small but important part of the backstory that explains why Buffy Summers is who she is. Hank isn't a demon or a fundamentally bad man. He's just a self-involved dad who wounds his child. As someone who had my own small experience of a father wound, I could sense the power of the role I was asked to play—so different from anything I'd done before. I wish I'd had more episodes, but of course, playing a neglectful and largely absent father meant I would not get much screen time.

I began my career with a major part on one of the most-beloved television dramas of the last fifty years. I moved on to play a loving, goofy husband on a light-hearted revival of an iconic sixties "girl power" franchise. In my third (and last) recurring role on a series, I played a very imperfect father figure in a show that revived and transformed the fantasy genre. Each time, I was there to support a young female protagonist as she overcame challenges and seized opportunities. I'm proud of that career arc. I'm proud too to have my very own Buffy trading card.

Buffy, the Vampire Slayer did not mark a triumphant return to acting. That chapter of my life was mostly done; this was one last chance to be part of a beloved series, and a chance to say good-bye to work in front of the camera. By the time I filmed my last episode of *Buffy*, I was certain my future lay behind the camera, finding new ways to tell powerful stories.

There was still work to be done.

CHAPTER 14
Feherty

I'M CONVINCED THAT IT WON'T BE LONG BEFORE EVERY HUMAN being with an Internet connection and a microphone will host a podcast. I admire everyone's confidence and belief that they have something to say—or more accurately, that they have something to say in a way that interests an audience. Hosting a talk show—whether the topic is sports, entertainment, or politics—is about much more than simply asking questions. A talk show host opens a door into the lives of their guests. It's knowing what questions to ask, and in which order. It's knowing when to press for more and when to back off. It's knowing when to lighten the mood and when to push through tension.

To put it gently, I've listened to podcasts and watched talk shows where the host had very few of these skills. It's not enough to be a good conversationalist. You need to invest in learning about the guest before the conversation begins so you can provide thoughtful context for the questions you ask. The goal is funny, revealing conversation that keeps an audience engaged and makes the guest look good.

Since I was first cast as Almanzo on *Little House*, I have appeared on many television and radio talk shows. In more recent years, I've been a podcast guest. I've been asked questions by many artful interviewers. I've also been queried by some who had no art at all. As a documentarian, I've done my best to ask the right questions to get answers I can use on screen to advance a story. Over time, I've become a student of that "art of asking." And in time, I would get a chance to work with and for a master of that craft.

On Monday, May 2, 2011, I was in my office at the Santa Monica Airport when my phone rang. On the other end, calling from Golf Channel headquarters in Orlando, was my friend and colleague Keith Allo. Since 1998, I had been getting calls from Keith that would open the door to unexpected opportunities; first in motor sports, later with the Olympics. Today's call would launch a television adventure related to golf—and to clever conversation.

"Do you know David Feherty?" Keith asked me.

"I don't," I told him.

After working with Keith for thirteen years, I knew there was no downside in answering questions honestly. "Fake it 'til you make it" is great advice in some areas, but not in this business. Better to be completely candid about what you don't yet know, and trust that you can quickly learn to know it. For Keith, what mattered was an appetite to grow, the ability to absorb, process, and organize information, and then present it all in a form that could captivate an audience.

"David Feherty is a former professional golfer from Northern Ireland, he's a great writer, and he's been a commentator on CBS's golf package for over twenty years. He's the funniest and most insightful voice working in golf. We're doing a talk show with him that's going to launch this summer."

"Congratulations," I told him. For so many reasons I was always rooting for Keith Allo. In my mind, I tried to imagine a Northern Irish accent.

"Would you be interested in producing it?"

This was Keith calling, so there was only one possible answer. "Yes," I told him.

I love sports, but I don't play golf. I don't follow the sport closely. I'd never heard of David Feherty. Oh, and one other thing: I'd never produced a talk show. What could possibly go wrong?

This job would be based out of Florida. That alone was going to be a big change for Katherine and me, but we'd both been in the entertainment business for our entire professional careers. We had both experienced ups and downs, as most everybody does. Doing this show was a huge opportunity for me to learn, grow, and contribute. Katherine understood that, and she supported me right from the beginning.

Five days after that phone call, I was on a flight to Orlando. I met Keith and his family for dinner that first night, and the next day traveled with our production manager, David Haas, to TPC Sawgrass, near Jacksonville. This is where I would meet David Feherty for the first time.

When Feherty walked into the bar for our initial meeting, his shirt was rumpled like he'd slept in it. It seemed he hadn't shaved in five days. He was meeting his new team for the first time, and it was revealing to me that he showed up to lunch just as he was. He hadn't even brushed his hair.

When Keith introduced me, David smiled warmly, shook my hand with just the right amount of firmness, and said with an unmistakable Irish lilt, "How you doin'?"

These were the exact words Michael Landon had said to me. It wasn't so much a question as it was an invitation. Feherty was creating a relationship with me with those first words; embracing me as a colleague, which immediately put me on his side. I realized he was saying, "I'm fine, and I want you to be fine too."

"How do you do?" is the way I was taught to begin conversations with new people. It's formal, perhaps even antiquated, but it's served me well for many years. On the other hand, the question doesn't create a connection as much as it establishes that I know how to behave when I meet a person for the first time. There's value in that, but for most of us, creating a relationship takes longer. David Feherty could create a connection instantly. As I got to know him better, I learned that yes, he always slept in his shirt, if he slept at all. That thick growth of beard might have taken five days for most men. For David, it was more like thirty-six hours.

Over the course of a long career, I've been around a lot of men and women with big, funny personalities. In my experience the common thread that unites those people is the need to be the center of attention. They need to establish right away that they are the "alphas" in the room. They need to hold the floor, to be the most present, the most engaged, and above all else, the funniest. If they can't hold your attention, they sometimes get desperate.

There was no doubt that David was funny. For most Americans his Irish cadence was funny regardless of what he said, but there was something else I could tell about David in a few minutes. As funny as he was, he didn't *need* to be funny. It wasn't a cultivated performance. It was an authentic identity.

Many years ago, thanks to auto racing, I got to spend time around the great actor Paul Newman. Anyone who ever watched Paul Newman couldn't take their eyes off him. He could hold the screen with the force of his personality. He could also turn "it" off. There were times I was around Newman, seemingly looking right at him, when he would disappear right before my eyes. I'd say to myself, "Where did he go?" only to turn around and see him riding away on his motor scooter. Newman could be mesmerizing, but when he didn't want to be noticed, he could take off his magnetism the way the rest of us take off a jacket.

Like Newman, David didn't need to hold the floor. He didn't

need to be the funniest person at the table, although he most certainly was. He had a series of one-liners and quips that could elicit laughter any time he wanted to refocus the energy in a conversation. It was always natural. He wasn't the least bit interested in proving himself the funniest man at the table.

As one of the two original producers of *Feherty* (along with Jason Harper), I could see that David's willingness to be *on* and *not on* was going to be a challenge for all of us who worked with him. I learned quickly that if David was excited by a guest, he could be incredibly funny and engaging, but if he wasn't excited, he couldn't fake being interested and intrigued. Authenticity is a great human quality—and it was precisely what his fans loved. The problem from a producer's standpoint quickly became evident to me: David isn't a performer; he's a *reactor*. The other person always drives the connection. If the guest was high energy, he'd be right there with them, and the conversation would be wonderful. If the guest wasn't a high-energy person, David would often come down to their level and the conversation could get dry and slow.

David always refused to push a dull guest, with one exception. That one break with habit came during the Ryder Cup in Chicago, when swimmer Michael Phelps was his guest.

It was the late summer of 2012. Michael Phelps was America's biggest Olympic star, and he had just come back from London, having added four more gold and two silver medals to his already historic cache of Olympic glory. When he arrived at the theater, it was clear that Michael was extremely stoned, just a toke or two away from being unconscious. David went to Michael's dressing room to introduce himself; Phelps could barely shake his hand or say his name. David was not unfamiliar with the effects of smoking funny cigarettes. He had seen performers be drunk or stoned backstage; he knew that plenty of people can transform from laconic to dynamic when they step in front of an audience. This was a live show with a big enthusiastic audience in the house, after all; David figured that the wild applause for an American hero would fire Michael up.

The crowd indeed roared when the great swimmer was introduced. As I watched Phelps amble onto the stage, I thought he was even more stoned than he'd been in the green room. He was an empty vessel—a one-man Cheech & Chong movie without the jokes.

David didn't get ruffled easily. At the same time, he'd never interviewed someone so utterly incapable of carrying on a conversation. It quickly became obvious that nothing we had planned for that opening segment was going to work, because Phelps simply wasn't there. David improvised and began doing his best imitation of Katie Couric, asking and answering his own questions. He was in survival mode. David had a savage sense of humor: he could easily have mocked Phelps, but he sensed he was dealing with someone struggling with a very real problem. Michael was also a valuable asset for NBC. At the same time, despite David's heroic efforts, the audience knew something wasn't right. The laughter got uncomfortable.

David dumped out of the segment early. After a commercial, he pivoted away from Phelps and quickly introduced Chicago's iconic superstar, Michael Jordan, who was waiting in the wings. I gave Jordan his cue to enter after David introduced him. I had never heard a roar like what this crowd gave Jordan. He stepped onto the stage like a man who was accustomed to being adored and took his time walking to the couch where David greeted him with a warm smile and handshake. Phelps got awkwardly to his feet, looking for all the world like a deer in the headlights. Jordan embraced him, then honored him with some very kind words about his place in the history of Olympic sports. The basketball legend was funny and charming. As the audience ate Jordan up, Phelps disappeared right in front of us.

If you'd asked me that night, I would have told you Phelps was done, both with swimming and a public life. He had spoken of retirement in London, but given enough time to assess his future without swimming, he made the decision to come back. I cheered hard for him as he won more gold in the 2016 Rio games. He was clean and sober, too, and I was heartened to see him back on the right track—or in the right lane.

Hosting a talk show isn't easy, though many people persist in believing it is. Very few who aspire to the craft can attract guests and audiences of any consequence. In the world of golf, because of his colorful history as a player, writer, and commentator, David is a rock star, albeit a reluctant rock star. It took me a long time to realize that was a key to his appeal. He didn't chomp at the bit to have a conversation with anyone. He liked talking, but he never gave the impression he craved it. Eagerness can easily slide into desperation. David was never close to desperate. He was himself—and gave his guests the permission to be themselves in return.

The people he most loved talking to fell into two categories. Those in the first group were his genuine friends like Lee Trevino, Tom Watson, Gary McCord, Ken Venturi, Sam Torrance, John Daly, Curtis Strange, Jack Nicklaus, Ian Poulter, Darren Clarke, Phil Mickelson, Condoleezza Rice, and former President George W. Bush. Their conversations were laced with stories and inside jokes that only good friends could tell each other. These segments made for great, and frequently hilarious, television.

The other category was composed of people that David did not know well but was fascinated by. This included the likes of Charles Barkley, Larry David, Bill Russell, Samuel L. Jackson, Matthew McConaughey, Steph Curry, Jordan Spieth, Bob Uecker, Lou Holtz, and Terry Bradshaw. In these shows David knew he was in the presence of singular cultural figures. David didn't know these celebrities well but found a way to ask probing (and frequently silly) questions that gave them each a chance to share something fresh and surprising about themselves. They knew that they wouldn't be judged. David radiated curiosity and acceptance of himself and everyone in his orbit.

No matter who the guest was, and whether he knew them personally or not, David was guided by a simple rule. *Feherty had guests, not victims.* There were no "gotcha" questions, and there were no traps. David wanted to leave every interview with a new friend. I think he largely succeeded in that goal.

There was only one interview that David really didn't want to do: Bill Clinton. David disagreed with Clinton's politics and didn't think much of how he'd behaved in his time in office. After five minutes in the room with the former president, however, David was totally enamored. If David Feherty was a star in his field, Bill Clinton was a gleaming galaxy of charisma. He was brilliant, funny, thoughtful, and a wonderful storyteller. I think David could've sat with him all day. We didn't break any news, but David gave his audience a wonderful opportunity to see an enormously polarizing political figure as a decent, accessible human being. I wish I could take credit for that conversation. That episode was produced by my very talented colleague James Ponti, who always had an uncanny way of getting to the heart of the person David was interviewing.

Feherty interviewed more than one former president. He also interviewed a future one, and that segment I did produce. In the summer of 2016, NBC Golf sent us to interview Donald Trump in his Manhattan home. Trump was already the presumptive Republican nominee; the morning before our interview, the Donald had gone on television and invited the Russians to release Hillary Clinton's thirty thousand emails—if, he said slyly, they had them.

I had gotten a kick out of Trump as the star of Mark Burnett's reality series, *The Apprentice.* Trump was cast (and I can't stress enough, he was *cast*) as the business genius mentoring New York's future billionaires. His breakdowns of contestant successes and failures in the boardroom at the end of each episode were fun. Trump's "You're fired!" at the end of each episode was television gold. It was very good reality television. Mark Burnett had created must-see TV, but even Mark had no idea what he was unleashing.

On this particular afternoon, David and (as he called us) his minions sat with the presidential candidate in his gold-leafed living room in Trump Tower. The view of Central Park was breathtaking. In prep for the interview, David and I had decided on a few questions. At one point, Feherty asked Trump how he felt about being "the man in the arena."

Feherty then read two (very long sentences) from Teddy Roosevelt's famous speech:

> *It is not the critic who counts; not the man who points out how the strong man stumbles, or where the doer of deeds could have done them better. The credit belongs to the man who is actually in the arena, whose face is marred by dust and sweat and blood; who strives valiantly; who errs, who comes short again and again, because there is no effort without error and shortcoming; but who does actually strive to do the deeds; who knows great enthusiasms, the great devotions; who spends himself in a worthy cause; who at the best knows in the end the triumph of high achievement, and who at the worst, if he fails, at least fails while daring greatly, so that his place shall never be with those cold and timid souls who neither know victory nor defeat.*

David did this sort of thing occasionally: reading a well-known quote to see what it would prompt. It often worked. This passage from our twenty-sixth president is one of the best-known pieces of American oratory; I've seen it quoted on posters hanging in countless offices.

After Feherty read the passage, Trump got excited. "I've never heard such a tremendous speech," he said. I almost fell off my chair. The candidate might just as well have said he'd never heard JFK's "Ask not what you can do for your country" line, or Dr. King's "Dream" speech. Trump wasn't joking. When the interview was over, he asked for a copy of "that great speech," saying he intended to use it himself. I handed him Feherty's interview notes. Trump folded them happily and put them in his suit pocket.

There were a few occasions where wonderful things were said in the moment only to be cut from the show. One involved Larry David, one of the great, distinctive comic voices of our time. Larry's brand is a playfully cultivated state of misery. I've never been able to watch Larry David in large doses, but he's a wonderful sketch comedian and a fascinating subject, filled with outrage and anxiety about everything. He is always in character. But when he came on our show, Larry made an uncharacteristic admission that caught all of us totally by surprise. As David was leading Larry through the highlights of his career, Larry paused and admitted that he was enormously grateful for the success he'd had with *Seinfeld, Curb Your Enthusiasm,* and so many other projects. This was news. Larry David was *grateful.* You could see it in his eyes. It was a humble and heartfelt moment. I was excited to include that moment in the show.

As a condition of doing the interview, Larry insisted that he be able to review and give notes on a rough cut of the show before it was completed. Keith Allo had never granted editorial approval of an interview to any guest. He'd reluctantly taken notes from Donald Trump after his first interview aired in 2012. Trump told Keith we were showing his old jet, not his new Boeing 757, and we didn't properly highlight the aircraft's elegant dishes and gold utensils. Those small changes were made, and they went into the archived version of the show for future airings. In contrast, Keith had granted Larry David the right to request changes before the show aired.

Larry had two notes. First, we had to shorten his pauses so the audience wouldn't see him thinking about his answers. Larry wanted to be seen as very quick on his feet. That was a good note because removing his pauses (referred to as "pull-ups" in the editing room) made the tempo of the conversation faster and funnier. The other note was more impactful. Larry insisted we cut what I knew was the most revealing moment in the conversation. We could not show his gratitude for his success.

Keith told me, "Larry's audience expects him to be miserable. He doesn't want them to think that he's genuinely happy about anything. Take out the gratitude."

I was not happy. "That comment is so humanizing," I pleaded. "No one has ever heard Larry David be grateful for anything."

"I get it," Keith responded calmly, "but misery is Larry's brand. Take it out."

Keith was the executive producer. He'd given his word to our guest, and he was going to keep it. At Keith's direction, our editor Andy Ebert deleted the gratitude exchange not only from the show but from all of Golf Channel's media servers so it could never be searched or randomly discovered by another producer. Feherty had no problem with the decision. He wanted great conversations, but David's larger commitment was to having "guests, not victims."

David was the star of his show but rarely made comments or offered notes about what was aired. He trusted us, which was a wonderful gift. There were other NBC personalities who micromanaged every aspect of their shows, and it could be exhausting, particularly when shows were on tight deadlines. The only time I got a call from David with a note came just ninety minutes before his interview with PGA Tour player Matt Kucher was scheduled to air.

"Deano, I need you to take something out of tonight's show."

I'd never heard those words from David before, and he instantly had my full attention. During the "cold open," which we shot boat-to-boat on a lake near Kuchar's home, David pulled down his pants and mooned an alligator that was swimming past him. We had blurred David's ass, but viewers would be able to see that he was giving the gator a good view. It was funny and totally consistent with Feherty's brand of humor.

"You can't show me mooning the alligator."

"Seriously?" I laughed. "You moon us every day." David wasn't laughing. There was a backstory. David had gotten in trouble at CBS for a magazine cover he'd done a year earlier. The shot showed him with his pants down, standing next to a toilet. "If CBS sees me with my pants down again, they'll fire me." There was no comedic lilt in his voice. He was serious.

For a split second, I thought, "Why is this *our* problem?" Our show is on Golf Channel. We weren't making *Feherty* for CBS. More relevant than that, we were under the gun. The show was airing in less than ninety minutes with a full quality control pass still to be done by Master Control before its 9 PM premiere. If a fix took just one minute too long, we wouldn't make air, and that would put me and our whole team at risk with Golf Channel and NBC Sports management. But Feherty, who never asked for anything, was stone cold serious, so I knew what we had to do. I called Keith immediately. He said, "Do it."

When I told Andy, that we had to "take out the moon" he pointed at the clock and said, "I'm not doing it. We won't make air." But even as he was complaining (and my good friend Andy loved to complain), he duplicated the sequence, did a quick lift of David's offending buttocks, and dropped in a shot of the alligator swimming past David's boat. The fix only took two minutes, but now we had to re-push the fixed show to Golf Channel servers, which happened only slightly faster than real time. It would be just over forty minutes. Then we had to do a complete quality control pass before air. We got everything done with three minutes to spare. That was the closest call Andy and I had in ten seasons of making the show, and as we walked out of the building to our cars, we shared a high five and laughed, grateful that we could do something for David when he really needed it.

In the talk show world, there's a lot of talk of production—the actual shooting of the interviews—and post-production, when the show is edited and finished. What doesn't get discussed nearly enough is pre-production. I'm biased, of course, because this has become my field of expertise, but I think most people who do this work would acknowledge pre-production is the most important phase of any show. This is the point that producers decide exactly what they are going to do, when and where they will do it, and who will be involved.

My primary task in the pre-production phase was to prepare and organize the research on the person David was interviewing, organize that material thematically into nine segments, and then brief David on that information before the start of the interview. This was not a perfect process. Our production associates could glean an overview of someone's life and career from a Wikipedia profile. More nuanced information would come from magazine articles, newspaper stories, and other video interviews, but the most interesting and usable information for a *Feherty* interview came from friends and colleagues of the guest who could share with us some unique aspects of his or her life and career.

If David knew the subject, those quirky insider details would come from him, and that invariably led to great television. For public figures with whom he had no prior relationship, it was usually no problem to find someone who knew something "spicy" about that celebrity—but again, we were looking for guests, not victims. The key was finding people who could share heartfelt, surprising insights without engaging in gossip or character assassination. Finding and contacting those insiders was the hardest and most time-consuming part of the pre-production process, but always yielded the best stuff.

Our pre-production and production phases were usually handicapped by the fact that our subjects were—by definition—busy people, and interviews often couldn't be booked until the last minute. An elusive subject would create a cascade of other issues. We almost always had too little time to research last-minute guests, scout the right location, and—most challenging of all—figure out the logistics of the activity that David and his guest would do together. That off-set activity would form the core of our packaging, rejoins, and bumpers—all industry terms for everything that marks a transition into or out of a segment. What I realized over time is that while I can get stressed out by pressure, I also thrive under it. I like the challenge of making things happen with a running clock while dealing with endlessly changing variables. Producing a show like *Feherty* gave me that challenge week after week.

Once we'd finished the production, we made the shows in the editing room. The *Feherty* team was blessed to have Golf Channel's most talented editors, Pat Devlin and Andy Ebert.

They were absolute masters of the latest technology, they each had encyclopedic knowledge of golf, uncanny memories of great moments, and above all else, knowledge of where those moments lived in the channel's enormous, ever-growing media asset library. The cherry on the sundae was that Andy and Pat were both exceptional storytellers with the ability to meld video, pictures, graphics, music, and conversation into watchable, entertaining programs.

As Andy and I worked together on show after show, I grew, as Feherty would say with a grin, to love him "like a sister." I trusted Andy with the vulnerability of my creative spirit more than any other human being I've known in my life, including Katherine or any member of my family. We laughed together, ate together, and vented our frustrations to each other. We could talk about life, our marriages, morality, politics, and sports, and we could sit next to each other silently for hours at a time as we collaborated on every detail of what went into our shows.

When making any show you're balancing creativity against deadlines. Editors and producers must have each other's backs. There can't be any fear of bad ideas or making mistakes. Everything is on the table all the time. We knew each other's strengths and weaknesses, and we trusted each other's sensibilities. In support of David's voice, I always wanted to be riskier (and bawdier) while Andy wanted to elevate the tone. I didn't always agree with Andy's desire to take the edge off things David would say, but I trusted his instinct to put us in the right place by the time we were done.

David Feherty is blessed with an enormous level of likability. He has the wonderful ability to observe and tease that makes his guests feel like buddies who are all in on the joke. Over time, I noticed that David was more relaxed and spontaneous with men than with women. David knew he pushed boundaries, and he was scrupulous about not crossing lines with women. Starting in 2017, with the advent of the #MeToo movement, I could see David start to monitor himself even more carefully in conversations with female guests. The reality is that David is the furthest thing from a predator—but he could see what was happening with the culture. He grasped instinctively that when you have a reputation for pushing the envelope, people might wonder what other lines you might cross. Watching David with his mother, which I had the opportunity to do both on our trips to Northern Ireland and during her visits to the States, there was no doubt that David both adored and respected women. That love and affection carry over to his wife, Anita, and to their daughter, Erin. Yet in the post-Harvey Weinstein era, you cannot be too careful, and I saw David's commitment to balancing that caution with his natural openness.

Two of my favorite episodes were David's conversations with Charlie Rose and Matt Lauer. Both gave us great interviews and were incredibly generous with their time. Each of these men were talented, popular fixtures on television, both largely supported by female staffs, and both beloved by their audiences. It was shocking to all of us when both men joined a club of famous entertainment figures facing allegations that they had misbehaved with women in the workplace. Overnight, iconic careers became cautionary tales.

Few figures in sports or broadcasting are more beloved for their flaws and failings than David Feherty. I break no news by sharing that David is a recovering alcoholic who also suffers from bouts of severe depression. He manages his pain, both physical and emotional, with humor, a nonstop schedule of service to others, and a daily cocktail of medications that could drop a charging rhino. He makes no attempt to hide his struggles with depression—or sobriety. Instead, he uses his demons to give voice to the daily struggles of millions of Americans. Rightly, they love him for it.

Having grown up in a family where heavy drinking was a regular feature of our social life, I learned about alcoholism all too early. But in our family, abusive consumption wasn't discussed or acknowledged because "nice people" don't talk about these things. I sat through countless dinners as a child watching the rest of my family ignore my grandfather's drunken, drooling belligerence. The lesson I got was that alcoholism couldn't be discussed even as it was happening right in front of me. That's no longer true, and we're better off for it. The courage of people like David has played a great part in building a more honest and healthy culture. I am honored that I collaborated with a man who lives his life committed to giving humorous voice to his pain as a way of helping others get through theirs. Producing David's show was a gift to me personally, and a way of closing a circle in my own life.

COVID-19 brought an end to *Feherty* in mid-2020. Nobody could travel, we couldn't book guests, and we knew full well the magic just wouldn't work over Zoom or Skype. After nine years and ten seasons, our wonderful run came to an end. We worked hard, met presidents, performers, and players of every sport. Our team got to deploy all our creative gifts (and discover new ones) in support of David Feherty's God-given gift for clever conversation. I will never not be grateful. Perhaps best of all, the show gave me one of the best friends I've ever had. The gentle spirit that was Andy Ebert lost his battle with cancer in December 2021. I miss him very much.

As public life returned post-pandemic, David left NBC to join the new Saudi-backed LIV Tour. There is occasional talk of putting the team back together and taking *Feherty* on the road again. If Keith calls, I'll be there. Whether that happens or not, let me finish with this: I was incredibly lucky to be part of a long-running TV show that will be my calling card for the rest of my life. I had five years on *Little House*, but nine traveling the world with David Feherty. In my entire creative career, my work on *Feherty* is the longest time I've spent on a single project. Keith Allo built a wonderful team, and in my heart I know that those eighty-plus shows mark the best work I've ever done.

CHAPTER 15

Number 1 in the Envelope

IN MY FAMILY, WE HAVE MANY COUSINS. MANY OF THESE COUSINS ARE very dear to me, even if I sometimes have trouble remembering exactly what sort of cousin they are. Are they my second cousin? Third? Fifth cousin, twenty-seven times removed? It is a blessing, I think, to have so many relatives that it's hard to keep track.

One particularly influential "second cousin, once removed" was Wolfgang Ehrensberger. Born in Hamburg, Germany, in 1924, he had served (reluctantly) in World War II. With Germany in ruins after its defeat, Wolfgang moved to Mexico in the early 1950s. He built a fabulously successful group of manufacturing companies that exported components for batteries and other electric devices all over the world. He became a very wealthy man—and in my family, a beloved arbiter of refined taste and all that was good.

During my teen years, Wolfgang was a frequent and always welcome visitor to Piedmont. He was a cousin to both my parents, and they each adored and admired him. When Wolfgang was with us, there was always dark rye bread in the pantry and a bottle of Campari in the bar. I never learned more than a word or two of German, but my mother made sure I pronounced our cousin's name correctly: *VOLF-gong.*

Wolfgang was serious about managing his companies, but he also had a childlike enthusiasm and appreciation for what he would call "really good" things: cars, homes, furniture, clothing, cameras, and fine art. Everything Wolfgang owned was carefully chosen to be of excellent quality. If he wanted a new shirt, he would research shirts to decide for himself which was the best one for him. He would closely review the styling, the quality of the fabric, the stitching, and the buttons to determine his choice.

When Wolfgang went out to take pictures, he didn't want to shoot a lot of film. He wouldn't have wanted ten thousand images on his phone. He wanted to take one perfect picture, and he would wait, sometimes for hours or even days, before squeezing the trigger on his Leica camera. There was a time when Wolfgang was one of the only amateur photographers in the world who was factory-supplied by Leica. He was that good.

Wolfgang loved to ski, he loved fine art, and he had a particular passion for things made of silver. That last passion was why he spent a great deal of time in Taxco—the famous silver capital of Mexico. Taxco was where he took me when I made my first trip south of the border. I had just graduated from high school, and my family thought it would do me good to spend some time with our beloved—and very sophisticated—relation.

On this trip to Taxco, we visited Wolfgang's old friend, Count Heinrich. (Yes, he really was from a German noble family.) On our second day in Taxco, after a spectacular lunch, the conversation turned to sex. Heinrich had recently married—for the fifth time—a woman more than twenty years his junior. He wanted us to know, none too subtly, that he was "still doing it." He and Wolfgang began to discuss the number of women a man should reasonably expect to bed over the course of his life. I blushed, as I so often did (and still do).

At seventeen, I was still a virgin. I was also completely in love with my high school girlfriend, Tracy Powell, who was a devout Mormon. For Tracy, then sixteen years old, the very natural desire for sexual intimacy was something that had to be resisted. In the heat of the moment, we sometimes came close to crossing the line, but looking back on those often-steamy nights now, I'm grateful that we never did. I didn't share Tracy's faith, but her beliefs were central to the integrity of who she was, and that simple reality was more important than anything else. After listening to these two elegant European gentlemen describe their loves and escapades, I told them in a very determined voice that I was sure Tracy and I would eventually marry. We'd have children, and we'd be together forever.

Heinrich laughed. "I have slept with eleven different women. You vill have your time, my boy." He poured another shot of tequila.

Cousin Wolfgang was too prudent to disclose a number, but his grin suggested he agreed with his friend.

I flared up in a mix of insecurity and judgment. "I'll never sleep with eleven different women," I told him with all the idealism only a smitten teen can muster. "I love Tracy, and I'll only sleep with her."

Wolfgang could see that I was on the verge of getting upset. "Dean, I know you are in love with Tracy. When you do sleep with her, just put a little piece of paper with the number 1 on it in an envelope. Mail it to your little old cousin so I can know you're growing up."

As I considered the request, Wolfgang winked at Heinrich. "And Dean, if by chance there should be others, just put more numbers on pieces of paper and mail them to me."

Tracy and I shared a wonderful first love, but as usually happens with first loves, we ended up going in separate directions. Some fifty years later, Tracy remains a touchstone in my life whom I will always treasure. When I did lose my virginity, it wasn't to her. And I never mailed that number to Wolfgang.

In the years after Tracy and I broke up, I dated other women, but none of those were terribly serious. I certainly didn't meet a girl I wanted to marry. I enjoyed having options, as many young people do. When I became a television star, suddenly positioned by the media as a teen idol, I was stunned to become an object for so many young women. There were pictures and gossipy articles in *Tiger Beat* and the *National Enquirer*. It was harmless fun, and I was connecting with girls and young women who were the core of our younger audience. This was an unexpectedly great part of my very unique job. For the most part, it wasn't real. Other times, it seemed wonderfully real, and I felt like a kid in a candy store. I met, dated, and played with a lot of attractive women. When I found myself judging the Miss America Pageant, I felt like I'd died and gone to heaven. Call it a cliché, but for a twenty-four-year-old guy who appreciated a certain kind of glossy feminine aesthetic, being in the Convention Center in Atlantic City was a week of incredible sensory overload. Despite all those amazing bodies in tight dresses and high heels, no one made me feel quite as Tracy had.

And then, it happened. On January 16, 1983, ABC aired a show called *Celebrity Daredevils*. You can still find the clip on YouTube: I climb up the outside of Caesar's Palace and am helped over the rail at the top by one of my boyhood idols, William Shatner. George Willig—better known as the "Human Fly" and famous for having climbed the World Trade Center—had trained me for my climb. The whole thing made my mother ill, but it was great television.

The night the show aired, the producers—Bob and Bunny Stivers—threw a dinner party. I wasn't seeing anyone, so I brought my little sister Meg, then a senior at UCLA, as my date.

It was a good thing I was with my little sister, as no other date would have forgiven the way my eyes kept going to one dazzling party guest: Mary Hart, then in her first full season as host of *Entertainment Tonight*. Mary was there on the arm of George Willig himself, but something told me they weren't a couple. Feeling bold, I checked with George before I approached Mary, and he kindly gave me the "all clear." My sister struggled unsuccessfully to control her amusement as I worked up the courage to ask Mary for her number and permission to call.

Driving home from the party, I couldn't stop thinking about Mary. She embodied my dream girl. Her energy was infectious, her sense of fun was unbridled, she had legs to die for, and her drive to succeed was all-consuming. I come from a family of strong women—and Mary was evidently that. She radiated fun, sexiness, and ambition. I desperately wanted to get to know her.

A few nights later, at Maurice's Snack 'n' Chat on West Pico, Mary and I had a candlelit dinner. Halfway through the meal, I felt Mary's foot caressing my calf under the table. What I first thought was an accident soon became unmistakably deliberate. From that first date, we plunged headlong into an intense, passionate relationship.

I was instantly head over heels in love with Mary. It was sexual, it was romantic, it was all-consuming. As the famous AC/DC song puts it, I was "thunderstruck." I was twenty-six; she was thirty-two and the sophisticated, dazzling, incarnation of every female fantasy I ever imagined.

The timing couldn't have been more perfect. For its ninth season *Little House* had been rebranded as *Little House: A New Beginning*, and I was one of the stars. Mary was an instant hit on *Entertainment Tonight*, and her own star was rising fast. In the eyes of the press, Mary and I were an "it" couple. I had never been with a woman who so clearly understood the importance of publicity and visibility, so we were everywhere. We went out multiple nights a week and were photographed in the best restaurants and at the biggest parties. We traveled to events all over the country on weekends. At one point, the *Hollywood Reporter*'s George Christy dubbed us "HOLLYWOOD'S MOST BEAUTIFUL COUPLE," which in a city filled with glamorous, photogenic people was quite a compliment. It also made sense to me.

Just as I was arriving at the apex of my popularity—and the peak of my relationship with Mary—unbeknownst to any of us, Michael had decided that the Ingalls family had done everything they could do as *Little House*'s leading family. That season he introduced two wonderful young actors, Jason Bateman and Missy Francis, whose presence and talent created opportunities for the kind of storytelling that had made the series so successful in the beginning. To create a new antagonist for the children after the departure of Alison Arngrim, Michael cast Allison Balson to play the character of Nancy Oleson, who turned out to be a much darker, victimized version of Nellie, perhaps best remembered for her signature accusation, "You hate me, you hate me!" It was fun to watch Katherine MacGregor, as Mrs. Oleson, actively recoil from this new character's troubled personality. Allison Balson was game, but she was in a tough spot. Replacing the humorous bad seed that was Nellie was a very tall order.

Later that year, we did "Days of Sunshine, Days of Shadow" to see, as our producer Kent McCray put it, "if the kids could carry the show." Those two episodes threw one crisis after another at Laura and Almanzo, and its high ratings gave *Little House* one final full season. I'll never forget the moment when my friend Rick Okie, our NBC programming executive, walked up to me on the stage and discreetly showed me a release from NBC that *Little House* would have a Season 9—with Melissa and me as number 1 and number 2 on the call sheet.

During that summer hiatus, my NBC deal was renegotiated, and we were off and running with storytelling refocused on the Wilders, the Olesons, and Mr. Edwards.

With the Ingalls gone, Michael introduced the Carter family, played by Stan Ivar, Pamela Roylance, Lindsey Kennedy, and David Friedman. I could tell when I met them on the first day of shooting for the ninth season that we were all going to get along very well. The Carters were moving into the Little House.

In retrospect, I wonder why the Wilders didn't move into the Little House. That might have made a more powerful connection for the audience, but I did end up wearing Michael's hat during that year, which I thought was an interesting though ill-conceived idea. But since a man's hat said a lot about him, and since that hat was Michael's, maybe the hope was that the audience might transfer some of the love they had for Michael to me.

We all had fun together that last season even as we were a bit disconnected from what we were doing. I particularly enjoyed the opportunities I got to act with and be directed by Victor French. Victor was always generous and fun to work with, and I could relate to him and Stan Ivar as peers. Melissa and I did well together. The relatively few romantic moments worked better. Melissa was dating now and had become much more comfortable with the intimacy of physical proximity.

I was number 2 on the call sheet and very publicly dating Mary Hart. At the time, it felt like a natural trajectory. I had no idea, nor did I care, how unreal or unsustainable it was. Mary and I had been together barely six months when I got a call from my brother on a Friday night. Scott told me his girlfriend, Katie, was pregnant, and they were getting married—the next day. "Bring Mary," my brother said. Mary and I flew to San Jose the next morning, rented a car, and drove to the bride's family home for a wedding that had been planned in a matter of hours.

As Mary and I sat by the pool in Katie's backyard, waiting for the simple ceremony to begin, Tracy Powell—still a dear friend to my entire family—walked over to say hello. The contrast between these two women was striking. Tracy was the all-American girl next door; Mary was the former Miss America semifinalist turned polished TV fantasy woman. Tracy and Mary were the two great loves of my life to that point. Seeing them together showed me in stark contrast who I had been—and who I was trying to be.

Back home in Los Angeles, I was so obsessed with Mary that I lost all sense of my professional obligations. I began missing early call times and showing up to work on the *Little House* set in clothes that I had worn to a previous night's event. More than once, our second assistant director, Brad Yacobian, looked at me with a mix of worry and exasperation, asking what he could do to get me to work on time. I'd always been the guy who showed up early—now, my head and my heart were elsewhere, and so sometimes, my body was too.

Mary and I had been together just over six months when I asked her to marry me. I flew to Fresno to ask her father for his blessing, and planned the proposal as best I could. But when I got down on my knee and asked the all-important question, I gave her diamond earrings instead of a ring. I was certain I wanted to marry Mary, but I didn't take the time to think through what it would mean to offer a woman something other than an engagement band. I thought the earrings were beautiful and special, perhaps more special than a ring. Obviously, I understand I was wrong. The handful of times I've told this story to female relatives and friends, they look aghast. How could I not know? Did no one help me? I have no one to blame but myself.

Mary said yes to my proposal. I would learn only later that she too had been shocked by the earrings. Maybe they fed her growing sense that I was not ready for marriage. As for me, I felt like the luckiest man in the world. I wanted everyone to know how happy we were.

Looking back, Mary's instincts were right. A big part of me wasn't ready for all that this entailed. As I sensed her doubts beginning to grow, my own insecurity began to flare. I started to feel anxious and jealous, two very unfamiliar and uncomfortable feelings. I am sorry to say that that anxiety led me to be critical of Mary, diminishing her talent and questioning why she needed everyone to see her million-dollar legs.

My insecurity was as much professional as personal. When we started dating, the entertainment press framed the relationship as "Mary Hart dating Dean Butler." I was the lead in the story of our romance, but there came a point when that framing flipped. Her star was ascendant as *Entertainment Tonight* became a cultural phenomenon. Meanwhile, the ratings for *Little House: A New Beginning* were in decline. Without Michael's on-camera star power, we weren't pulling the audience as we had before. My worries about my career fed my envy of Mary's, and that in turn damaged our relationship.

The end of my engagement to Mary Hart came shortly after the explosions that punctuated *Little House*'s "Last Farewell." I'd had time to prepare myself for the end of *Little House*. The end of the engagement blew a hole in my life that I didn't recover from for several years. Mary wept as she broke things off, saying over and over, "Dean, you're so young." I was only five and a half years her junior, an age gap that would have been completely unremarkable if I had been the older one. As it was, though, it wasn't a bullshit excuse. I really was too young for Mary, unready for a full-fledged partnership.

The obvious irony here is that I was "too young" for the love of my life, while many people considered me "too old" to play Melissa Gilbert's husband on camera. Obvious irony was no consolation. I was devastated. I went away for the weekend so that Mary could move her things out of my house. When I came home that Sunday night she was gone, and I felt like my life as I had known it was over. That's hyperbole, but it's what it felt like. The first week after she left, I got into two car accidents because I couldn't focus on driving.

I don't regret anything that happened. I think everyone deserves at least one relationship that drives them just a little bit insane. In retrospect, the heat and intensity of my nights with Mary stand in humorous contrast to my sweet and chaste on-camera marriage. After all these years, I'm able to laugh at the young man who dragged himself reluctantly out of Mary's bed to make his way to Stage 15 to film a very different bedroom scene, perhaps one with Almanzo and Laura eating popcorn, their bodies not touching, both in modest flannel. In retrospect, I can laugh with gratitude. It's taken me a long time to get there!

I dated other women after Mary. I met many wonderful women. I didn't find anyone I wanted to marry, and I didn't much worry about it. My younger brother and sister both married young and, soon thereafter, became parents. Part of me knew that wasn't going to be my story, and I tried not to put pressure on myself. I was focused on my career, but when that started to flounder in the early 1990s, I made what I can only describe as the greatest mistake of my life.

As I've mentioned, I've generally gone for women just a little bit older than me. I've always been intrigued by that confidence, that self-possession, that strength. I broke that pattern a few times, but only once was it truly disastrous. I met a striking young blonde in a hair salon in Studio City. I was reeling from one unsuccessful audition after another, and I was getting a haircut that I hoped would give me a little boost of much-needed confidence. I allowed myself to be charmed and flattered by the pretty girl sitting across from me. It didn't take more than a few minutes for her to tell me that she had been a beauty queen and that she was an aspiring actress.

This young woman, eleven years my junior, clearly couldn't see the hot mess that was sitting right in front of her. The near-instant relationship that began after that encounter in the hair salon led to one colossally bad decision after another, all culminating in a bizarre wedding halfway across the country that I was too numb to stop. This young woman was struggling with her career just as I was. We had no work, few prospects, and very little in common other than mutual need. Our families and friends saw this relationship for the mistake it was, but they were powerless to stop it. You may already know this, and I certainly know it now, but it's a truth bomb worth repeating: getting married is not a way to fix your life. A successful marriage between two healthy people offers countless opportunities for humor, love, intimacy, and acceptance. When I met she who was briefly my first wife, I was so drained by my own sense of failure that I had little love to give. I certainly had almost no humor or acceptance of her or myself.

As I write this, I think back to something my father shared with me many years ago about flying. He had over seven thousand hours as a pilot. By his own admission, he had done some crazy things in airplanes and survived. I had witnessed a few of them myself, including the ranch plane crash. "It's not the first mistake that kills you," he said. "It's the third." The first mistake can be corrected, but a second mistake magnifies the first mistake, and the third mistake makes the first two unrecoverable. That's true in the cockpit, and it's true in relationships. Far too often, we double down on our errors. It's certainly what happened in my first marriage.

There's no need for me to share my first wife's name or to say much more about our story. I take full responsibility for having made a foolish mistake at a very vulnerable time in my life. I have nothing negative to say about this woman. I will say that in hindsight, I am grateful for what this brief and disastrous marriage taught me about myself. I've gotten a lot of public love and affection over the years because I come across to many as a version of an ideal man. A lot of good people and opportunities have come my way because of that perception. For all the nice qualities that I genuinely possess as well as project, I can also be thin-skinned, short-tempered, judgmental, and a whole host of other unattractive qualities. This ill-considered first marriage held up a mirror for me to the parts of myself that aren't so nice. Just as the colossal heartbreak of my broken engagement with Mary led to some great growth, so too did this wildly difficult (and again, blessedly short) first marriage lead me to do work I might not otherwise have done.

I have not spoken to the woman who was my first wife since we walked out of the lawyer's office for the final time. Wherever she is and whatever she's doing, I wish her nothing but peace and happiness.

In the months after that divorce, I sometimes thought of my conversation with Wolfgang and Heinrich. At eighteen, I was so sure of what my life would be. I was certain I'd be married to Tracy and have children. Now, I was divorced, hitting forty, and struggling both professionally and personally. I thought of how Heinrich and Wolfgang had laughed at me. They hadn't been unkind. They just knew what life would likely bring. Perhaps, they knew that if I was lucky, life would in its own sweet time bring me someone like Katherine Cannon.

I first met Katherine on the set of *Little House* when she came to read for Michael to play Merlin Olsen's love interest on his *Little House* spin-off, *Father Murphy*. I remember seeing her for the first time as she stepped out of our makeup trailer. She was beautiful, but there was something about her beyond her beauty. There was a smart, sporty, sassy quality about her that caught my attention.

After Katherine was cast and started working, I remember countless members of the cast and crew remarking about how good she was with Merlin Olsen and all the kids. I ran into her at lots of company events, and once we did a recording session together of songs we were going to sing on New Year's Eve at the Orange Bowl Parade in Miami. I listened in the green room as Katherine belted out a very fine "Put on a Happy Face" from *Bye Bye Birdie.*

At that Orange Bowl event, I met Katherine's young son, Colin. In the parade, she and Colin rode a float that looked like the Eiffel Tower; she sang to her son while dressed as a French girl, complete with a beret. I was with a date that weekend, so Katherine and I didn't really talk, but years later, after we started seeing each other, she said that she felt a connection when we made eye contact at the hotel pool. I just remember she had a wonderful style about her, a playful twinkle in her eyes, and a fabulous smile. That was my good memory of Katherine Cannon. We wouldn't see each other again for a long time.

Nearly fifteen years later, our paths crossed again at a commercial audition. I had been officially divorced for a year.

"Dean?" It was a familiar voice behind me. When I turned around, there was beautiful Katherine Cannon, looking tan, fit, and spectacular in a wonderful pink suit that showed off her pretty legs.

"You were sitting in front of me hunched over into yourself," Katherine remembers. "You didn't look very happy to be there." Her memory is correct. I wasn't.

"But when you turned around and looked at me, your sad face turned happy. 'Oh, hi,' you said."

There was a lot in that "Oh, hi." I do not exaggerate when I say that in an instant I felt myself coming out of the dark cloud I had been in for several years. There wasn't a lot of time to talk, but when I asked, "Can I call you?" Katherine gave me her number. After the audition, I went straight home, dialed her number, and left a message. Within a few minutes, she called me back, and we set a time a few days later to meet for coffee at her house.

I didn't book the commercial, but that day I found the doorway to the rest of my life.

I still remember sitting for the first time in what is now our kitchen and watching her make coffee for us. She had on a beautiful pair of brown slacks, a crisp white tailored blouse, and simple silver jewelry. The simple necklace and bracelet looked almost familiar; in retrospect, perhaps it was a sign from Taxco and my very wise cousin Wolfgang. I recall thinking Katherine looked like a woman who knew exactly who she was. As I watched her move, and listened to her voice, I knew she was a woman I wanted to know better.

After drinking coffee from a pair of blue mugs that still sit on our kitchen pantry shelf and catching up on fifteen years gone by, we walked outside to say goodbye on the steep driveway of her garage. With me standing on the low side, it was like she was standing on an apple box that put us face to face. It felt good to be looking straight into Katherine's good, honest eyes and be so close to that bright, pretty smile. We didn't kiss, but when we hugged, we held onto each other for a long time. That silent hug in the late afternoon sunshine in the spring of 1996 marked the start of our journey. We've been together ever since.

Like me, Katherine was drawn to acting in high school. She was inspired by her drama teacher, Judy Farrell, the wife of future *M.A.S.H.* star Mike Farrell. She would work at the Laguna Playhouse and later at the Pasadena Playhouse before being put under contract by Universal Studios, where she did *The Survivors* with Lana Turner and then did *Fool's Parade* with Jimmy Stewart for Columbia Pictures. Later, Katherine would play opposite Michael Nouri in the feature film *The Hidden*. My girl also worked extensively on television, including guest starring roles in *Gunsmoke, The Streets of San Francisco, Matlock, Black Sheep Squadron, Battlestar Galactica, Magnum P.I.,* and *Murder, She Wrote*. Her star turns on television include *Can Ellen Be Saved?, High Noon, Part II: The Return of Will Kane, Will: G. Gordon Liddy,* and *Father Murphy* (where I met her for the first time). Katherine's last recurring role was on the influential hit series *Beverly Hills 90210*.

Katherine was married for nine years to Richard, a commercial director. They had their wonderful son, Colin. After their amicable divorce, Katherine lived and worked as a single parent—all the while hoping to find someone with whom she could share her life.

If it's true that three mistakes can kill you, it might also be true that three good decisions can transform your life for the better. My three good decisions are that I turned around, I called, and I made a date. The lucky part for me was that I made those decisions with Katherine Barry Cannon.

Katherine was the first woman I had known in my adult life who was truly emotionally compatible to build a life with me. Yes, there were fireworks and there was attraction, but there was much more. She had the emotional skills to build something enduring, and at last, so did I. So often I've said to her about our relationship, "It feels like we've been together since yesterday and forever." It's fresh like we began only yesterday, and yet so committed that it feels like forever.

A relationship can't solve career problems. I was still floundering when we got together, but in Katherine I found a woman who had absolute faith in me. Her certainty that things would work out built my confidence. She had been working in Los Angeles longer than I had, and she knew the highs and lows of an actor's life better than I did. Through the ups and downs, she had always done many other things. She'd been a script supervisor, a production accountant, an agent, and a hand model. Even when she was enjoying on-camera fame and success, she had done other things "just in case." As a single mother, she had no room for vanity in her decision-making. Her example helped me overcome my stubborn pride about looking for work outside of acting.

A lot of actors and actresses struggle with the fear of failure, particularly if they've had some success. It's such rarefied air when you're in it that it's agonizingly hard to admit that you are not there anymore. Katherine didn't have the time or patience for that self-indulgent agonizing. Her wise and realistic view of life and career was a game changer for me, and I would not have had the career I've had these past twenty-eight years without her.

When Katherine and I decided to move in together, the question was where. My house in the Hollywood Hills or Katherine's in Westwood? For Katherine, with Colin still at home, it was her house or nothing. I rented my place, and we set out to combine our two households into one without giving anything up. Katherine was incredibly patient as one item after another came off the moving truck. By the time my movers left, there was barely room to close the front door. It was obvious that we each needed to part with some things to get to a home that was comfortable and welcoming for both of us.

Giving things up wasn't easy, but learning to live with Fred was harder. Fred was Katherine's cat, and he was furious that I had invaded his space. More than once, Fred threw up on my computer keyboard. He saw where I put my attention, and he decided to send me a message. I was apoplectic with rage the first time, and incandescently angry the second.

Katherine saw the problem. "You're too uptight. Fred's telling you to lighten up." I didn't like hearing that, but I knew she was right. After buying a second keyboard, so I'd have a spare, I did lighten up around Fred. Lo and behold, the cat stopped regurgitating on my keyboard. Katherine was right, as usual.

It took me a long time to propose marriage to Katherine. Not because of any doubt, but because I was gun shy after my first divorce. At some point, however, I accepted that I was in a different place and with a very different woman. On January 21, 2001, in front of a very small group at the Hotel Bel-Air, Katherine and I exchanged the vows we had written ourselves. As we stood there in front of a justice of the peace, I knew with total calm and clarity that the commitment I was making to Katherine on that day would last. I knew that we'd always find a way to get from here to there, wherever "there" might be. And we'd do it together.

PRAIRIE MAN

Like most couples, we've had our challenging moments, but there has never been a doubt that we could and would weather any storm. We thrive together because we believe in each other, and we can laugh together—at least, most of the time. The ability to laugh may seem like a simple thing, but it was new for me, and it has been a key ingredient in the success of our marriage.

We don't have children together, but we do have a beautiful white and tan Cavachon named Benny. Benny is blend of the Bichon Frise and Cavalier King Charles Spaniel, and he is adorable. While I'd grown up with dogs, I had no idea how all-consuming our dog would be. To be precise, I had no idea how intensely Katherine was going to bond with Benny, and vice versa. Benny is a four-legged love affair for both of us. One of the great gifts of Benny is being able to share him with our two grandchildren, Sam and Romy, who have so joyously come into our lives thanks to Colin and his marriage to Kim.

One of my favorite things about being a bonus grandfather to Sam and Romy is sharing with them our Christmas traditions, especially our tree and special stand. Every year the grandkids come over to help us decorate, and as the years go by, we'll be counting on them to do more and more of the decorating for us. They'll be ready, as they've got the Christmas touch.

The Roeding family Christmas tree stand was built in 1910 for my grandmother and her sister Dorothea by my great-grandfather, Henry Roeding. He was inspired by a Christmas display in the window of the City of Paris department store in San Francisco's Union Square. Henry Roeding was a master craftsman and applied his talents to create the Christmas log that is our family's treasured tradition. It looks like a cutout of a large redwood tree trunk with a miniature snow scene on the top and Santa's workshop carved inside. The original stand was copied for my mother and her sister in 1934, and again for me, my brother, and sister in 1965. In 1985, I made my own version of the stand, and through the years I've made nearly twenty others for family members and friends. Sam Haskell still has the one I made for him in 1988. If I can still use a hammer and saw, I'll make one each for Sam and Romy when they strike out on their own.

My cousin Wolfgang died in 2014. I didn't update him much over the years on the ups and downs of my romantic life, but if he were still with us, I would very much like to send him a scrap of paper in an envelope. I'd write the number 1 on it, for my beautiful Katherine, and the beautiful life we have built together.

CHAPTER 16

Little House Battles, *Little House* Legacy

THIS BOOK IS MY MEMOIR. IT IS NOT A COMPREHENSIVE HISTORY OF *Little House on the Prairie*. At the same time, I started this book with the thought of the fiftieth anniversary of the television series very much in mind. *Little House* isn't just something I did for a few seasons in my twenties; it remains a vital part of my life. Along with many other people, I've devoted many years to keeping the *Little House* legacy alive to be enjoyed by new generations of fans. And I'm keenly aware that there are painful conflicts around the TV series that go back decades. With all that in mind, I feel an obligation to address at least a few aspects of our show's history.

The biggest fans of *Little House on the Prairie* generally fall into two categories. Either they are passionate disciples of the hugely successful Laura Ingalls Wilder novels that she wrote (with the help and support of her daughter Rose), or they are fans who came to the *Little House* phenomenon by way of television. The most passionate book aficionados are often (though not always) dismissive of the series because it didn't adhere strictly to what Laura wrote. In my experience, series fans enjoy the books, if they've read them—but they invariably miss Albert or the Garveys or Hester Sue or any of a dozen other characters that came straight from the imagination of Michael Landon.

The debate goes back to the genesis of the TV series. Should the show adhere strictly to Laura's books, or should it use Laura's family as the emotional foundation of the episodes, while also incorporating new characters and an original storyline? That debate drove a wedge between the two men most responsible for bringing *Little House* to television. That divide remains a source of tension and genuine pain half a century later. I have experienced that tension myself, and to the best of my ability, I want to play a part in healing it.

When you watch our show, you'll see the name Ed Friendly listed in the credits. There would be no *Little House on the Prairie* on TV, at least not as we've known it, were it not for Edwin S. Friendly, Jr. Ed Friendly was born in 1922 and raised in an affluent family in New York City. As a boy, Ed spent summers in Idaho, where he learned to ride horses and fell in love with the beauty, freedom, and adventurous spirit of the American West. Home movie footage I've seen of him on horseback and working calves showed him to be an energetic and enthusiastic boy. After Pearl Harbor in 1941, Ed joined the army and served through the duration of the war, rising from private to captain. As the baby boom kicked off after the war, Ed began his career in New York advertising. He later moved into network television, first in ad sales at ABC, then as a contract producer at CBS, and later as a programming executive at NBC responsible for primetime offerings like the *Bob Hope Christmas Specials*, the *Macy's Thanksgiving Parade*, and other entertainment featuring the likes of Frank Sinatra and Sammy Davis Jr.

In 1967, Ed left the networks and went independent, forming Ed Friendly Productions. He partnered with comedy giant George

Schlatter to create the hit comedy-variety series *Rowan & Martin's Laugh-In. Laugh-In* was topical and irreverent. Even Richard Nixon, before Watergate took down his presidency, wanted to appear on *Laugh-In.* The show's memorable take on the pop culture phrase of the day was delivered by Nixon as a question: "Sock it to me?" It was, perhaps, a foreshadowing of what would happen with the former President and Ed's next project: *Little House on the Prairie.*

As Ed's son, Trip Friendly, tells it, the story began when the family was living in Beverly Hills, and Ed's daughter, Brooke, was home from school with a cold. Ed came in to say goodbye before leaving for the office and found sixteen-year-old Brooke reading one of the Laura Ingalls Wilder books.

"Why are you reading *Little House?*" Ed asked. "Those are children's books."

"Oh, Daddy," she said enthusiastically, "I love these books. I read them every year."

On his way out the door, Ed remarked to his wife, Natalie, his surprise on finding their teenage daughter reading *Little House.*

Natalie wasn't surprised. "I grew up on the *Little House* books," she reminded him. "I've always loved them. I've told you for years that they'd make a wonderful television series."

Laugh-In was winding down. Ed was looking for a new project. The next day, he flew to New York on a business trip—and brought a borrowed copy of one of the *Little House* books with him on the plane. Trip says his father hid the book inside a *Time* magazine, not wanting the other first-class passengers to see him engrossed in a children's book. By the time the flight landed, Ed had fallen in love with Wilder's story and vision. From a phone booth at the airport, he called his attorney to find out who held the rights to the *Little House* books.

That call led to a series of meetings with Roger Lea MacBride, Rose Wilder Lane's adopted grandson, who lived in Charlottesville, Virginia. Rose inherited the rights to the *Little House* books from her mother, but with no children of her own, Rose bequeathed the rights to all their works to Roger MacBride upon her death in 1968. After protracted negotiations in both Virginia and Beverly Hills, Roger MacBride sold Ed Friendly the film and television rights to all the *Little House on the Prairie* books in the summer of 1972. The right to develop a TV series secured, Ed got straight to work.

From the beginning, Ed Friendly knew he wanted the series to mirror the detail of Laura's books. The first writers he hired to develop a pilot didn't capture his vision. He eventually found Blanche Hanalis, who had successfully adapted the wonderful children's novel *From the Mixed-Up Files of Mrs. Basil E. Frankweiler* for the small screen. Hanalis had also written teleplays for the hit series *The Courtship of Eddie's Father*. Blanche Hanalis and Ed Friendly worked on the *Little House* script together, reviewing and revising at Ed's kitchen table.

Once he was satisfied with what he had, Ed sent the pilot script to the networks. The response wasn't good: he was told that it was too "old-fashioned" for contemporary audiences. While still in the process of trying to sell the pilot, Ed and Natalie watched and loved an episode of *Bonanza* called "The Wish." Ed noted that the episode had been directed by Michael Landon. Ed knew, as everyone did, of Michael's talents as one of the show's stars; he hadn't realized Michael also had formidable behind-the-camera skills. Ed called his close friend, Lorne Green, who played *Bonanza*'s family patriarch, Ben Cartwright. Green confirmed for Ed that Michael's directing talents were genuine.

On a Sunday morning in 1973, Ed's daughter, Brooke, drove up the streets of Beverly Hills to deliver a copy of the *Little House* script to Michael Landon's home on Tower Road. Hours later, Ed's phone rang: it was Michael, inviting himself over to the Friendly home. That afternoon in Ed's kitchen Michael made his pitch: he not only wanted to direct the *Little House* pilot, but he wanted to star in it too.

This was perfect timing for Michael. After fourteen seasons as one of the most popular shows on television, *Bonanza* had just been cancelled. Michael was a hugely popular actor who had also proven that he could produce, write, direct, and edit. Those four skills are the holy grail of television drama showrunning. When Michael and Ed Friendly brought the *Little House* script to NBC, they came in as one of the stars of *Bonanza* and one of the executive producers of *Laugh-In*, arguably two of the network's most successful series of the past decade. Both these men were ready to bring all their talents to bear on this script for *Little House on the Prairie*. While the script and the Laura Ingalls Wilder source material were stylistically taking NBC back to an era all the networks were leaving behind, it was wonderful, and Michael Landon would deliver an audience. What did NBC have to lose? At the very least, the network would have a family-friendly movie of the week starring one of its biggest homegrown stars. NBC gave Ed and Michael the green light to produce their *Little House on the Prairie* movie.

I never met Ed Friendly, and of course I wasn't present during production of that first movie or the early seasons of the series. I don't know how long it took for conflict to develop between Ed and Michael, but Melissa Gilbert had a sense of it. She told me in a telephone conversation for this book: "I knew something happened when we were shooting the pilot. I think at one point Ed wanted us kids barefoot, and Mike got mad because there was snow. And he said, 'I'm not making the girls walk barefoot.' "

Despite the tension that was rapidly growing between them, Ed Friendly and Michael Landon delivered a hugely successful pilot. When it aired in March 1974, it got huge ratings—and was the highest-testing pilot in NBC history. The network picked up the show the week after it aired, asking Michael and Ed to deliver twenty-two episodes for a full season, starting on September 11. The two executive producers had less than six months to deliver.

The best account of the conceptual planning and physical work to move from pilot to series comes from the show's production manager/producer (and Michael's closest friend) Kent McCray. I highly recommend reading *Kent McCray: The Man Behind the Most Beloved Television Shows*. Kent's book is a master class from a man who had an all-consuming and encyclopedic love of production, the people he worked with, and an extraordinary temperament that enabled him to make it all look astonishingly easy—which it wasn't. Between March and September 1974, Ed, Michael, and Kent were able to turn to dozens of known, proven, and trusted collaborators to open production offices, hire writers and crew, break stories, write scripts, acquire studio space, design and build interior and exterior sets, and fill out the cast—all essentially from a standing start. Each step included hundreds of details and decisions that had to come together perfectly to make it all work.

Ed Friendly wanted the series to mirror the *Little House* books in tone and content. Michael's vision was more emotionally driven than the *Little House* books, and he was unyielding. Each man saw the show as his baby. Melissa remembered, "I think there was literally a physical altercation at some point. Which looking back on it, I think the one person you don't want to get into a physical altercation with is probably Michael Landon."

I've told the story of Michael throwing me across the barn. I can't imagine getting into it physically with Michael and expecting to win.

As that first season moved from concept to camera to air, there were numerous accounts in private letters and the press detailing that Ed Friendly was growing increasingly frustrated with what he saw as a lack of fidelity to the Laura Ingalls Wilder novels. Ed and Roger MacBride submitted as many as a dozen script ideas based on events from Laura's early novels, and they were all rejected. I think we'd all love to see these—but unfortunately, they are lost. Trip Friendly has looked for his father's scripts without success.

Roger MacBride was on Ed's side. While he was extremely bullish on the pilot, once the first season's episodes began airing, his view changed. Despite the high ratings, Roger MacBride was quoted in the press as being deeply disenchanted with Michael Landon's vision. MacBride claimed, "The series is a weekly package, unrelated to [Laura's] books; it's an outrageous copy of *The Waltons*." Roger went on to assert that Landon's *Little House* "has no fundamental guts to allow it to last."

The first season ended with the show on top of the ratings— and the bad feelings between Ed and Michael at a boiling point. Before leaving for his annual family vacation in Hawaii, Michael reached out to NBC with a message that *Little House* could continue with him or with Ed, but not with both. Series television was and still is a showrunner's medium; it's about stories and execution and creating content that grabs and holds an audience's attention. Despite all his passion, devotion, and commitment to the project, Ed was also a seasoned television executive who knew all too well how the business worked. It's hard for me to imagine that Ed believed that he could win a fight against Michael Landon for control of *Little House*.

Ed Friendly was a rights holder, he was a dealmaker, and he clearly saw the potential of *Little House* to succeed as a television series, but his public persona and creative track record were no match for Michael Landon's status as an elite showrunner and the face of NBC's newest prime-time hit.

In his unpublished memoir, Ed wrote, "Rather than fight these day-to-day battles in which there are no real victors, I prefer to address myself to fresh creative projects. I am looking forward to a very productive year."

Ed Friendly retained his rights, which allowed the *Little House* series to be produced, and he created an opportunity to do *Little House* his way twenty years after production on the original series ended. In 2005, he produced a six-part adaptation of two of Laura's earliest books for ABC's *Wonderful World of Disney*. As anyone who has watched that more recent mini-series knows, it reflects a very different vision for *Little House* from the one Michael created. It is, as Ed wanted, more rigorously faithful to the source material. Audiences have decided for themselves which vision was most effective.

Since Ed's passing in 2007, his son, Trip Friendly, has taken the reins of Friendly Family Productions and has devoted himself to honoring both his father's vision and the works of Laura and Rose Wilder.

As I grew in my confidence behind the camera, it made sense for me to work with Trip to help expand the public understanding of the *Little House* books. It was a natural fit for me to make a documentary about Laura Ingalls Wilder.

The documentary *Little House on the Prairie: The Legacy of Laura Ingalls Wilder* was produced by my company for Friendly Family Productions. Throughout the making of the film—of which everyone involved should rightly be proud—I had to deal with my own nagging sense that I had made an unfavorable production deal with Friendly Family Productions. After completion of the film, a dispute ensued which was resolved amicably through mediation. It remains a considerable source of pain to many that these stories about family devotion have torn so many relationships apart. I accept with regret that I was centrally responsible for my conflict with Friendly Family Productions.

I note too that this same documentary impacted another important relationship. Robin Bernheim, whom I'd known since *Forever* (pun partly intended), was a dear friend. I sang with Stephanie Zimbalist in Robin's wedding to David Burger. We celebrated holidays together. Katherine and I watched Robin and David's daughter, Katie, grow up. Robin had helped get me a writing assignment on William Shatner's *TekWar.*

I was fortunate that Robin willingly came on board the *Little House* documentary as a gesture of our friendship. However, as the director I made changes to several scenes without consulting Robin first. With our relationship strained, Robin and I had a complete falling-out over another *Little House*-related project, *Pa's Fiddle: The Music of America,* which I wanted to do for PBS. Conflicts have a way of snowballing, especially when pride, sweat, and artistic vision are on the line.

I wish now that I'd had the capacity to step back, take a deep breath, and take the long view with both Friendly Family Productions and Robin Bernheim. Katherine had counseled me against getting into a conflict with anyone over a show. I was strongly advised by literary agent Mitchell Stein to compromise with Robin. Hindsight, as the old saying goes, is 20/20. Katherine was right. At the time, I was too dug in to shift my perspective, and in both cases the cost of my misjudgment was an important relationship.

Perhaps the issues became so bitter because the stakes felt so high. So many of us care so much about how we can best honor the extraordinary legacy of Laura Ingalls Wilder! Fans of the show and of the books may not always overlap, but they all deserve new content about the world that Laura described. I hope we continue to be able to create and produce more to delight the millions of stakeholders. I've sincerely and lovingly tried to do my part, however imperfectly. One project of which I'm especially proud is my work with Rick Okie co-producing *Pa's Fiddle: The Music of America.* It would become a live show, a PBS broadcast event, and a wonderful recording.

Pa's Fiddle was inspired by a series of recordings that ethnomusicologist Dale Cockrell had created after discovering the 127 different songs that Laura had referenced in the *Little House* books. I first met Dale in the summer of 2010 at the inaugural Laura Ingalls Wilder academic conclave "LauraPalooza" in Mankato, Minnesota. In our first meeting, Dale told me he had a theory: though Laura didn't start writing her books until she was sixty-five, she was able to recall her youth so vividly by tapping into her memories of the music Pa played on his fiddle. I was instantly fascinated. This was an idea worth exploring.

My friend Chris Schueler connected me to producer Tony Tiano, who had produced many successful shows for PBS. Tony's Santa Fe Productions agreed to partner with my company, Peak Moore Enterprises, to develop and produce the show. Tony made an introduction for us to PBS, and Rick Okie and I flew to New York and pitched *Pa's Fiddle*: *The Music of America* in detail. They bought it in the room.

We hoped to film the show at Nashville's historical Ryman Auditorium, but the cost of that space was prohibitive. Our director Ryan Polito and supervising producer Jillian Ellis encouraged us to consider other options. Producing is about making financially responsible choices that maximize outcomes, and we knew we had to be able to shoot a beautiful show within our modest budget. Jillian eventually found us the Loveless Barn in Hendersonville, Tennessee. It felt perfect, with a rustic, intimate atmosphere ideal for a *Little House* themed event. Along with wonderfully high ceilings that could accommodate extensive lighting, there was enough floor space to build a thrust stage and provide seating for 120 invited *Little House* friends. We would shoot with six cameras, and our partner Compass Records would do the high-end audio recording that would support the TV show, the CD, and the DVD.

All the advance work on my end was done from long distance while producing *Feherty* in Orlando for NBC Golf. I had great faith in Jillian Ellis, Ryan Polito, and our show producer, Tisha Fein, to pull all the elements together, and just days before the shoot we gathered everybody at Randy Scruggs' Nashville studio to rehearse the music with our lineup of singers and musicians.

Pa's Fiddle would feature genuinely legendary talent, including Randy Travis, Ronny Milsap, Natalie Grant, Ashton Shepherd, Rodney Atkins, The Roys, and the a capella quintet Committed.

It's rare to be around such accomplished artists. You know how good they are when they can deliver fully realized performances with little or no formal rehearsal. Our Pa's Fiddle Band was led by Randy Scruggs (son of the great Earl Scruggs) on acoustic guitar with Matt Combs on fiddle, Dennis Crouch on stand-up bass, Hoot Hester on mandolin, Shad Cobb on banjo, and Chad Cromwell on drums. While we knew some of the artists by their considerable reputations, Rick and I hadn't met any of them in person until they walked into the studio to rehearse.

With the band in place, one by one, our talent came in to sing. The beauty of the performances gave Rick and me shivers. We were completely overwhelmed by how well all of this had come together. My friend Chris Schueler shot some terrific "behind the scenes" video for a *Making of Pa's Fiddle* documentary being produced by Middle Tennessee State University. I wish more elements from that documentary could've made their way into our final PBS show, but the network only wanted music.

At noon on a cold January day, we took possession of the Loveless Barn. It was the day before the show. Fifty people descended on that space to set up—and we were gone thirty-six hours later. That's how tight it was; there was barely time to breathe, much less rest. Our budget from PBS was so small that Tony Tiano and I each put in thirty thousand dollars of our own money to get the show over the finish line. PBS aired the show to considerable acclaim. Compass Records did a wonderful job with the audio recording. Although the pictures are beautiful, I think the CD captures the evening best.

DEAN BUTLER

I dedicated *Pa's Fiddle: The Music of America* to Michael Landon. I would never have been able to do a project about the music of *Little House* without the faith Michael had to cast me as Almanzo Wilder three decades earlier. It's not a stretch to say that without *Little House*, I wouldn't have done most of the things I've done in my professional life. Because of all that *Little House* gave me, I have spent many years doing all that I can to try to give more of *Little House* to its legions of fans. I was excited to produce *Pa's Fiddle* and *Little House on the Prairie: The Legacy of Laura Ingalls Wilder*, and the 2008 video *Almanzo Wilder: Life Before Laura* because I wanted to do my part to deepen our understanding of (and devotion to) the world described in those wonderful books—and on our equally wonderful show.

In the summer of 2018, many of us heard rumblings from our friend William Anderson about a producer named Christopher Czajka and a project he was developing about the life and career of Laura Ingalls Wilder for PBS. That got my attention because PBS had given audiences the Ken Burns documentary *The Civil War*—the very documentary series that had first sparked my interest in producing.

Melissa Gilbert, Alison Arngrim, and I were honored to be interviewed for the resulting episode of PBS's *American Masters* which was called "Laura Ingalls Wilder: Prairie to Page." The show offered us yet another opportunity, in an important forum, to connect our series to the themes of the Wilder novels. "Prairie to Page" was beautifully produced and focused on Laura's life, her journey as a writer, the themes of her books, and her little-known collaboration with her daughter, Rose Wilder Lane.

In the weeks that followed its premiere we learned that "Prairie to Page" was on its way to becoming the most watched episode in the history of the *American Masters* series, yet more proof of the enduring appeal of the *Little House* books. The show's success was particularly gratifying to Chris Czajka because he had fought with his superiors at PBS to sell Laura Ingalls Wilder as a worthy *American Masters* subject. The powers-that-be at PBS didn't think anyone would care about this writer of children's books. I'm sure, like so many others through the years, they were surprised by Laura's ongoing appeal.

I was gratified to see that "Prairie to Page" had similarities in content and style with *Little House on the Prairie: The Legacy of Laura Ingalls Wilder,* which I produced and directed for Friendly Family Productions years earlier. After seeing what Chris and the *American Masters* team did with a considerably larger budget, I was very pleased with what we achieved with our show.

Little House is the gift that keeps on giving. Laura Ingalls Wilder was a Pioneer Girl. Thanks to Michael Landon, I'm humbled and proud to call myself a Prairie Man.

Conclusion

IT IS 1998, AND I AM WITH MY FRIEND AND EXECUTIVE PRODUCER Keith Allo in South Florida. We're in Miami shooting Champ Car racing at the Homestead Motor Speedway. As Keith and I step into our hotel elevator, heading out to dinner, a woman does a double take. She hesitates, then speaks to me.

"I know you. You're Almanzo."

Keith looks at me and then back to the woman and asks, "He's *who?*"

The woman smiles. "He's Almanzo, from *Little House on the Prairie.*"

Keith replies, "Um, he's Dean Butler. He's my producer."

"Maybe, but he's also Almanzo from *Little House.*" The woman is certain. I am busted.

As she gets off the elevator, the woman says, "Good night, Manly."

Keith laughs, "*Manly?*"

"I'll explain it later."

"*Are* you Almanzo from *Little House on the Prairie?*" Keith asks.

I'm not sure I'll still have a job if I answer honestly, but I can't lie. Not now. Not about this.

"Yeah, Keith, sorry. I am."

I didn't get fired. I think Keith thought it was cool that I hadn't used that credit on my resume to get the job. At the time, I wasn't actively trying to hide from my *Little House* history, but I wasn't exactly embracing it. I thought I needed to focus on what I could do now, and not what I had once been. The encounter in the Miami elevator showed me that I couldn't hide my past. There's a difference between trying to use an old role as leverage—and pretending that part of your life never existed.

Since that night, I've never tried to hide from my background. I've embraced that I was Almanzo, and I've grown ever more grateful for my chance to be a part of such an enduring part of American popular culture.

Television has changed a great deal in the fifty years since *Little House* debuted in 1974. It has changed a great deal over the course of my TV career, which began only shortly after our series first hit the airwaves. The technology has changed enormously, as has the number of choices confronting the average viewer. In the 1970s, when my career began, there were three networks—now, thanks to streaming, there are many hundreds of programming options. And in the 1970s, when my career began, most faces on American TV looked like mine.

Fifty years ago, American television was nearly all-white. America was also a much whiter country. The ethnic balance of the entire western world is shifting fast, and television is catching up. American popular entertainment is much more diverse in both faces and themes than it was when I began. I'm in my late sixties now, and I have peers who wring their hands and complain about how much has changed. They don't think it's for the better. From my perspective, their anxieties are a total waste of time and energy. It's happening. The question is how we will address it. My hope is that as an industry and a nation we will gracefully embrace changes that are right in front of us. Current evidence of those "graceful embraces" are scant, however, because an older generation of leaders sees it as their responsibility to protect the status quo. That's as much a commentary on who makes the decisions in entertainment as it is on politics.

I see how much the world has changed since 1974, and I see how much I took for granted as a white actor from a comfortable background. I have always embraced the new and the cutting-edge when it comes to technology. I've reached a point in my life where I do the same when it comes to the social and cultural changes going on around me. Resisting the call of the young for more representation seems as silly as still insisting on using a rotary dial phone. More members of my generation need to be a little less afraid, and a lot more welcoming.

If the world has changed a lot in the past fifty years, it's a safe bet it will change a lot more in the next fifty. For me the most important question for this book is, will people still be watching our *Little House on the Prairie* family fifty years from now, on devices yet to be invented? I don't know, but I hope so. I always harken back to Michael's confident declaration that people would still be watching *Little House* long after we're all gone. If Michael was right, I think the case for *Little House*'s ongoing success can be found in the circumstances of its initial success fifty years ago.

> *Back then, we said that if a show's not sexy enough; if it's not edgy; if it doesn't have half-dressed women or men without their shirts on, nobody will watch it.*

Those are the words of my friend and colleague, Sam Haskell, who has been a straight A student of television since his boyhood in Amory, Mississippi. As one of the industry's top packaging agents, Sam helped bring to television iconic programming like *The Fresh Prince of Bel Air*, *The Cosby Show*, and *Everybody Loves Raymond*. Today Sam is an Emmy-winning producer of heartwarming family entertainment for Warner Brothers Television.

Sam is the personification of the old saying, "you can take the boy out of the country, but you can't take the country out of the boy." He remains one of my best and most trusted friends, and he has an excellent insider's perspective on *Little House*'s history. Sam has reminded me many times that when it premiered in 1974, a lot of young and hip television executives were wagering on the series' quick failure. The show's setting and themes didn't fit into their sexy, edgy worldview. They were saying to themselves, according to Sam, "Nobody wants to watch this simple family in a covered wagon out in the middle of nowhere celebrating Christmas with tin cups, shiny pennies, and candy canes. I guarantee they said, 'Whoever bought that show is going to get fired.'"

Sam and I laugh a lot at how wrong "they" were.

The *Little House* series arrived on American TV at a challenging time for our nation. Gas prices were soaring. Inflation was running upward of 11 percent, we were headed toward a historic defeat in Vietnam, and the Watergate scandal was toppling the Nixon presidency. Nixon became the first president to resign just over a month before the series debuted. Americans needed comfort, they wanted a distraction, and they wanted a window into a happier, more optimistic America. Michael Landon delivered all that and more.

For years after it debuted, *Little House* was NBC's only successful series. CBS had *M.A.S.H*, *One Day at a Time*, *All in the Family*, and *The Waltons*. ABC had *Happy Days*, *Laverne & Shirley*, *Welcome Back, Kotter*—and *Monday Night Football*. NBC had *Little House* and not much else. NBC would dominate the mid-1980s with its famous Thursday night comedy lineup, but a decade earlier, it regularly languished in third place behind its rivals. That the network's only consistent hit wasn't sexy or edgy or controversial made *Little House* an even more surprising triumph for the last-place network.

As Sam and I—and perhaps you—agree, *Little House* was successful because it genuinely touched the hearts of its audience.

It made them laugh, it made them cry, it made them think, and it helped people of all ages, particularly parents, consider what kind of human beings they wanted to be and the messages they wanted to give their children. I don't think it's an exaggeration to say that *Little House on the Prairie* and its Depression-era colleague, *The Waltons*, define the "warm and fuzzy best" of television's family drama genre.

We all come from families: some big, some small, most dysfunctional in some respects—and loving in others. There's an endless appetite to see family love and family conflict represented on television. In the years since *Little House* hit the air, we've seen shows like *Family, thirtysomething, Eight Is Enough, Parenthood, Seventh Heaven,* and *This Is Us* offer us optimistic and moving perspectives on family. We've also seen "guilty pleasure" homages to wealth, power, greed, and great dysfunction. *Dallas* and *Dynasty* lead us to *The Sopranos, Empire,* and *Succession.* Loving or murderous, laughing or backstabbing: everyone loves family drama.

My friend Sam likes to distinguish the heartwarming shows from "good trash" like *Falcon Crest* and *Knots Landing.* "Those shows represented everything most people weren't, but we were still intrigued by them," he says. Most of us want our pulpy and absurd distractions as well as comforting reassurance about hope, character, faith, and love; plenty of *Little House* viewers also enjoyed the darker, soapier shows like *Dallas.* The difference is, there's relatively little audience for *Dynasty* and *Dallas* today—but there still is for *Little House.* Sam has a theory: "I'm into genealogy and ancestry. I know the lines of my family and how far back they go, and I think lots of people loved to think that their ancestors faced and overcame challenges as the Ingalls family did, with strength, courage, grace, and resolve."

I think Sam has hit on the reason *Little House* has thrived for half a century and why it will thrive for fifty years more. There are very few shows in the history of the medium, and none today, that allow us to consider the impact of life choices so clearly. *Little House* is not nuanced. It paints clear, universally accessible pictures of actions and consequences. Through its archetypal characters *Little House* offers examples of morally uplifting behavior with no murky justifications for bad behavior. *Little House* offers a standard that is both lofty and attainable. It tells us who we were, and who we still could be.

After that moment in the Miami elevator, I realized it was time to openly recommit to my part in *Little House* history. In the early 2000s, I began to do appearances again for the *Little House* community, returning to the real Walnut Grove for their summer pageant, *Fragments of a Dream*. By 2006, I was folding *Little House* into my work as a producer by making DVD bonus content for NBC Home Entertainment. After that, it was the *Little House*-themed documentaries and the PBS music special. Regardless of whatever else comes along in my life, through highs and disappointments, there is always the gift of *Little House*. There are always more stories to be told, new fans to meet, and new perspectives to realize about our very special show.

Over the years, I've been eaten alive by mosquitos again and again at that Walnut Grove pageant. *Little House* cast members have gone to Walnut Grove and joined with fans, young and old, for fortieth and forty-fifth anniversary celebrations of the series. I will be in Walnut Grove again, being bitten by golf-ball-sized mosquitos, for the fiftieth anniversary celebration of the series in 2024. And who knows? If luck holds, I'll be at celebrations after that as well. I know this: the show will live on after I'm gone.

In the meantime, I'm honored to support the *Little House* legacy. I'm honored to affirm the timeless appeal of the series, the genius of Michael Landon, my immediate and extended *Little House* family, and of course, the brilliance of Laura Ingalls Wilder. There has been other work of which I'm proud, but *Little House on the Prairie* is my place in television. I'm always home there, as I am with my flesh-and-blood family, and as I am in my always-new romance with Katherine.

As I come to the end of this story, I am conscious that it is—as Laura Ingalls Wilder said of the books we all love—"the truth, but not all the truth." There is more that I'm not sharing, partly for reasons of space, partly because of failing memory, and partly because some stories deserve to stay untold. I can't begin to know what conclusions you will draw about me after reading this volume, but as Reverend Terry Cole-Whittaker often said, "What you think of me is none of my business." On the other hand, I do hope you enjoyed the stories I've shared. It's been a fun journey remembering so many people and places. It's been a pleasure to pay tribute as best I can to those who have given me this wonderful life—and this special place in television history.

My earliest childhood dreams were of being a policeman, a fireman, or a pilot. I could easily see myself in a navy-blue cop's uniform or on a fire truck or in the cockpit of an airplane. My dreams grew as I got my first cowboy hat and boots and learned to ride horses in the hills overlooking San Francisco Bay. The dreams evolved more as I played football and basketball with my brother and dad, watched *Lost in Space* and *The Wild, Wild West* on TV and took my first art class. Then came my first play, my first kiss, my first on-stage solo, and that little movie the guys and I made in eleventh grade about the mob. I'm fortunate that I grew up in a family of dreamers, raised by a large and loving group of people with the capacity and commitment to nurture my hopes and possibilities.

Unless I was going to hurt myself or others, nobody ever said, "You can't do that." There are many gifts, material and intellectual, that can be given to a child during their formative years, but the freedom to dream and try without restriction may be among the most important blessings we can receive in our entire lives. Turning dreams into reality is rarely easy, and it's not enough to encourage kids to follow their bliss. You need to remind them of the virtues of hard work, tenacity, and patience. You need to encourage self-confidence. And you need to give them the tools to cope with setbacks and failures. I am so fortunate to have grown up with people who gave me the tools to succeed—and to adapt and survive when success didn't come easily.

I recently joined the *Little House* Fiftieth Anniversary Celebration Committee, where I've had yet more chances to connect with *Little House* colleagues and fans who continue to celebrate our series with a fervor that is wonderfully affirming. As part of our preparations for a Simi Valley celebration scheduled to take place in March 2024, we took the Warner Brothers studio tour. I've been in this industry a long time, but I still enjoy the same things tourists enjoy; I highly recommend taking the tour if you find yourself in L.A. As part of that Saturday afternoon on the back lot, groups were invited onto sound stages that were active for different shows filmed during the week.

It was a thrill to remember all the things I had done in this place. *The New Gidget* was shot on a stage close to where the studio tour went that day. We shot scenes for *Little House* on Warner Brother's western street. There is much that has changed regarding cameras, sets, and lighting through the years, but now as in the past (at least until artificial intelligence takes over), actors still must come onto a sound stage—and supported by talented crews—fully commit themselves to turning scripts into engaging entertainment for audiences. If all the pieces line up just right, actors, writers, and crews might create something with a core of humanity and truth that audiences will love for years and years to come. It's a kind of immortality for actors that few other professions, other than musicians and elite athletes, ever experience. We didn't achieve that immortality with *The New Gidget*, but not because everyone didn't give it their best. I'm not sure it happened with *Buffy, the Vampire Slayer* either, but there is no question after fifty years that we all hit a home run with *Little House on the Prairie*.

Acting, like life, is a team sport. I have been part of many wonderful teams in my career, none quite as magical or as enduring as the one Michael Landon and Kent McCray put together all those years ago. I'm grateful to be growing older alongside so many of my fellow cast and crew. We still look great, as far as I'm concerned, and we're still a family.

As for me, I've survived bee stings, sunburns, cancer scares, losses of loved ones, career reverses, and heartbreaks, but I'm still here and as I've said throughout this book, I'm grateful: grateful to my large multigenerational family, my teachers, mentors, partners, and—most importantly—the people who appreciated the work that has given my life purpose. I'm still meeting them, joined with members of our *Little House* cast, to honor the work and the people, living and past, who made it all happen.

I am a son, a brother, a husband, an uncle, a cousin, and even a grandfather. I'm an actor, a producer, a director, and now you might even consider me a writer. For some I'm an afterthought, and for others I might be an inspiration. But when the lights go out and I'm alone with myself and my thoughts, I'm a sixty-eight-year-old man who loves and is loved by a wonderful woman, who every day feels incredibly lucky to have had the life I've had.

My commitment is to keep getting up every day and living my life with goodness and purpose. I'm going to keep supporting Katherine and our family. I'll continue developing documentary projects. I want to grow as a voice-over artist, and I'd like to act again, if the right opportunity comes along. Regardless of how any of that works out, I will always be a Prairie Man, devoted to an experience that has brought to my life every wonderful thing I have.

I began writing this book on a stormy January morning. I finish it on a warm July afternoon.

It's been seven months of getting up before the sun, walking the dog, making coffee, settling quietly into our dining room, turning on my MacBook Pro, and recounting the events of my life. I'm glad to be done, but part of me will miss this writing routine.

If I were a different man, I'd celebrate finishing this book with a round of beers or a glass of very good, very old Scotch. Because I'm me, I'm going to treat myself to a pint of Rocky Road ice cream. I think I've earned it.

As I finish my story, I imagine I'm somewhere else, somewhere not very far away. I'm on the set at MGM, sitting at Charles and Caroline's dining table. I'm not typing on a laptop but writing with pen on paper. I have just finished this manuscript, and somehow in this daydream, it's already bound in leather. I stand up and carry my book to a shelf. Waiting on that shelf are the books you already know. There's *Little House in the Big Woods, On the Banks of Plum Creek, Farmer Boy*, and all the other beloved works of Laura Ingalls Wilder.

Next to these are the books written by the cast and crew who have been such a big part of my life. There sit Melissa Gilbert's books, Alison Arngrim's, and there are books by Karen Grassle and Kent McCray, Wendi Lou Lee and Charlotte Stewart, Melissa Francis and Ketty Lester. They've all loved *Little House* and been shaped by it; they've each told their stories and offered their recollections. It's my turn to join them here and add my voice to theirs in this chorus of memory.

I put my book next to theirs, step back, and under my breath, say a quiet, heartfelt "thank you."

Acknowledgments

There is a long list of special people who I want to thank for their influences on my life and this memoir. I want to start with my editor at Kensington Publishing, John Scognamiglio, who received my book proposal from his published author and my friend, *Waltons* star Mary McDonough, read it, and reached out less than twenty-four hours later with a firm offer to publish it. After I got up off the floor, I connected John to my agent Danita Florence and literary attorney, Andrew Zucker, who put all the details together.

When I sat down to write, I began by interviewing people who really understood the story of my life and the details of special moments in my career. That list includes my first cousin Hugo Schwyzer, who is an expert on our family history; my friend of over forty years, Sam Haskell; and Melissa Gilbert, the woman to whom I am forever linked because of her beloved portrayal of Laura Ingalls Wilder.

I also had conversations with everybody's favorite "Nasty" Nellie Oleson, Alison Arngrim; *Little House* casting director Susan Sukman McCray, who more than anyone else was responsible for putting me in the room with Michael Landon; my friend and former NBC programming executive Richard C. Okie; *Little House* historian William Anderson; and *Little House on the Prairie* film and television rights holder, Trip Friendly. I also spoke to

ACKNOWLEDGMENTS

my favorite Gidget, Caryn Richman, and our *New Gidget* show-runner, Larry Mollin, about our days on the beaches of Southern California.

After that, it's all about giving thanks to my family, friends, teachers, mentors, and other creative collaborators, beginning with two who made my life possible, my parents Peter and Marianna Butler, who are the foundation of what makes me me; my brother, Scott Roeding Butler; and my sister, Margaret Marian Butler Michaels. I couldn't be more grateful for the foundational love and guidance of my grandparents Arthur Moore and Margaret Roeding Moore Chickering and her second husband, Allen Lawrence Chickering. Throughout my life I've been shaped, balanced, and affirmed by my mother's sister, Alison Moore Schwyzer, as well as her sons Hugo and Philip and their children. My appreciation of our large multigenerational family was cemented when I was a boy by my great-aunt Margaret McClure, my beloved aunt Dorothea Bishop, and her son Thomas B. Bishop. In addition, I will never forget my aunt Marybelle Doub and my cousin Philip Doub. My brother-in-law, Noell Michaels, has been a constant source of stability, kindness, and familial commitment throughout his marriage to my sister and their children, Thorne and Caroline, are and will be a positive force in our family for the rest of their lives, as will my brother's sons—Jack, Ted, Mike, and Rick—along with their spouses and children.

Outside of my immediate family, the relationships I've had with Tracy Powell, Chris Schueler, Rick Okie, Keith Allo, Rick Livingston, and Nikki Alpert have touched my life in incalculable ways with their love, kindness, and intelligence.

For the lessons I received about country life and hard, smart work I will never forget Mission Peak's "Marlboro Man" Ed Chadbourne, Pat Bordy, and Glenn Jones.

While I was never a stellar student, I'll always be grateful to my earliest teachers and leaders at Wildwood Elementary School;

ACKNOWLEDGMENTS

Richard Rosenquist, Miss Enlow, Miss Bouey, Mrs. Higgins, Mrs. Treadwell, Miss Oldham, and Mrs. Thomas. At Piedmont High School I was nurtured by John Morrison, Tom Goldstein, Dale Porter, Jane Nelson, James Killian, Diane Courtois, Lewis Hutchinson, Edward Hallman, James Cochran, Bob Muenter, Clark Ransom, Leonard Waxdeck, Alan Harvey, and Charles Harris.

I am also grateful for the friendship, kindness, and inspiration of my schoolmates, including David Bowman, Jayne Rutledge, Rebecca Powell, Bill Harris, Jay Tyler, Linda Ricksen, Loring Barker, Joe Leadem, John Moxon, Don Curotto, George Christopoulos, Jim Kinney, Ellen Chan, Dave Branson, Jan Hjorth, Ken Stanley, Debbie Robinson, Susan Fleming, Bill Knowland, Marla Ferrell, Kathy Finney, John Dorward, Mary Anne Dorward, Bruce Turner, Brad Howard, Josh Bernstein, Barbara Strain, David Livingston, Margaret Ferguson, and my most important childhood friends Mary Anne Vochan and Perry, Christopher, and Sally Dreiman.

At University of the Pacific, in addition to my friend Chris Schueler, there are more special individuals who have impacted my life and career, including Laura Roberts, Warren Kelly, Stanley McCaffrey, Don DeRosa, Judy Chambers, Diane Philibosian, Cy Kahn, William Wollack, Lou Nardi, Dennis Jones, Gary Armagnac, Dave Streeter, David Giovannoni, Dave Baer, Alan Cook, Stewart Cooper, Jim Meade, Bill Coen, Kelli Page, and Janice Wagner.

Between college and career life there were no influencers more important to me than Don Dorward and my first agent, Ann Brebner.

Once I got started, the people of enormous significance in my life include Stephanie Zimbalist, her father Efrem Zimbalist Jr., John Korty, John Friedrich, Ina Bernstein, John Kimball, David Westberg, Jon Feltheimer, Robin Bernheim, Jodie Knofsky, Rosemary O'Brien, Jay and Rosemary Asher, Mary Hart,

ACKNOWLEDGMENTS

Cheri Ingram, Deidre Hall, Kathy Ireland, Jason Winters, Erik Sterling, Jon Carrasco, Stephen Roseberry, Steve Rosenbloom, Michael Sterling, and supporting the publication of this memoir, Harlan Boll, Ann Pryor, Lou Malcangi, and Michael Roud.

In my *Little House* family the people who most impacted my growth and opportunity and who can't be thanked enough for their kindness, patience, and trust are Michael Landon, Melissa Gilbert, Kent and Susan McCray, Rick Okie, Karen Grassle, Melissa Sue Anderson, Robin and Rachel Greenbush, Alison Arngrim, Bill Claxton, Maury Dexter, Ted Voigtlander, Haskell Boggs, Brad Yacobian, Katherine MacGregor, Lucy Lee Flippen, Charlotte Stewart, Victor French, Merlin Olsen, Richard Bull, Kevin Hagan, Dabbs Greer, Jonathan Gilbert, Pam Roylance, Stan Ivar, David Friedman, Lindsey Kennedy, Shannen Doherty, Charlotte Yerke, Gladys Whitten, Whitey Snyder, Miles Middough, David Rose, Marvin Coil, John Loeffler, Vince Guttierez, Don Balluck, Chris Abbott, Danny Doucette, Brandon Tartikoff, and Jeanette Hektoen.

The *Gidget* years brought a whole new group of special people to whom I owe my thanks, beginning with my favorite Gidget, Caryn Richman, and extending to William Schallert, Sydney Penny, Lili Hayden, Jill Jacobsen, David Preston, Don Stroud, Harry Ackerman, Ralph and Rebecca Riskin, Henry and Paul Seigel, Mort Marcus, George Zatezlo, Larry Mollin, Ted Lange, Roger Duchowny, Fred Mollin, Ken Koch, Dean Torrence, Jan Berry, Randell Kirsch, Gary Griffin, Heinz Von Schuler, Ricardo Altieri, and so many more.

When my energies turned unexpectedly toward the theater, I offer thanks for the trust and support of *West Side Story* director Alan Johnson, Lauri Landry, Steve Blanchard, Irving Seiders, the entire 1988 *West Side Story* Japan Tour company, Carol Burnett, Glenn Casale, John McDaniel, David Galligan, Bill Hutton, Frank Levy, Kay Cole, and Michael Lamont.

On Broadway my massive thanks go to Stephen Sondheim,

ACKNOWLEDGMENTS

James Lapine, Joanna Merlin, Paul Gemignani, Chuck Wagner, Robert Westenberg, Chip Zien, Marin Mazzie, Colleen Fitzpatrick, Kay McClelland, and Adam Grupper.

My teachers and creative collaborators who offered me their wisdom and experience through the years include Peggy Feury, Darryl Hickman, Milton Katselas, Jeffrey Tambor, Nathan Lam, Seth Riggs, Dee Marquit, Jay Asher, and Dr. Dale Cockrell.

In my producing life I have enormous gratitude for the support and generosity of Chris Schueler, Keith Allo, Alex Gittinger, Greg and Wayne Gears, Steve Gilson, Paul Block, Glenn Wiley, Scott Liggett, Ed Friendly, Trip Friendly, Rebecca Friendly, the Laura Ingalls Wilder historical sites, Anthony Tiano, Ryan Polito, Tisha Fein, Jillian Ellis, Bill Morris, Martin and Tobias Ehleben, John Moranville, David Feherty, Jay Kossoff, Molly Solomon, Jason Harper, my dear departed friend Andy Ebert, Pat Devlin, James Ponti, Ryan Griffiths, Courtney Vargas, Jimmy Roberts, and all the talented people at NBC Sports and Golf, whose professionalism inspires me every day. Thanks also to Coach Susan Summons, who has kept me on task with an important project about the history of women's basketball that I'm committed to making before I'm done.

Recently I have been impacted by and am grateful to more members of the *Little House* family, including Ken and Karen Carre, Wendi Lou Lee, Jennifer Donati, Eric Caron, Orlando de la Paz, Arlene Toro, Jack Bishop, Nick and Ruth Ann Johnson, Becky Jones, Kathi Van Etten, Daniel Jordan, Todd McGraw, Derek Hecker, Jenn Brallier, and so many others whose love and commitment help keep *Little House* alive for millions of devoted fans all over the world.

I owe my most heartfelt thanks to my beautiful girl, Katherine, whose love and patience provide a safe harbor for all my dreams. Katherine's parents, Tom and Catherine, accepted me when I stepped into their daughter's life a quarter of a century ago, as did her ex-husband Richard, her brother Richard, her

ACKNOWLEDGMENTS

niece Amber, her son Colin, his wife Kim, our in-laws Marc and Deb, and later Sam and Romy, our beautiful grandchildren.

There are surely many more people whose names should be included here, including the legions of fans—most significantly, my devoted Austrian fan, Martha Keller, who through the years has sent me incredible supplies of chocolate during the holidays—as well as members of Dean's Divas. I'm sure many more names will pop into my head after this book goes to print. For anyone I omitted here, I offer my karmic appreciation for your understanding.